DRAGON AGE™

MAGEKILLER

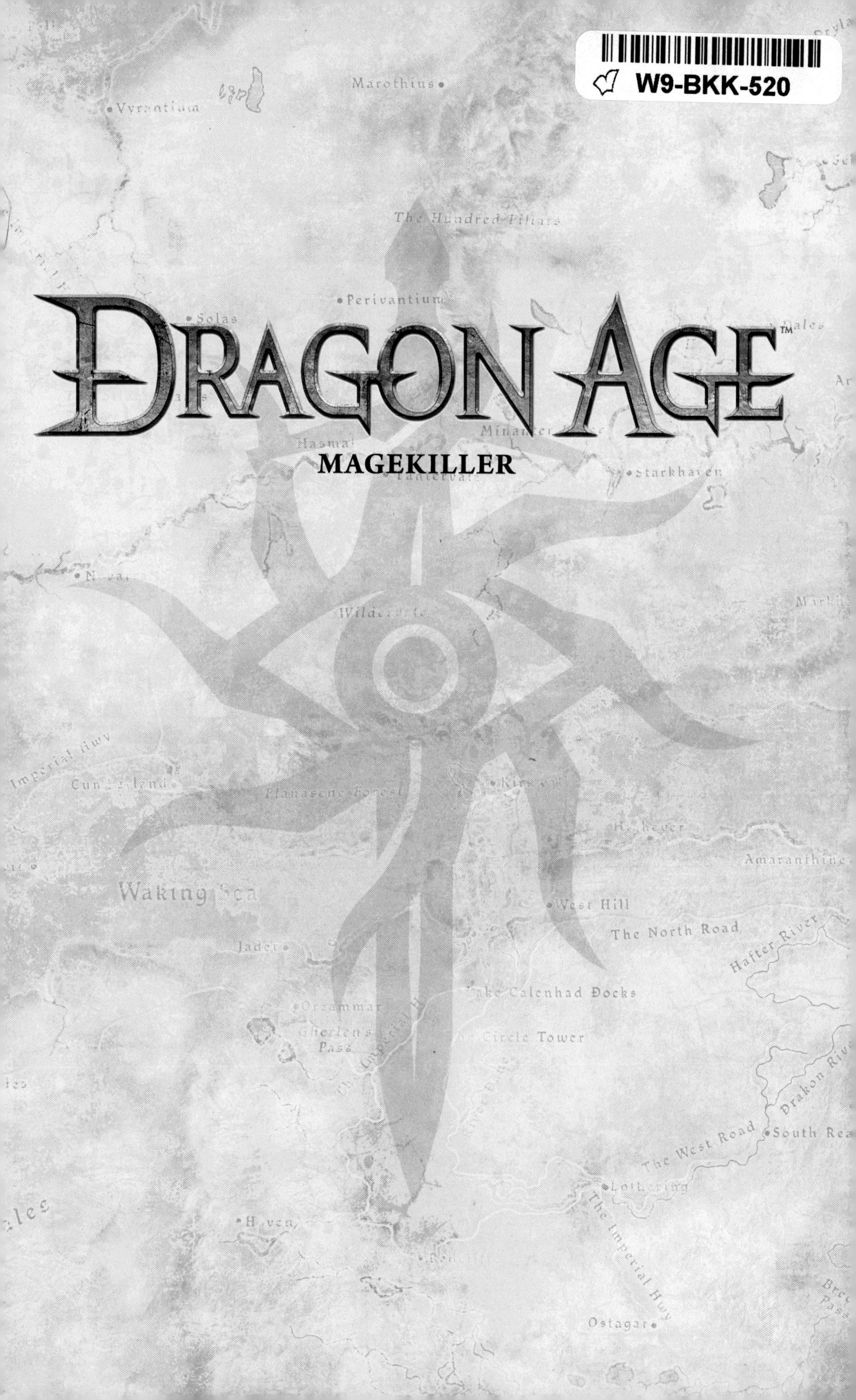

Marothius
Vyrantium
The Hundred Pillars
Perivantium
Solas
Starkhaven
Wildervale
Imperial Hwy
Planasene Forest
Kirkwall
Amaranthine
Waking Sea
West Hill
The North Road
Hafter River
Jader
Lake Calenhad Docks
Orzammar
Gherlen's Pass
Circle Tower
Drakon River
The West Road
South Reach
Lothering
The Imperial Hwy
Ostagar

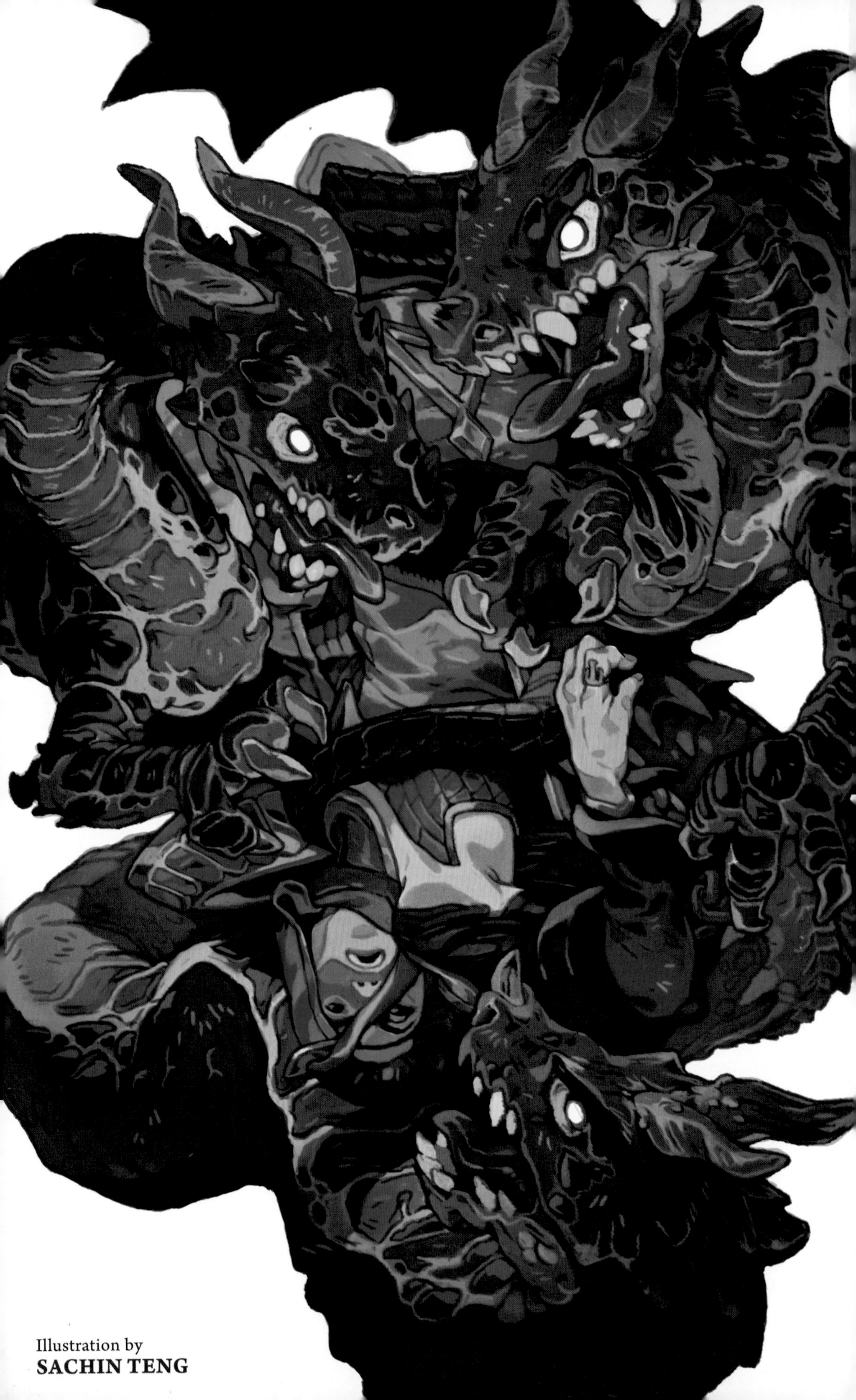

Illustration by
SACHIN TENG

Dragon Age™
MAGEKILLER

Script
GREG RUCKA

Pencils
CARMEN CARNERO

Inks
TERRY PALLOT

Colors
MICHAEL ATIYEH

Lettering
MICHAEL HEISLER

Front Cover Art
SACHIN TENG

President
MIKE RICHARDSON

Editors
PATRICK THORPE and **DAVE MARSHALL**

Assistant Editors
ROXY POLK, RACHEL ROBERTS, and **CARDNER CLARK**

Collection Designer
SARAH TERRY

Digital Art Technician
ALLYSON HALLER

SPECIAL THANKS TO BIOWARE, INCLUDING: **Nick Thornborrow**, Concept Artist • **Patrick Weekes**, Lead Writer • **Matthew Goldman**, Art Director • **Mike Laidlaw**, Creative Director • **Aaryn Flynn**, Studio GM, BioWare Edmonton **Chris Bain**, BioWare Business Development

International Licensing: (503) 905-2377 | Comic Shop Locator Service: (888) 266-4226

DRAGON AGE: MAGEKILLER

This volume collects issues #1 through #5 of the Dark Horse comic-book series *Dragon Age: Magekiller*.

Published by
Dark Horse Books
A division of Dark Horse Comics, Inc. | 10956 SE Main Street | Milwaukie, OR 97222

DarkHorse.com | DragonAge.com | BioWare.com

First trade paperback edition: July 2016
ISBN 978-1-61655-634-1

10 9 8 7 6 5 4 3 2 1
Printed in China

Neil Hankerson Executive Vice President **Tom Weddle** Chief Financial Officer **Randy Stradley** Vice President of Publishing **Michael Martens** Vice President of Book Trade Sales **Matt Parkinson** Vice President of Marketing **David Scroggy** Vice President of Product Development **Dale LaFountain** Vice President of Information Technology **Cara Niece** Vice President of Production and Scheduling **Nick McWhorter** Vice President of Media Licensing **Ken Lizzi** General Counsel **Dave Marshall** Editor in Chief **Davey Estrada** Editorial Director **Scott Allie** Executive Senior Editor **Chris Warner** Senior Books Editor **Cary Grazzini** Director of Print and Development **Lia Ribacchi** Art Director **Mark Bernardi** Director of Digital Publishing **Michael Gombos** Director of International Publishing and Licensing

Library of Congress Cataloging-in-Publication Data

Names: Rucka, Greg, author. | Carnero, Carmen, illustrator. | Pallot, Terry, illustrator. | Atiyeh, Michael, illustrator. | Heisler, Michael, illustrator. | Teng, Sachin, illustrator.
Title: Dragon age : magekiller / script, Greg Rucka ; pencils, Carmen Carnero ; inks, Terry Pallot ; colors, Michael Atiyeh ; lettering, Michael Heisler ; front cover art, Sachin Teng.
Description: First trade paperback edition. | Milwaukie, OR : Dark Horse Books, 2016. | "This volume collects issues #1 through #5 of the Dark Horse comic-book series Dragon Age: Magekiller."
Identifiers: LCCN 2016003488 | ISBN 9781616556341
Subjects: LCSH: Magic--Comic books, strips, etc. | Graphic novels.
Classification: LCC PN6728.D68 R83 2016 | DDC 741.5/973--dc23
LC record available at http://lccn.loc.gov/2016003488

Illustration by
SACHIN TENG

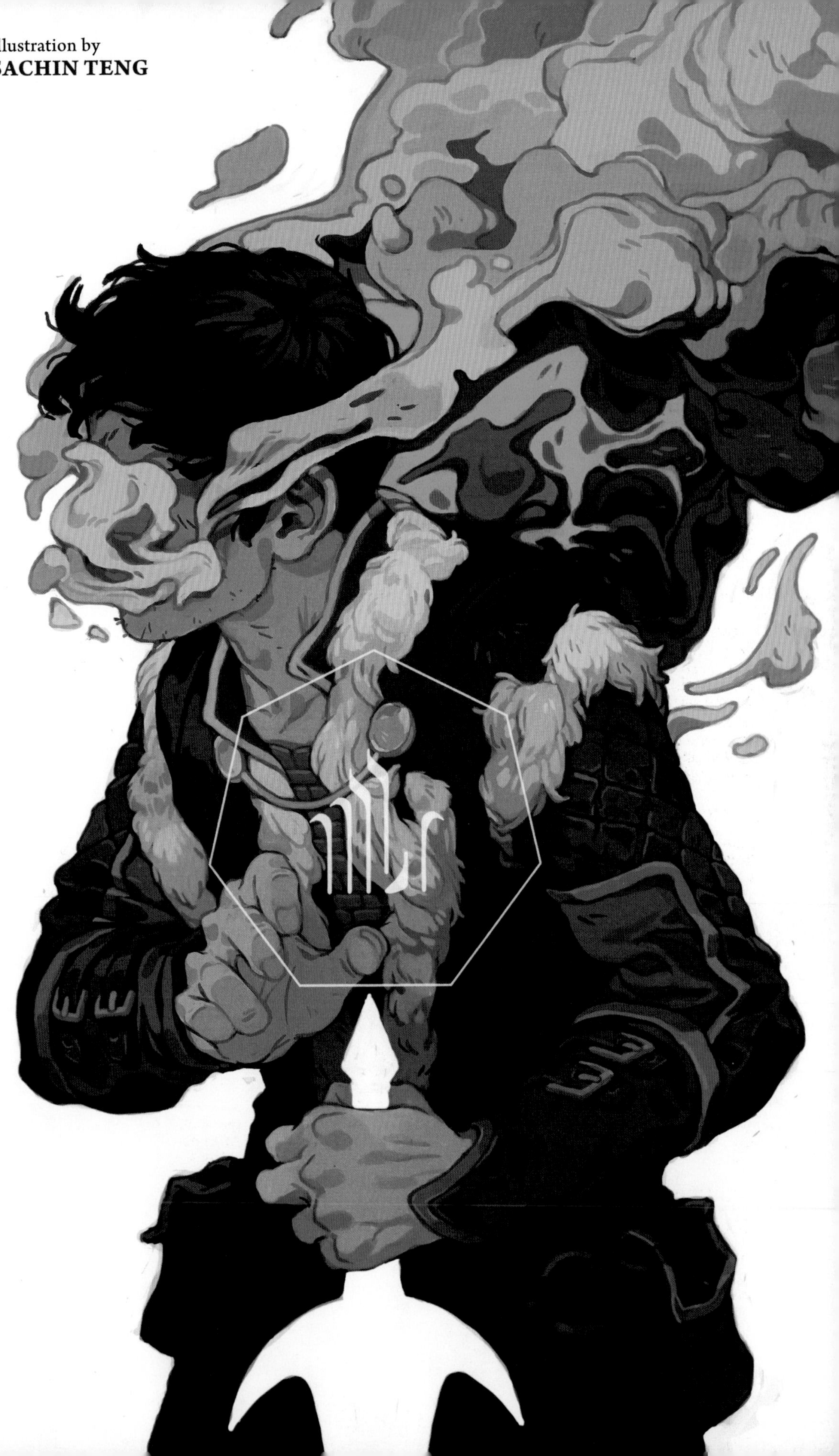

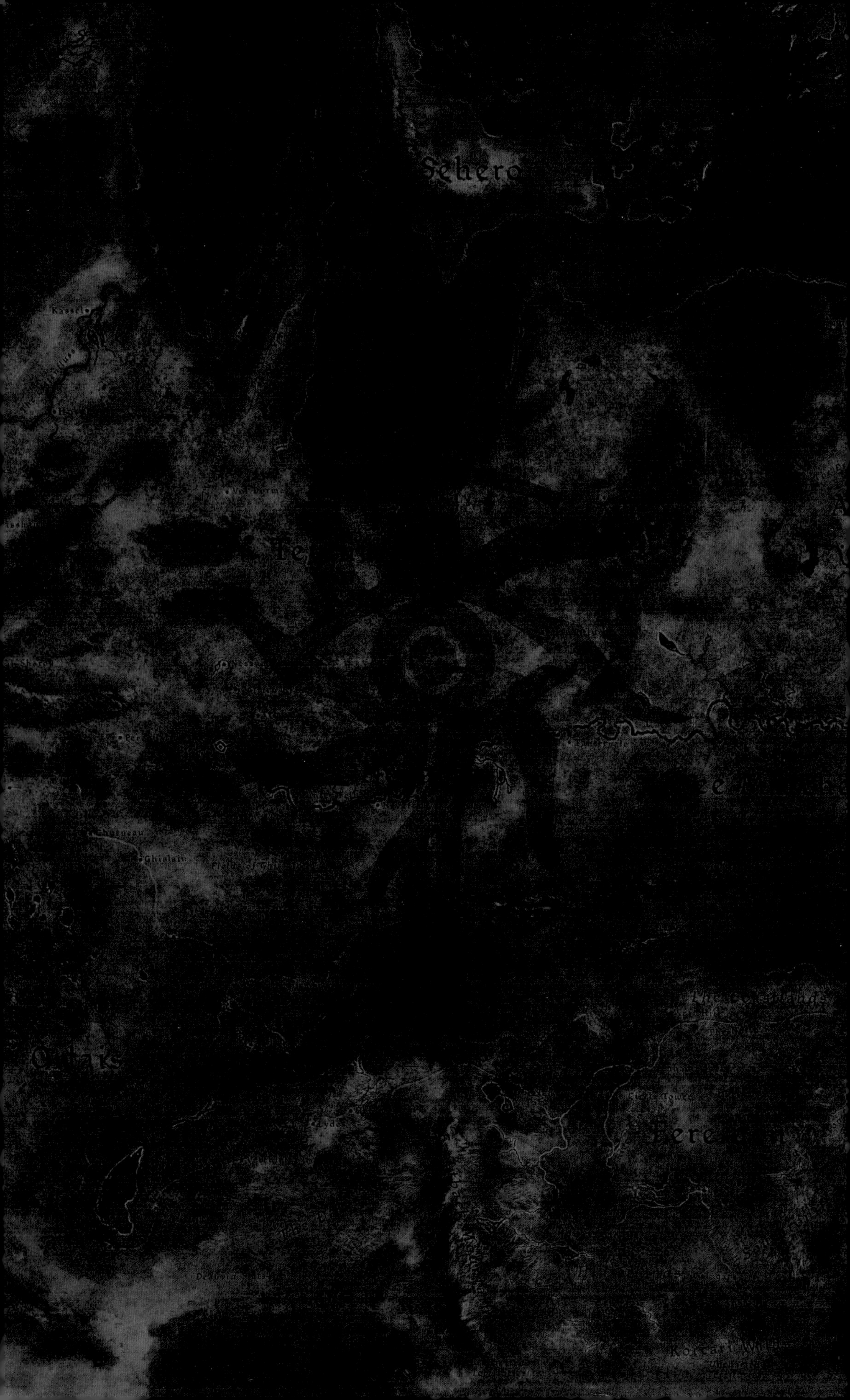

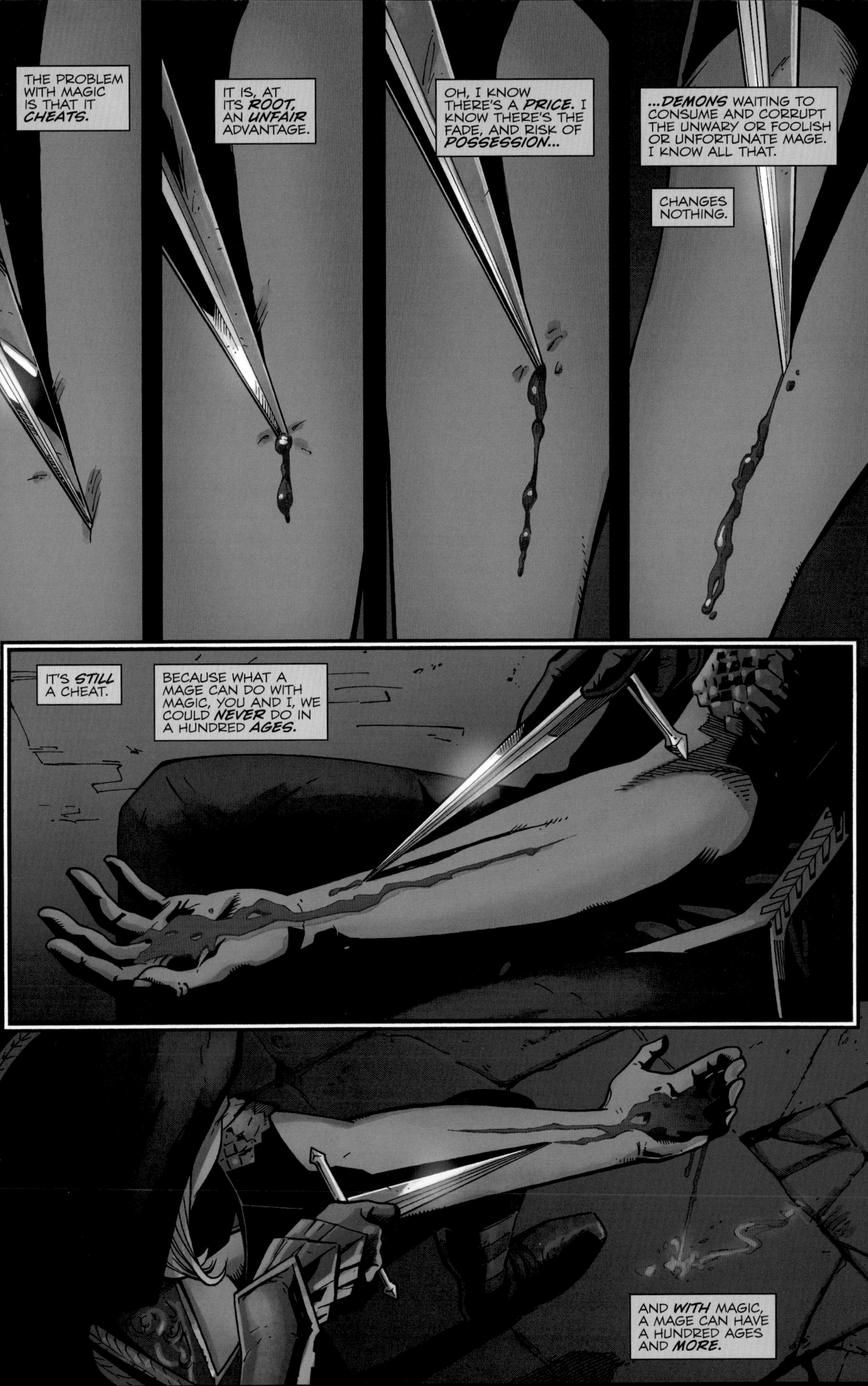
THE PROBLEM WITH MAGIC IS THAT IT CHEATS.
IT IS, AT ITS ROOT, AN UNFAIR ADVANTAGE.
OH, I KNOW THERE'S A PRICE. I KNOW THERE'S THE FADE, AND RISK OF POSSESSION...
...DEMONS WAITING TO CONSUME AND CORRUPT THE UNWARY OR FOOLISH OR UNFORTUNATE MAGE. I KNOW ALL THAT.
CHANGES NOTHING.
IT'S STILL A CHEAT.
BECAUSE WHAT A MAGE CAN DO WITH MAGIC, YOU AND I, WE COULD NEVER DO IN A HUNDRED AGES.
AND WITH MAGIC, A MAGE CAN HAVE A HUNDRED AGES AND MORE.

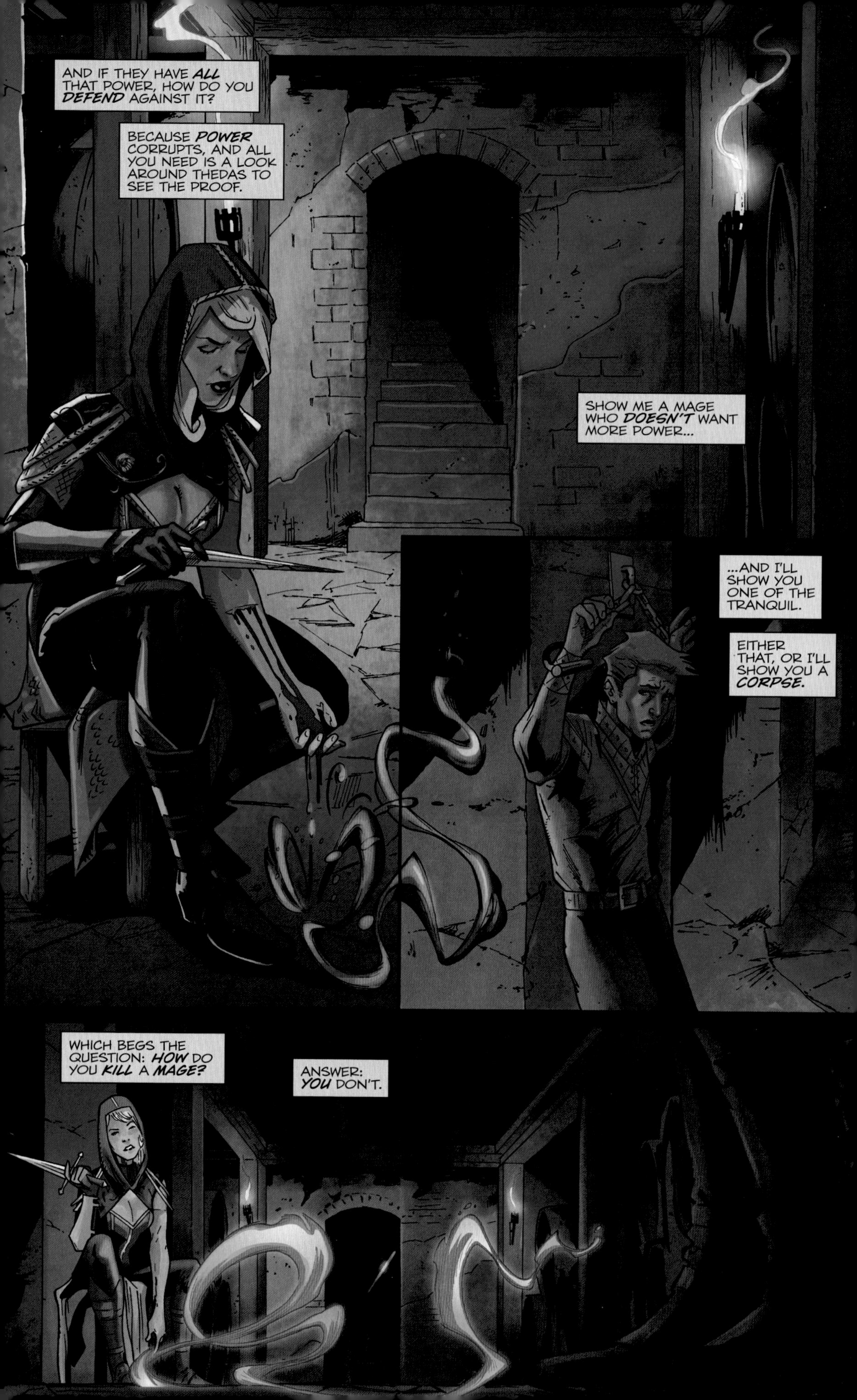
AND IF THEY HAVE ALL THAT POWER, HOW DO YOU DEFEND AGAINST IT?
BECAUSE POWER CORRUPTS, AND ALL YOU NEED IS A LOOK AROUND THEDAS TO SEE THE PROOF.
SHOW ME A MAGE WHO DOESN'T WANT MORE POWER...
...AND I'LL SHOW YOU ONE OF THE TRANQUIL.
EITHER THAT, OR I'LL SHOW YOU A CORPSE.
WHICH BEGS THE QUESTION: HOW DO YOU KILL A MAGE?
ANSWER: YOU DON'T.

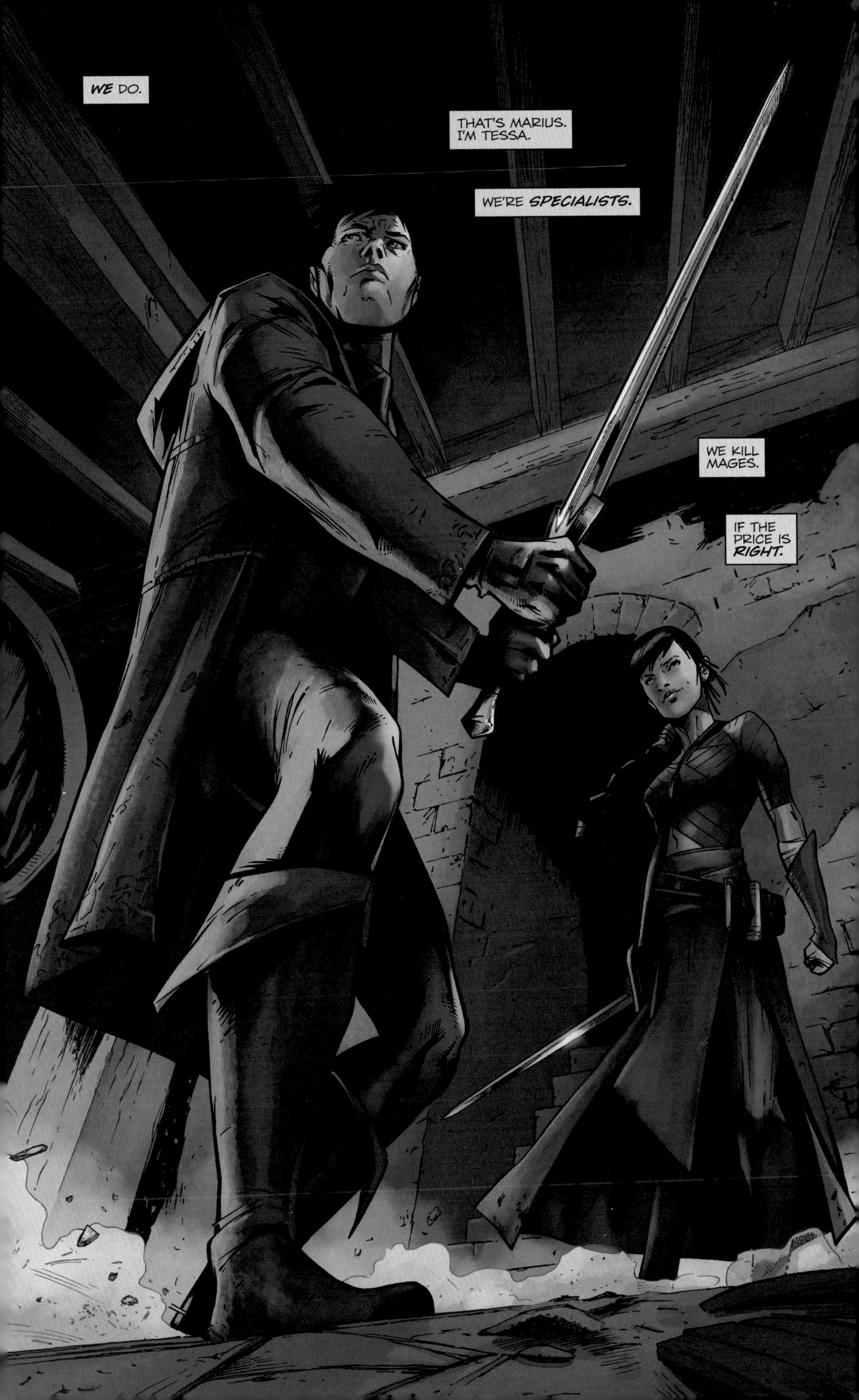
WE DO.
THAT'S MARIUS. I'M TESSA.
WE'RE SPECIALISTS.
WE KILL MAGES.
IF THE PRICE IS RIGHT.

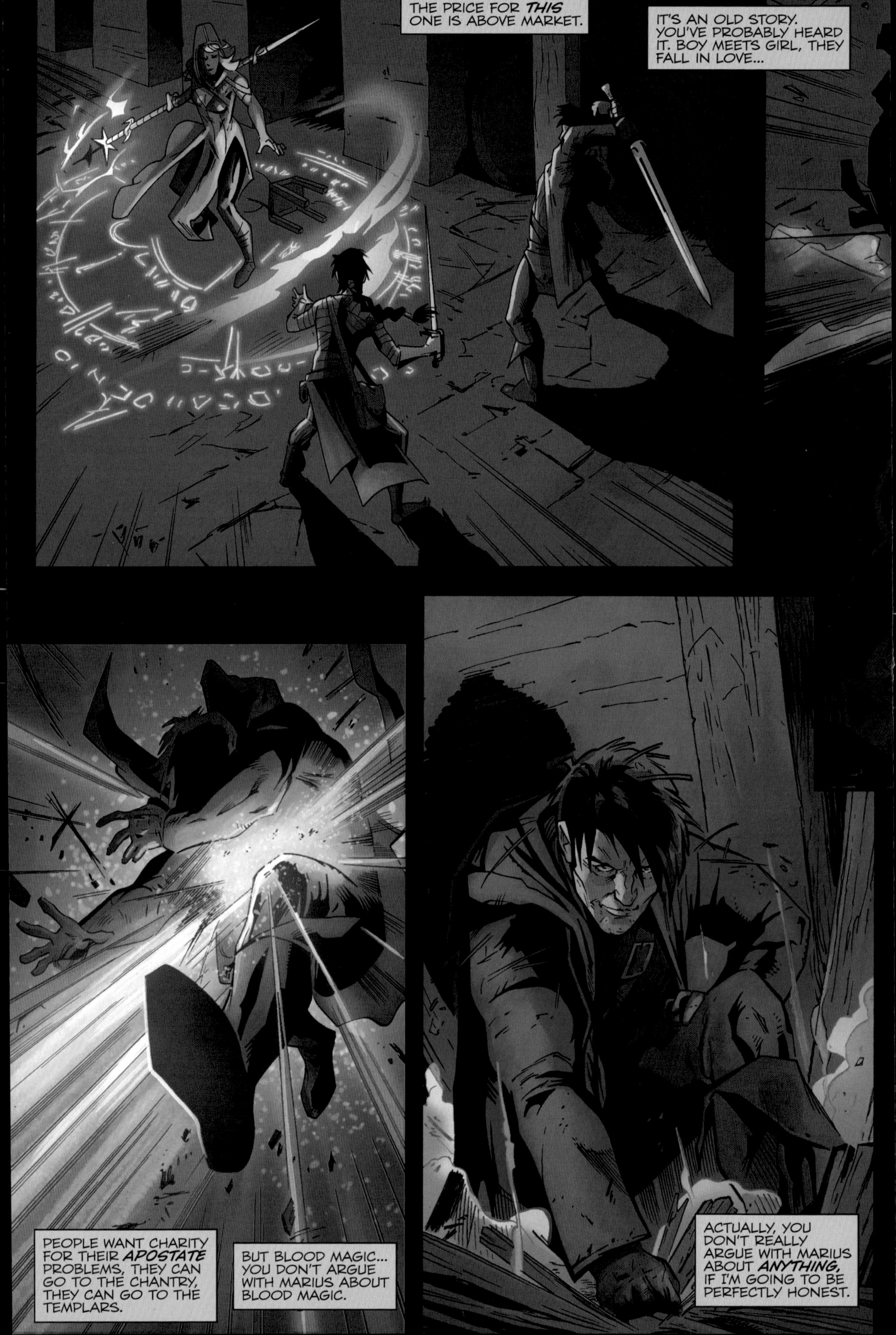

THE PRICE FOR THIS ONE IS ABOVE MARKET.
IT'S AN OLD STORY. YOU'VE PROBABLY HEARD IT. BOY MEETS GIRL, THEY FALL IN LOVE...
PEOPLE WANT CHARITY FOR THEIR APOSTATE PROBLEMS, THEY CAN GO TO THE CHANTRY, THEY CAN GO TO THE TEMPLARS.
BUT BLOOD MAGIC... YOU DON'T ARGUE WITH MARIUS ABOUT BLOOD MAGIC.
ACTUALLY, YOU DON'T REALLY ARGUE WITH MARIUS ABOUT ANYTHING, IF I'M GOING TO BE PERFECTLY HONEST.

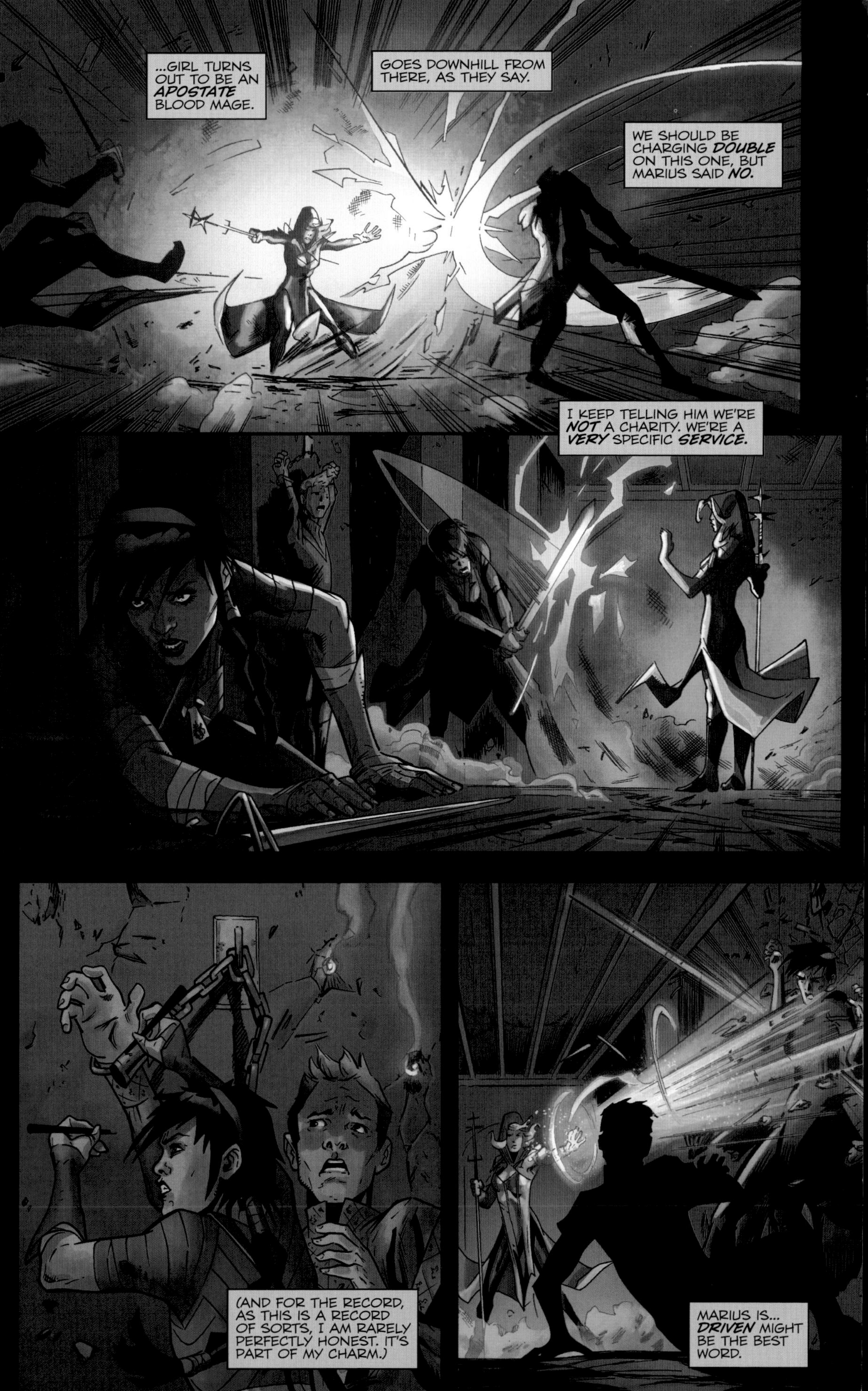

...GIRL TURNS OUT TO BE AN ***APOSTATE*** BLOOD MAGE.
GOES DOWNHILL FROM THERE, AS THEY SAY.
WE SHOULD BE CHARGING ***DOUBLE*** ON THIS ONE, BUT MARIUS SAID ***NO.***
I KEEP TELLING HIM WE'RE ***NOT*** A CHARITY. WE'RE A ***VERY*** SPECIFIC ***SERVICE.***
(AND FOR THE RECORD, AS THIS IS A RECORD OF SORTS, I AM RARELY PERFECTLY HONEST. IT'S PART OF MY CHARM.)
MARIUS IS... ***DRIVEN*** MIGHT BE THE BEST WORD.

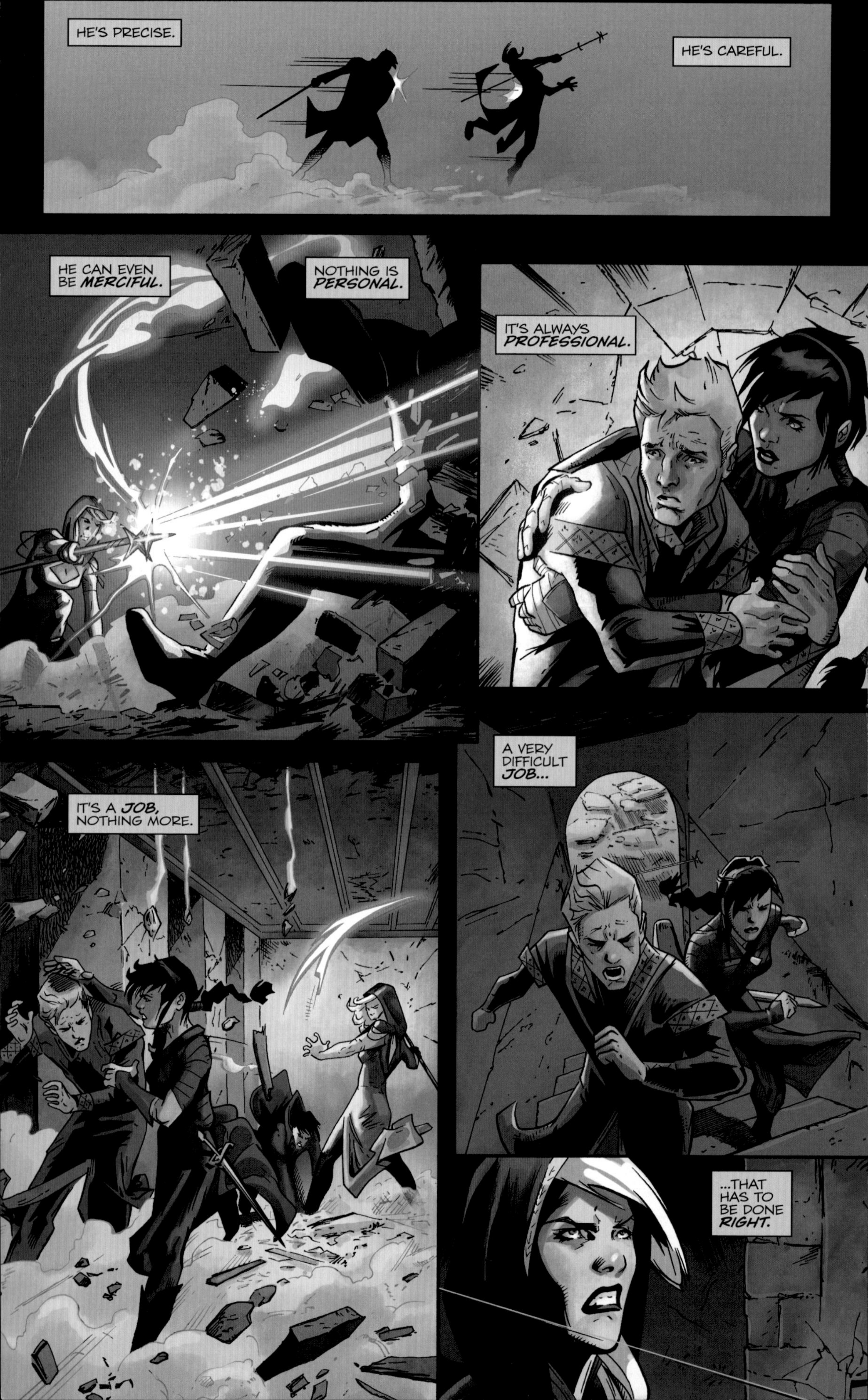
HE'S PRECISE.
HE'S CAREFUL.
HE CAN EVEN BE MERCIFUL.
NOTHING IS PERSONAL.
IT'S ALWAYS PROFESSIONAL.
IT'S A JOB, NOTHING MORE.
A VERY DIFFICULT JOB...
...THAT HAS TO BE DONE RIGHT.

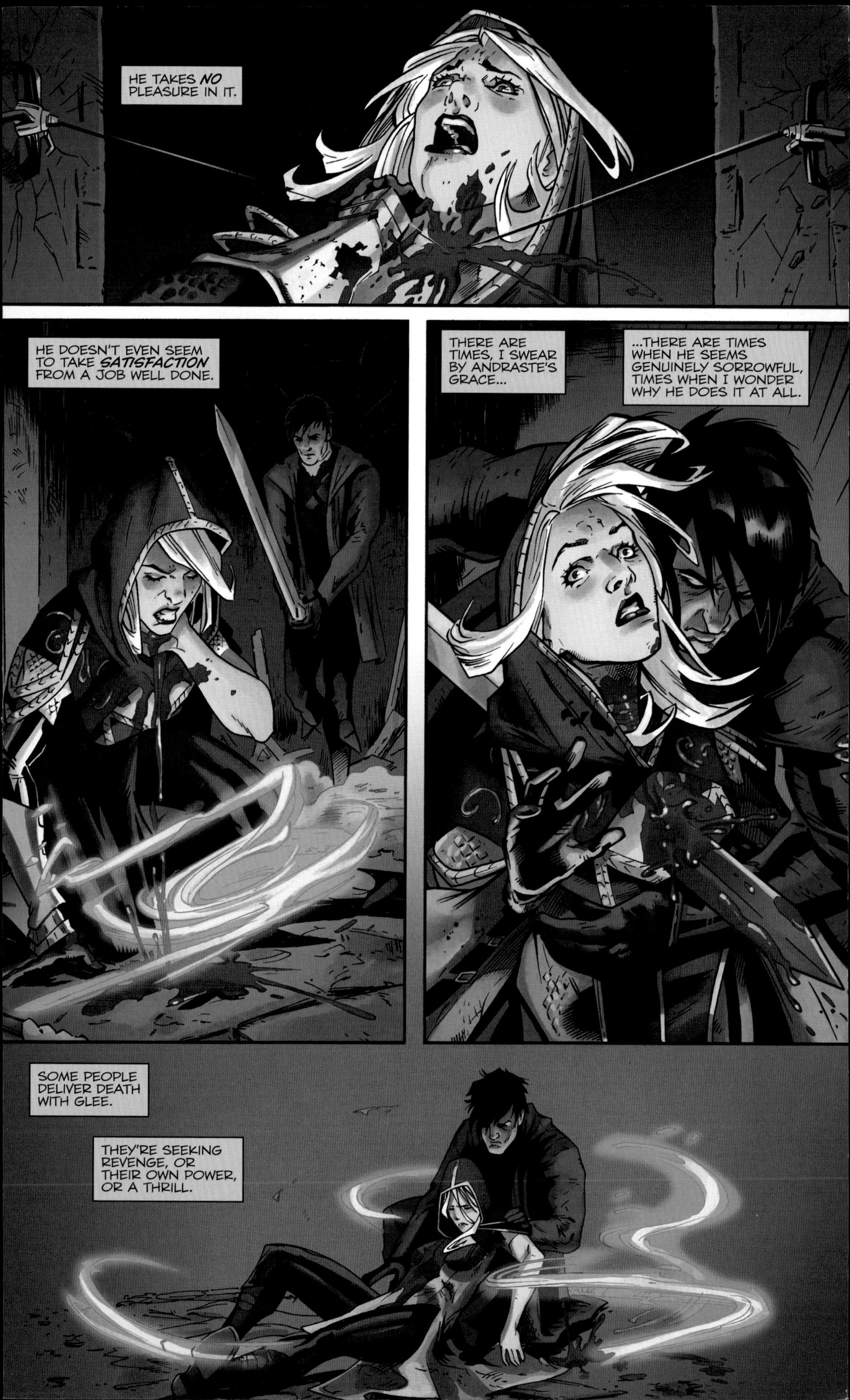
HE TAKES *NO* PLEASURE IN IT.
HE DOESN'T EVEN SEEM TO TAKE ***SATISFACTION*** FROM A JOB WELL DONE.
THERE ARE TIMES, I SWEAR BY ANDRASTE'S GRACE...
...THERE ARE TIMES WHEN HE SEEMS GENUINELY SORROWFUL, TIMES WHEN I WONDER WHY HE DOES IT AT ALL.
SOME PEOPLE DELIVER DEATH WITH GLEE.
THEY'RE SEEKING REVENGE, OR THEIR OWN POWER, OR A THRILL.

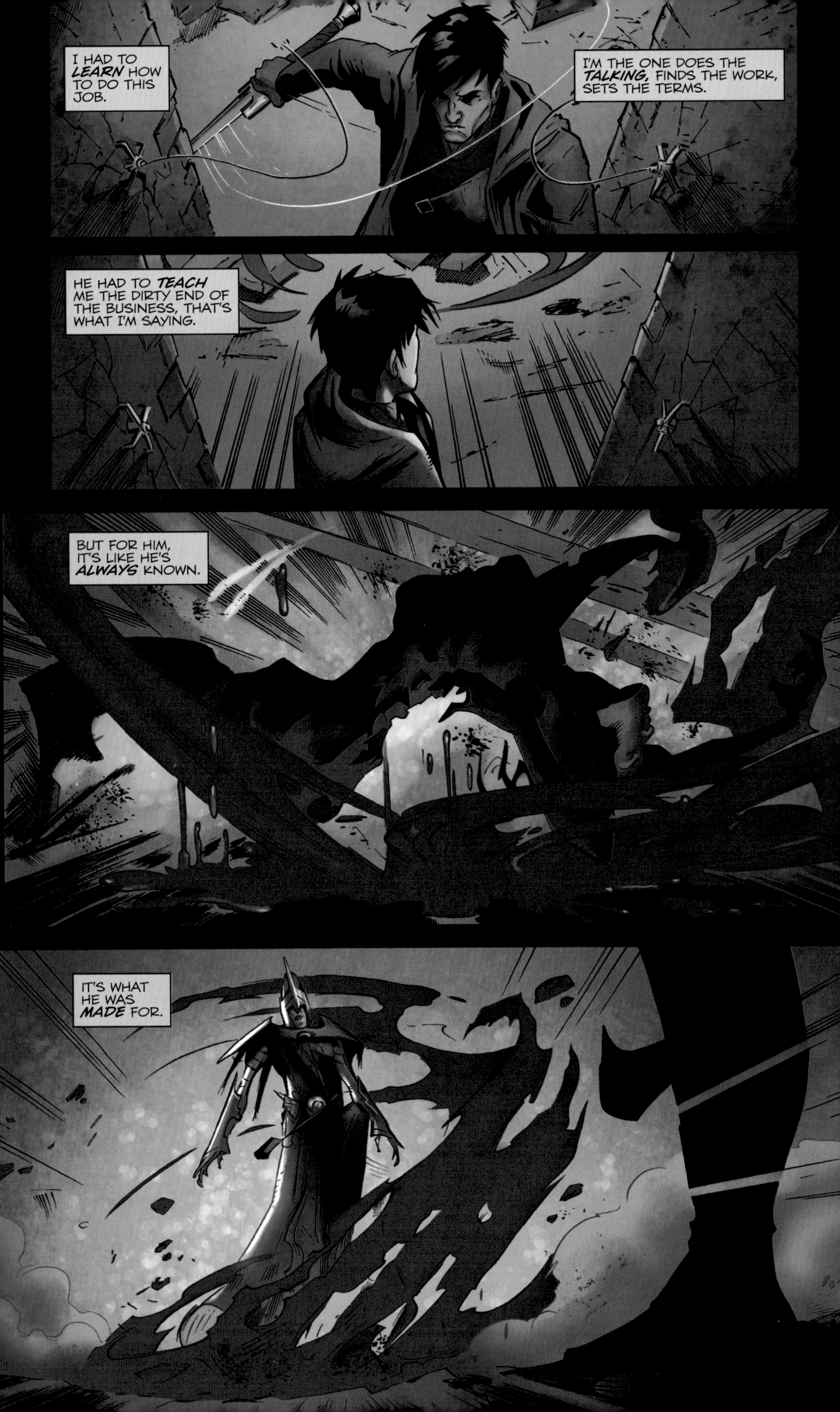
I HAD TO LEARN HOW TO DO THIS JOB.
I'M THE ONE DOES THE TALKING, FINDS THE WORK, SETS THE TERMS.
HE HAD TO TEACH ME THE DIRTY END OF THE BUSINESS, THAT'S WHAT I'M SAYING.
BUT FOR HIM, IT'S LIKE HE'S ALWAYS KNOWN.
IT'S WHAT HE WAS MADE FOR.

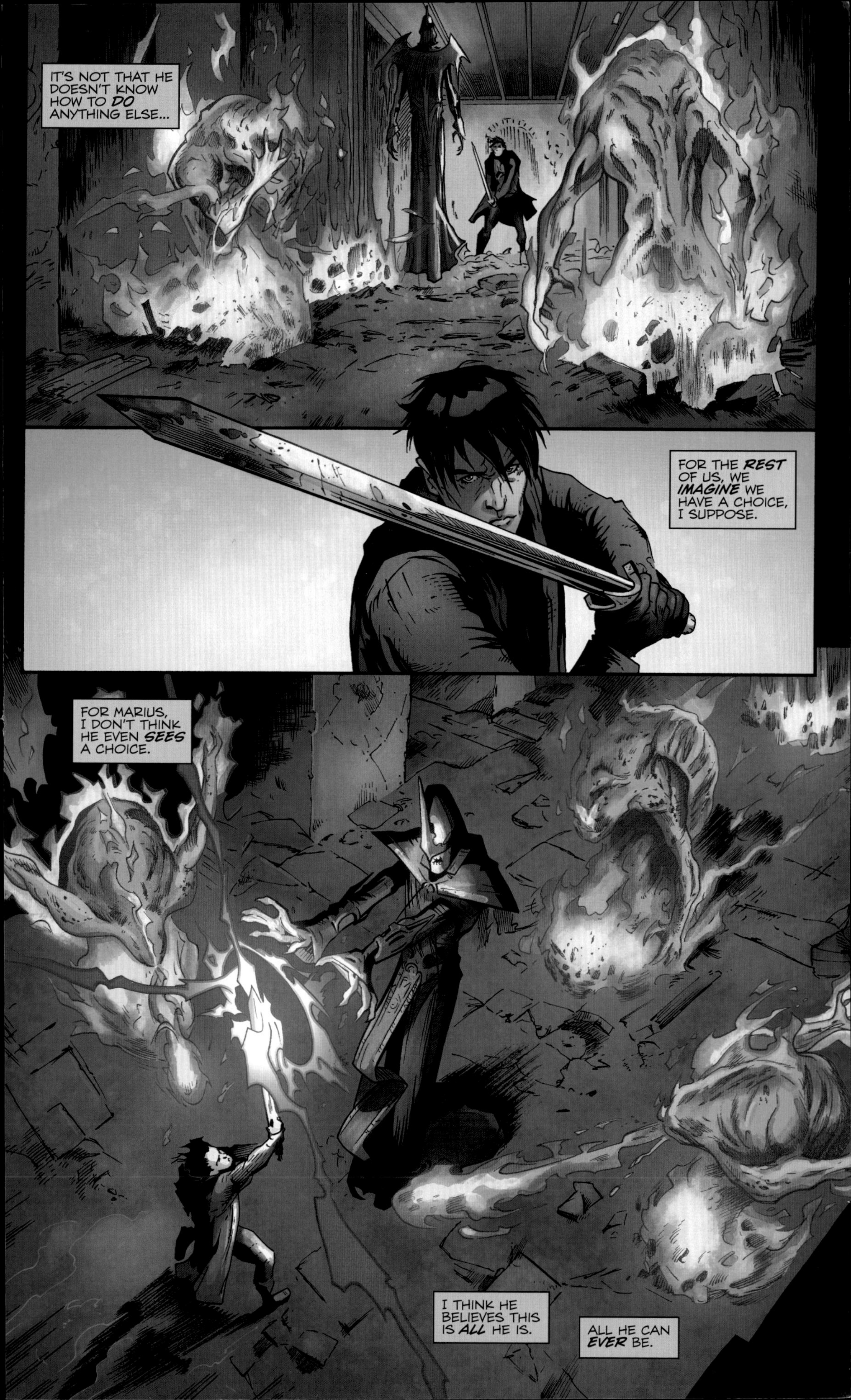
IT'S NOT THAT HE DOESN'T KNOW HOW TO DO ANYTHING ELSE...
FOR THE REST OF US, WE IMAGINE WE HAVE A CHOICE, I SUPPOSE.
FOR MARIUS, I DON'T THINK HE EVEN SEES A CHOICE.
I THINK HE BELIEVES THIS IS ALL HE IS.
ALL HE CAN EVER BE.

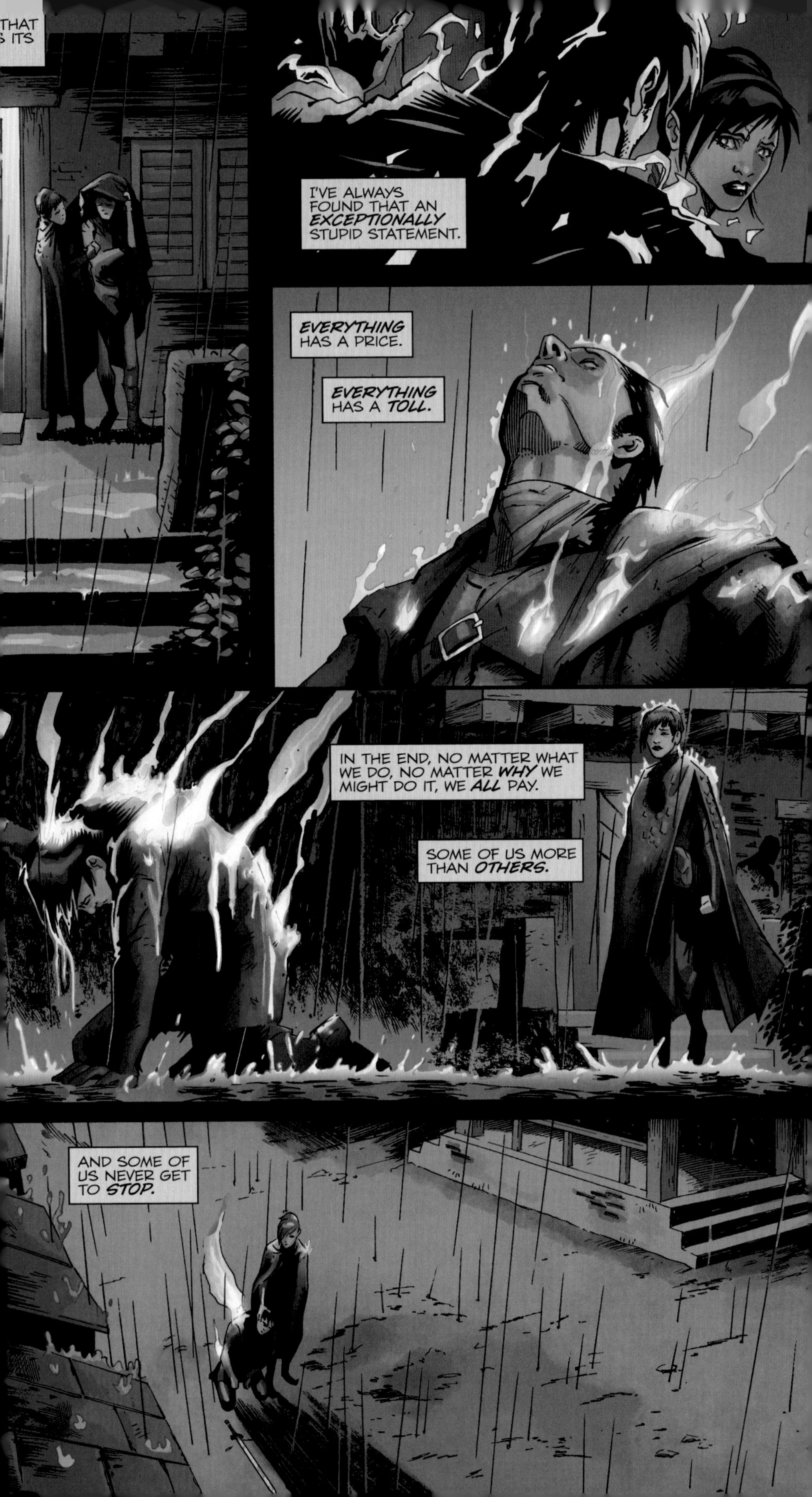
THAT
ITS
I'VE ALWAYS FOUND THAT AN EXCEPTIONALLY STUPID STATEMENT.
EVERYTHING HAS A PRICE.
EVERYTHING HAS A TOLL.
IN THE END, NO MATTER WHAT WE DO, NO MATTER WHY WE MIGHT DO IT, WE ALL PAY.
SOME OF US MORE THAN OTHERS.
AND SOME OF US NEVER GET TO STOP.

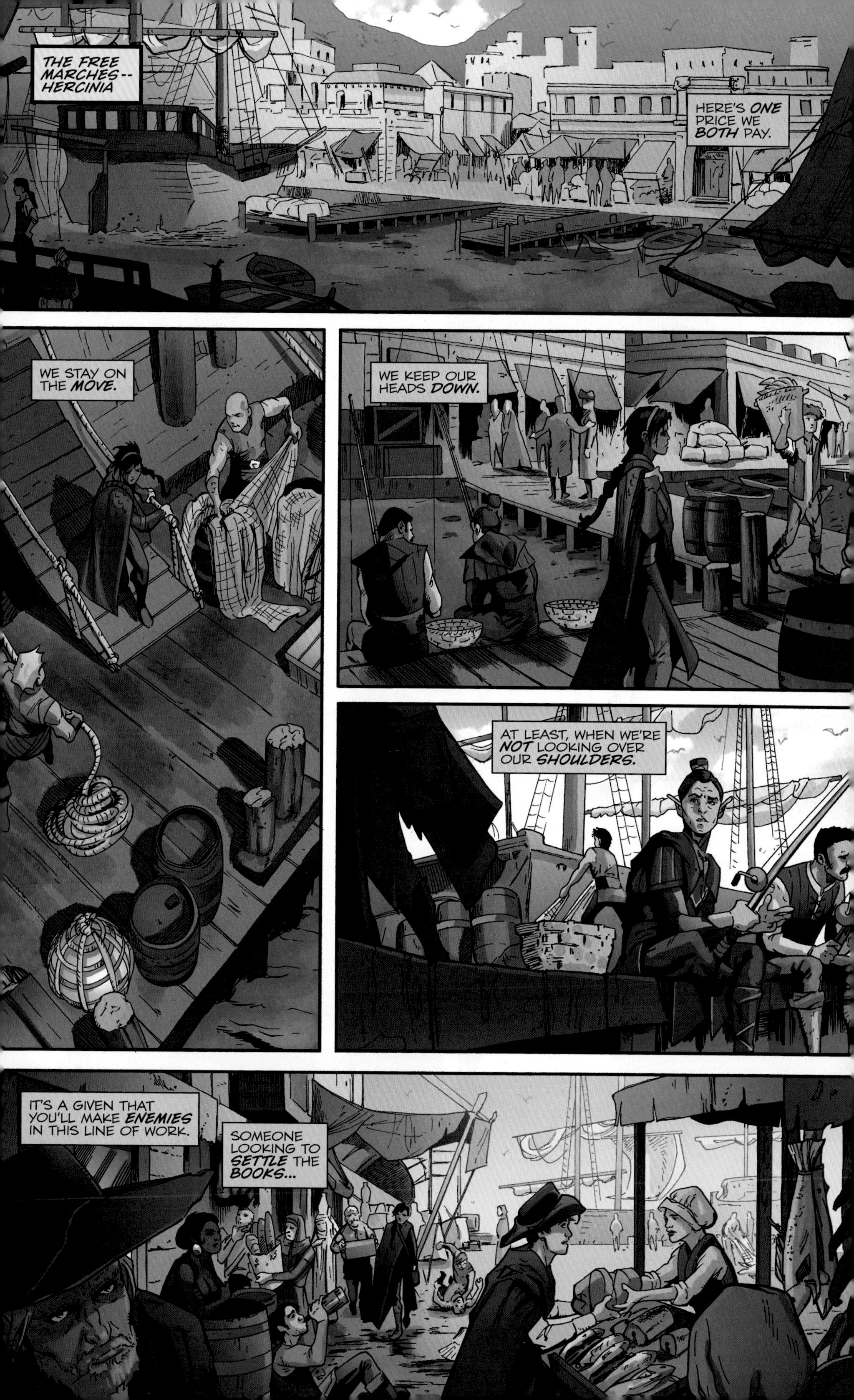
THE FREE MARCHES--HERCINIA
HERE'S ONE PRICE WE BOTH PAY.
WE STAY ON THE MOVE.
WE KEEP OUR HEADS DOWN.
AT LEAST, WHEN WE'RE NOT LOOKING OVER OUR SHOULDERS.
IT'S A GIVEN THAT YOU'LL MAKE ENEMIES IN THIS LINE OF WORK.
SOMEONE LOOKING TO SETTLE THE BOOKS...

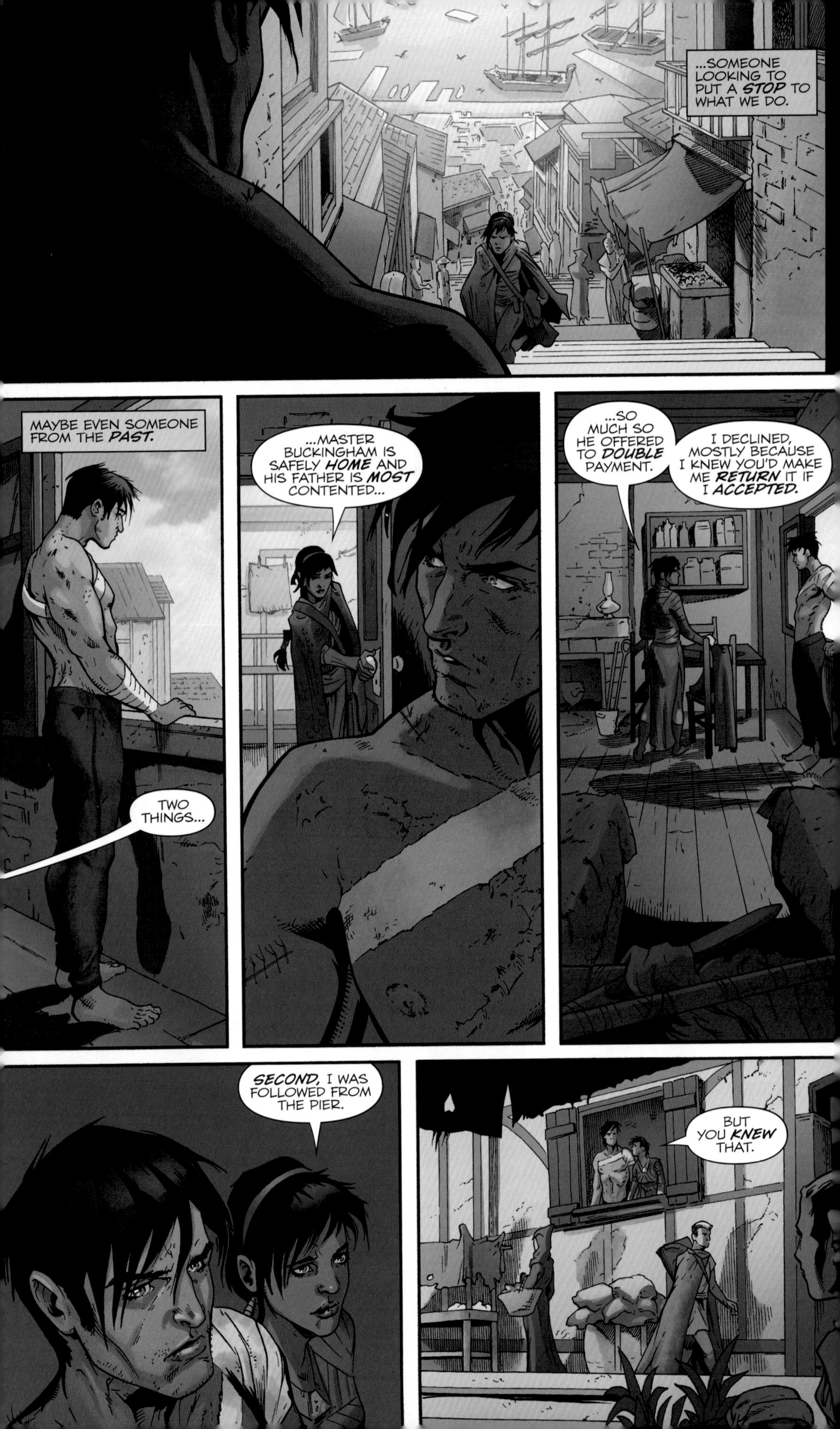
...SOMEONE LOOKING TO PUT A STOP TO WHAT WE DO.
MAYBE EVEN SOMEONE FROM THE PAST.
TWO THINGS...
...MASTER BUCKINGHAM IS SAFELY HOME AND HIS FATHER IS MOST CONTENTED...
...SO MUCH SO HE OFFERED TO DOUBLE PAYMENT.
I DECLINED, MOSTLY BECAUSE I KNEW YOU'D MAKE ME RETURN IT IF I ACCEPTED.
SECOND, I WAS FOLLOWED FROM THE PIER.
BUT YOU KNEW THAT.

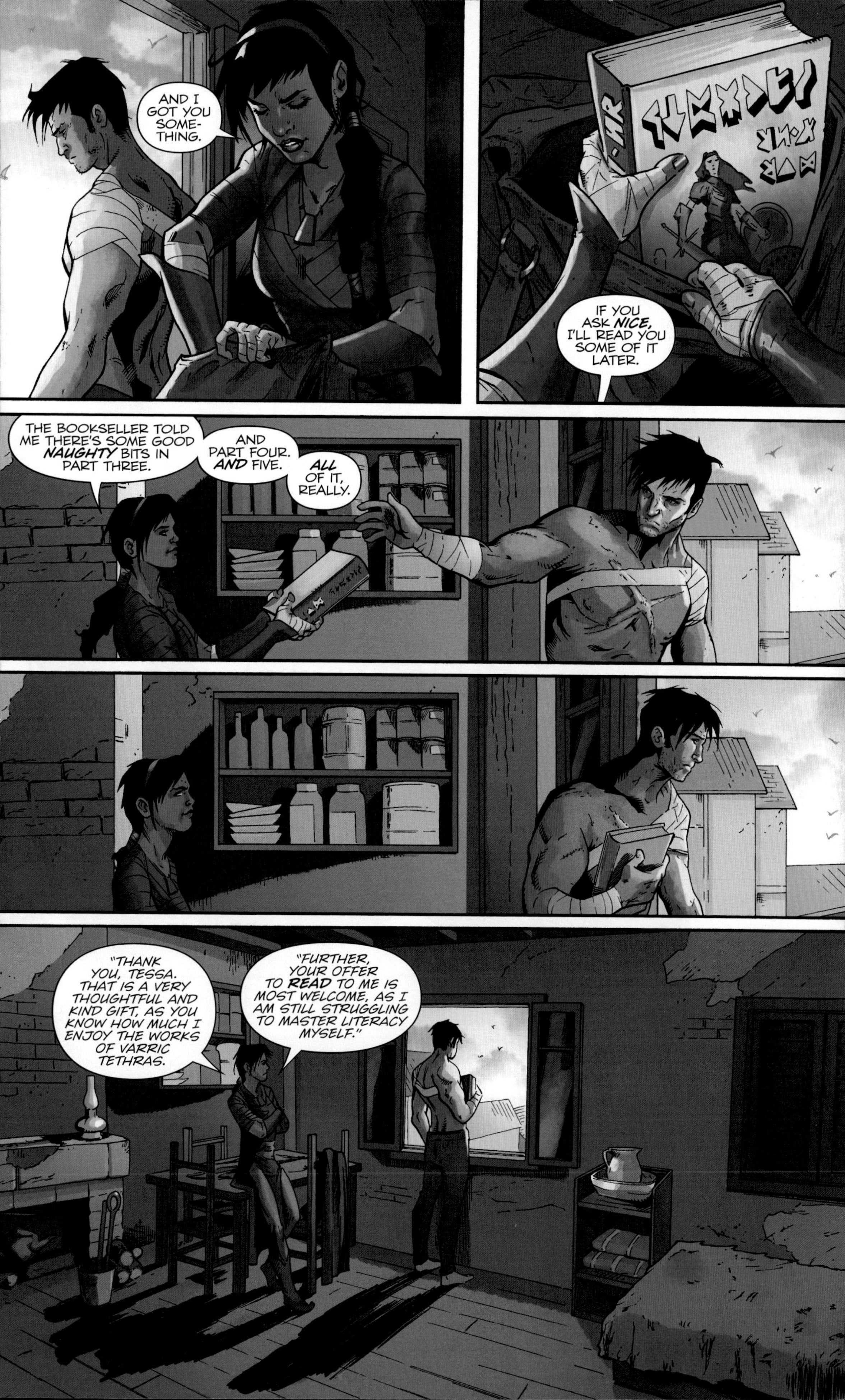
AND I GOT YOU SOME-THING.
IF YOU ASK NICE, I'LL READ YOU SOME OF IT LATER.
THE BOOKSELLER TOLD ME THERE'S SOME GOOD NAUGHTY BITS IN PART THREE.
AND PART FOUR. AND FIVE.
ALL OF IT, REALLY.
"THANK YOU, TESSA. THAT IS A VERY THOUGHTFUL AND KIND GIFT, AS YOU KNOW HOW MUCH I ENJOY THE WORKS OF VARRIC TETHRAS.
"FURTHER, YOUR OFFER TO READ TO ME IS MOST WELCOME, AS I AM STILL STRUGGLING TO MASTER LITERACY MYSELF."

WHY, THINK NOTHING OF IT, MARIUS, MY FRIEND!

I SAW IT FOR SALE AND THOUGHT IMMEDIATELY OF YOU.

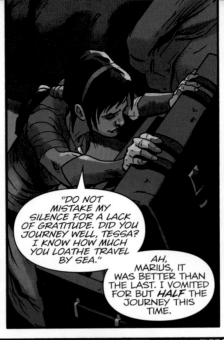

"DO NOT MISTAKE MY SILENCE FOR A LACK OF GRATITUDE. DID YOU JOURNEY WELL, TESSA? I KNOW HOW MUCH YOU LOATHE TRAVEL BY SEA."

AH, MARIUS, IT WAS BETTER THAN THE LAST. I VOMITED FOR BUT *HALF* THE JOURNEY THIS TIME.

"I'M SORRY TO HEAR THAT, TESSA..."

"...MAYHAPS YOU WOULD LIKE SOMETHING TO SETTLE YOUR STOMACH? I SHALL ASK VEYNA TO BRING US SOME BROTH."

THAT'S VERY KIND OF YOU, MARIUS, BUT I THINK I'M ALL RIGHT...

...AND AS IT IS, I BELIEVE WE'RE ABOUT TO HAVE *COMPANY.*

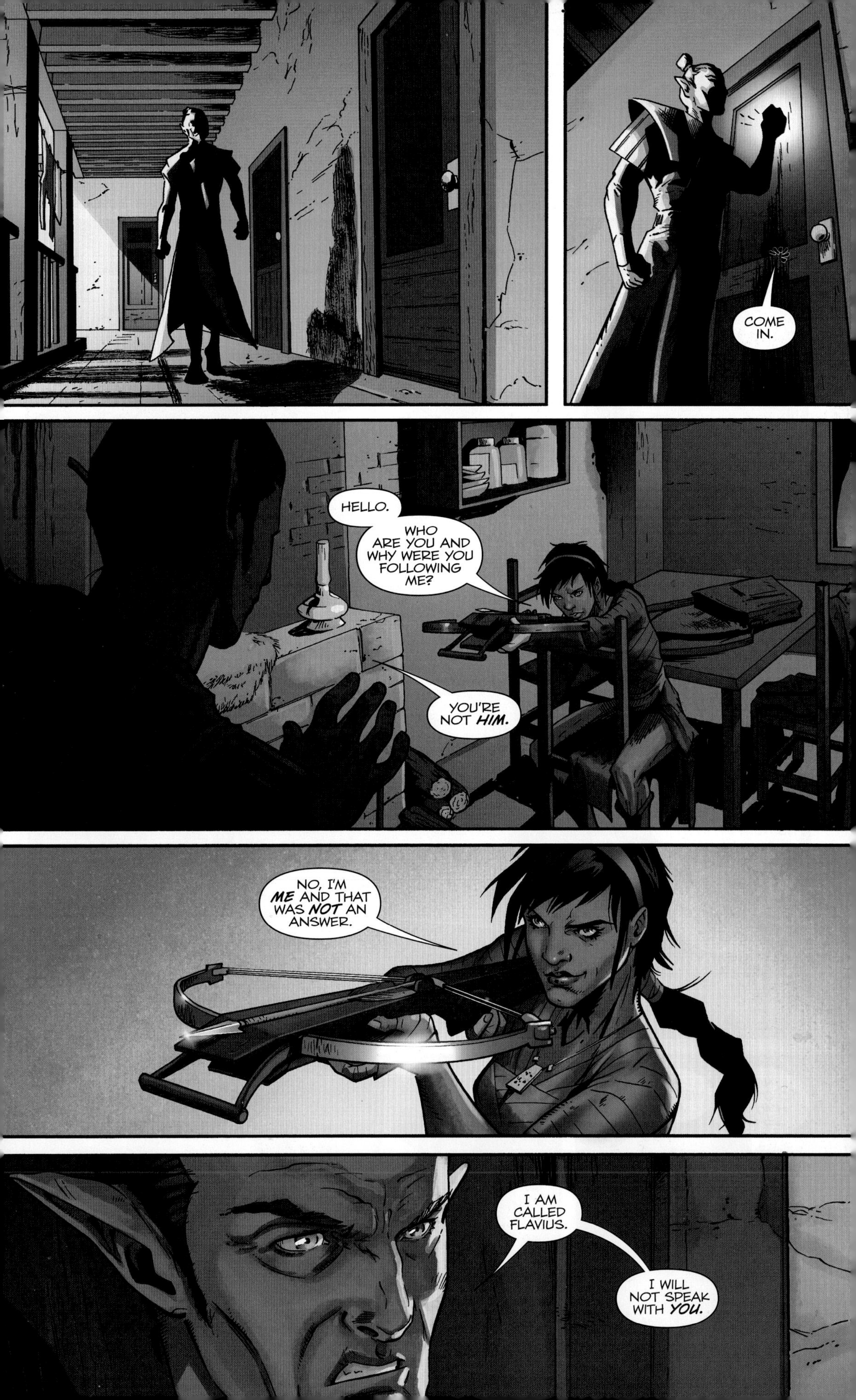
COME IN.
HELLO.
WHO ARE YOU AND WHY WERE YOU FOLLOWING ME?
YOU'RE NOT *HIM.*
NO, I'M *ME* AND THAT WAS *NOT* AN ANSWER.
I AM CALLED FLAVIUS.
I WILL NOT SPEAK WITH *YOU.*

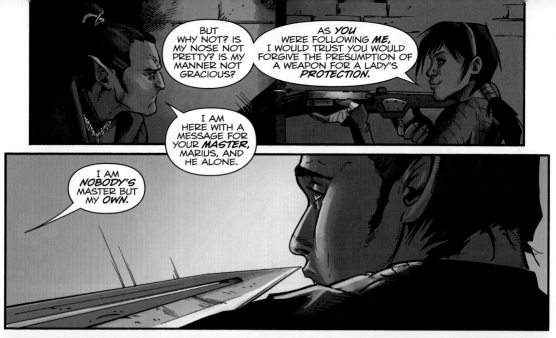

BUT WHY NOT? IS MY NOSE NOT PRETTY? IS MY MANNER NOT GRACIOUS?

AS *YOU* WERE FOLLOWING *ME*, I WOULD TRUST YOU WOULD FORGIVE THE PRESUMPTION OF A WEAPON FOR A LADY'S *PROTECTION*.

I AM HERE WITH A MESSAGE FOR YOUR *MASTER*, MARIUS, AND HE ALONE.

I AM *NOBODY'S* MASTER BUT MY *OWN*.

I KEEP NO SLAVES, AND DO NOT SUFFER THOSE WHO *DO*.

TO SOME, A LIFE IN SERVICE IS NEITHER INSULT NOR *SHAME*.

YOU WILL PARDON ME IF I HAVE CAUSED OFFENSE. THAT WAS *NEVER* MY INTENT.

NOT TO OFFEND *HIM*, AT LEAST.

SHALL WE TRY THIS AGAIN?

PERHAPS THAT MIGHT BE FOR THE BEST.

I COME WITH AN OFFER OF WORK. IN TRUTH, I COME WITH A *PLEA* FOR *HELP* FROM MY *OWN* MASTER.

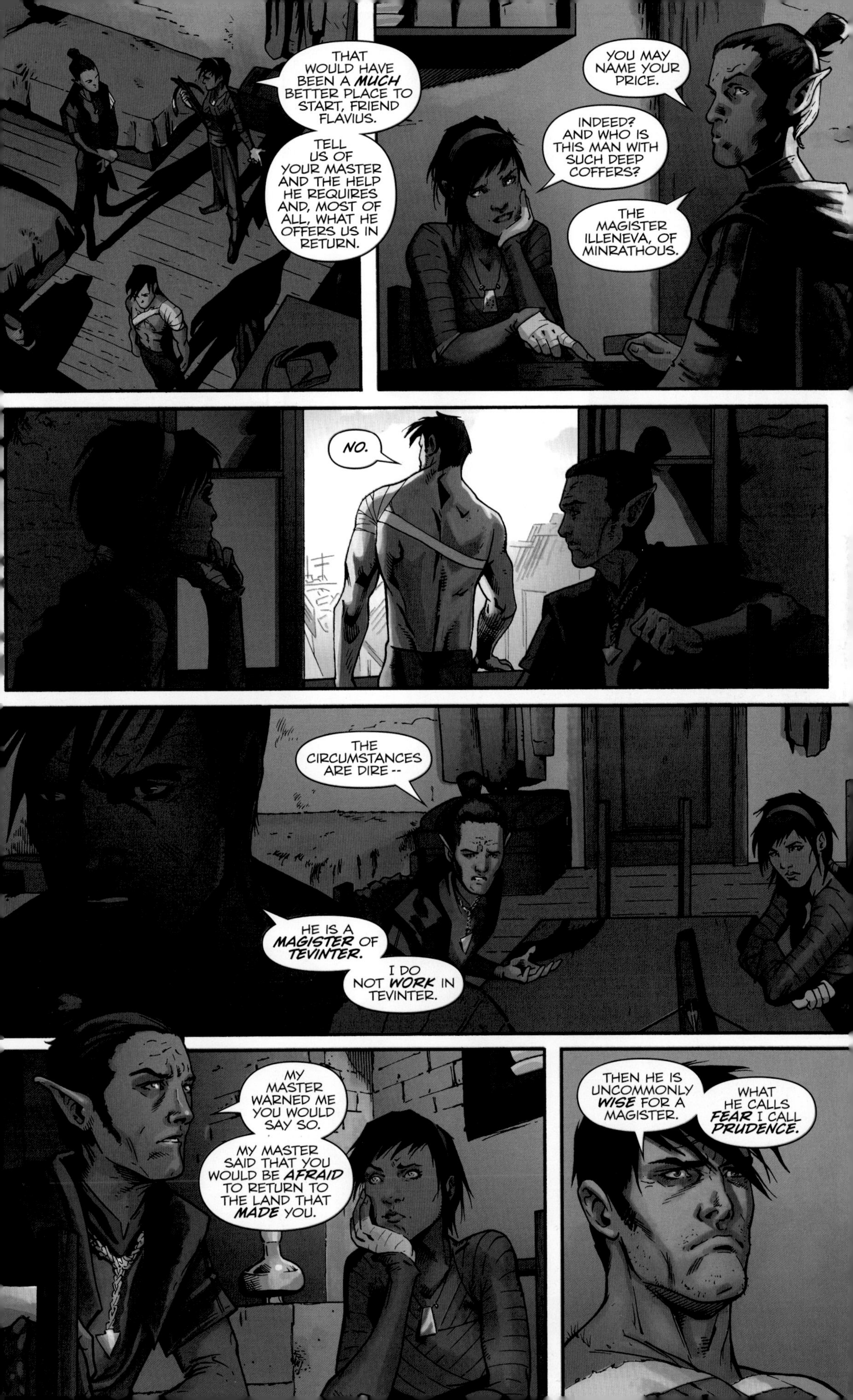
THAT WOULD HAVE BEEN A MUCH BETTER PLACE TO START, FRIEND FLAVIUS.
TELL US OF YOUR MASTER AND THE HELP HE REQUIRES AND, MOST OF ALL, WHAT HE OFFERS US IN RETURN.
YOU MAY NAME YOUR PRICE.
INDEED? AND WHO IS THIS MAN WITH SUCH DEEP COFFERS?
THE MAGISTER ILLENEVA, OF MINRATHOUS.
NO.
THE CIRCUMSTANCES ARE DIRE --
HE IS A MAGISTER OF TEVINTER.
I DO NOT WORK IN TEVINTER.
MY MASTER WARNED ME YOU WOULD SAY SO.
MY MASTER SAID THAT YOU WOULD BE AFRAID TO RETURN TO THE LAND THAT MADE YOU.
THEN HE IS UNCOMMONLY WISE FOR A MAGISTER.
WHAT HE CALLS FEAR I CALL PRUDENCE.

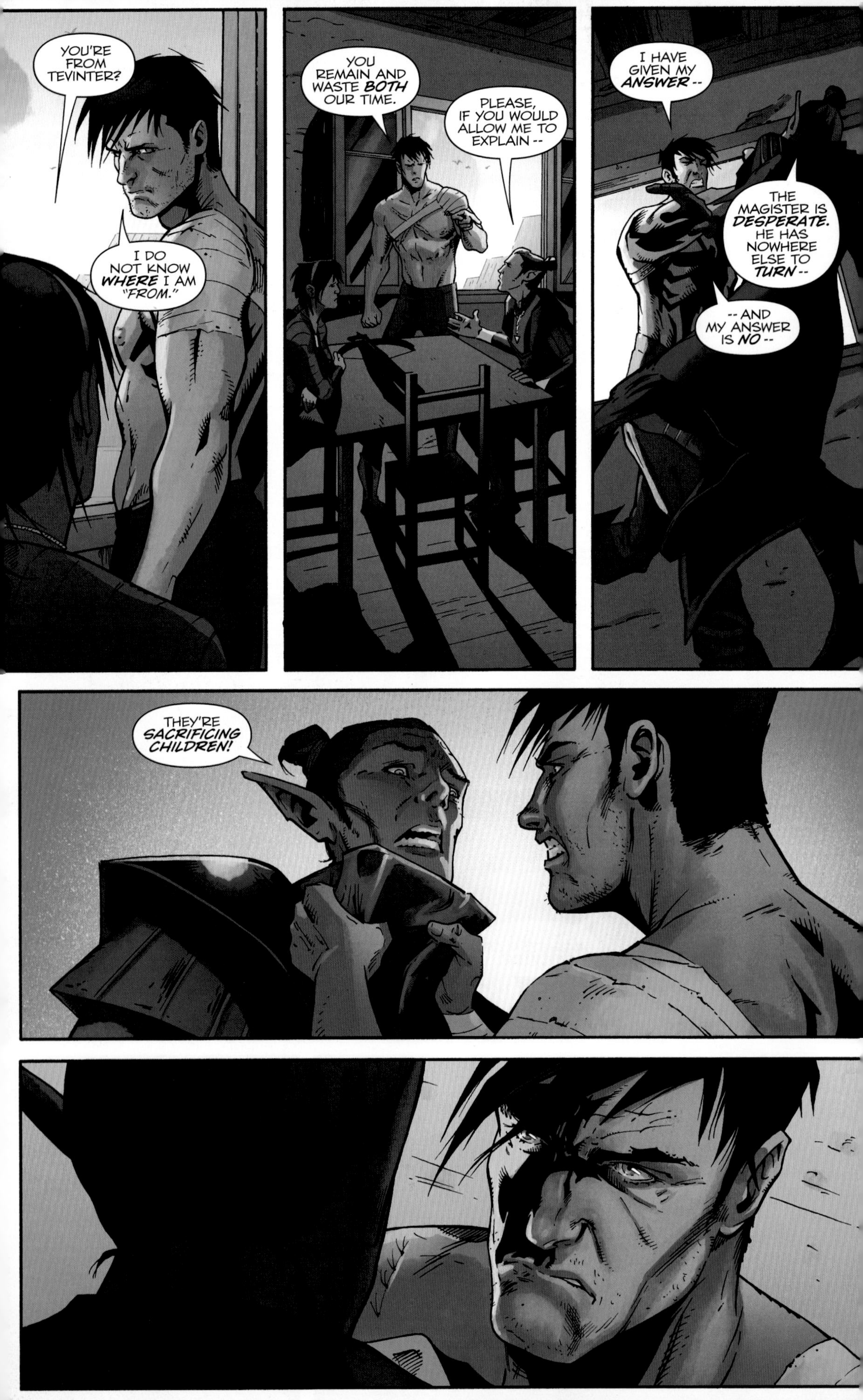
YOU'RE FROM TEVINTER?
I DO NOT KNOW WHERE I AM "FROM."
YOU REMAIN AND WASTE BOTH OUR TIME.
PLEASE, IF YOU WOULD ALLOW ME TO EXPLAIN --
I HAVE GIVEN MY ANSWER --
THE MAGISTER IS DESPERATE. HE HAS NOWHERE ELSE TO TURN --
-- AND MY ANSWER IS NO --
THEY'RE SACRIFICING CHILDREN!

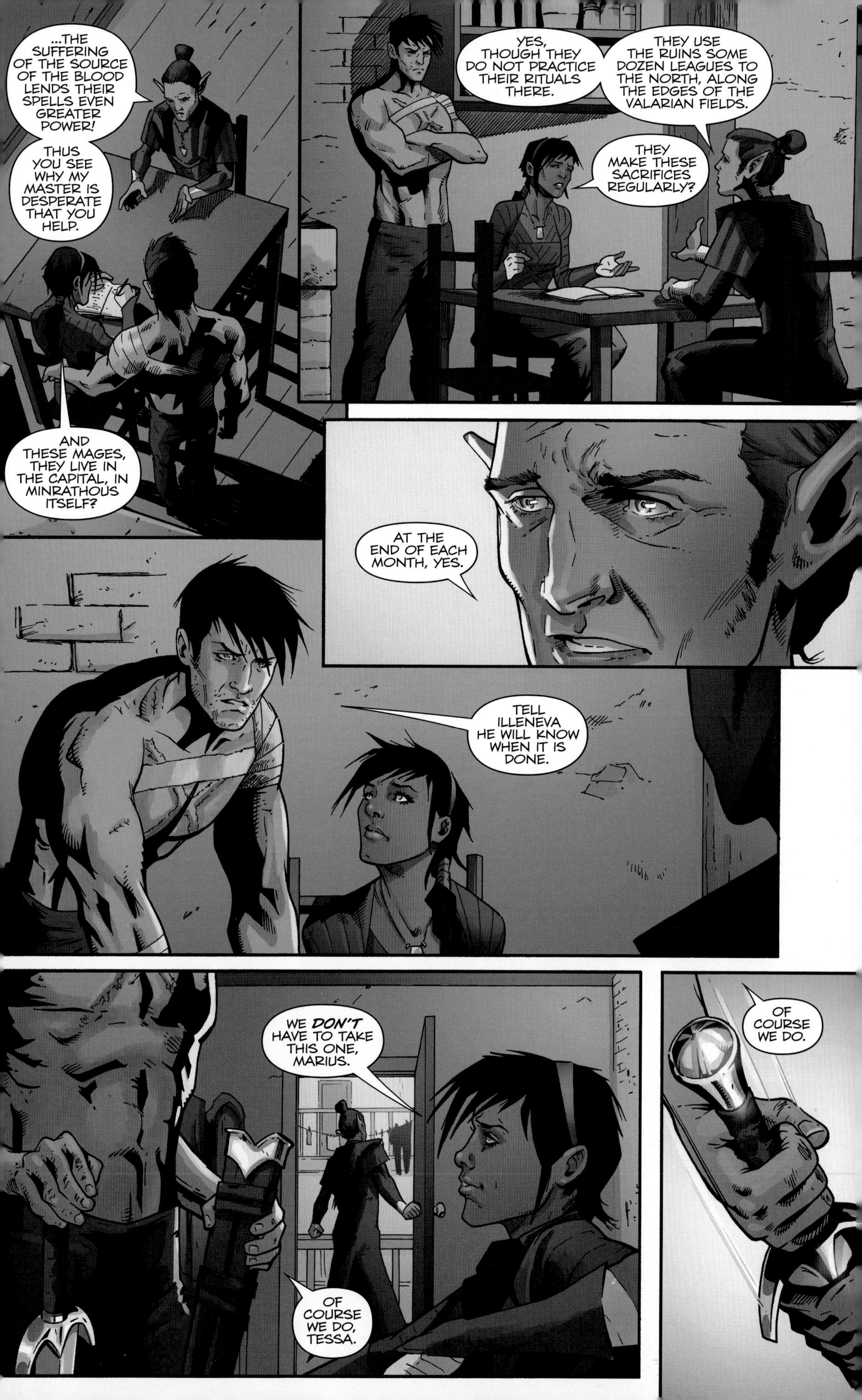
...THE SUFFERING OF THE SOURCE OF THE BLOOD LENDS THEIR SPELLS EVEN GREATER POWER!
THUS YOU SEE WHY MY MASTER IS DESPERATE THAT YOU HELP.
AND THESE MAGES, THEY LIVE IN THE CAPITAL, IN MINRATHOUS ITSELF?
YES, THOUGH THEY DO NOT PRACTICE THEIR RITUALS THERE.
THEY USE THE RUINS SOME DOZEN LEAGUES TO THE NORTH, ALONG THE EDGES OF THE VALARIAN FIELDS.
THEY MAKE THESE SACRIFICES REGULARLY?
AT THE END OF EACH MONTH, YES.
TELL ILLENEVA HE WILL KNOW WHEN IT IS DONE.
WE DON'T HAVE TO TAKE THIS ONE, MARIUS.
OF COURSE WE DO, TESSA.
OF COURSE WE DO.

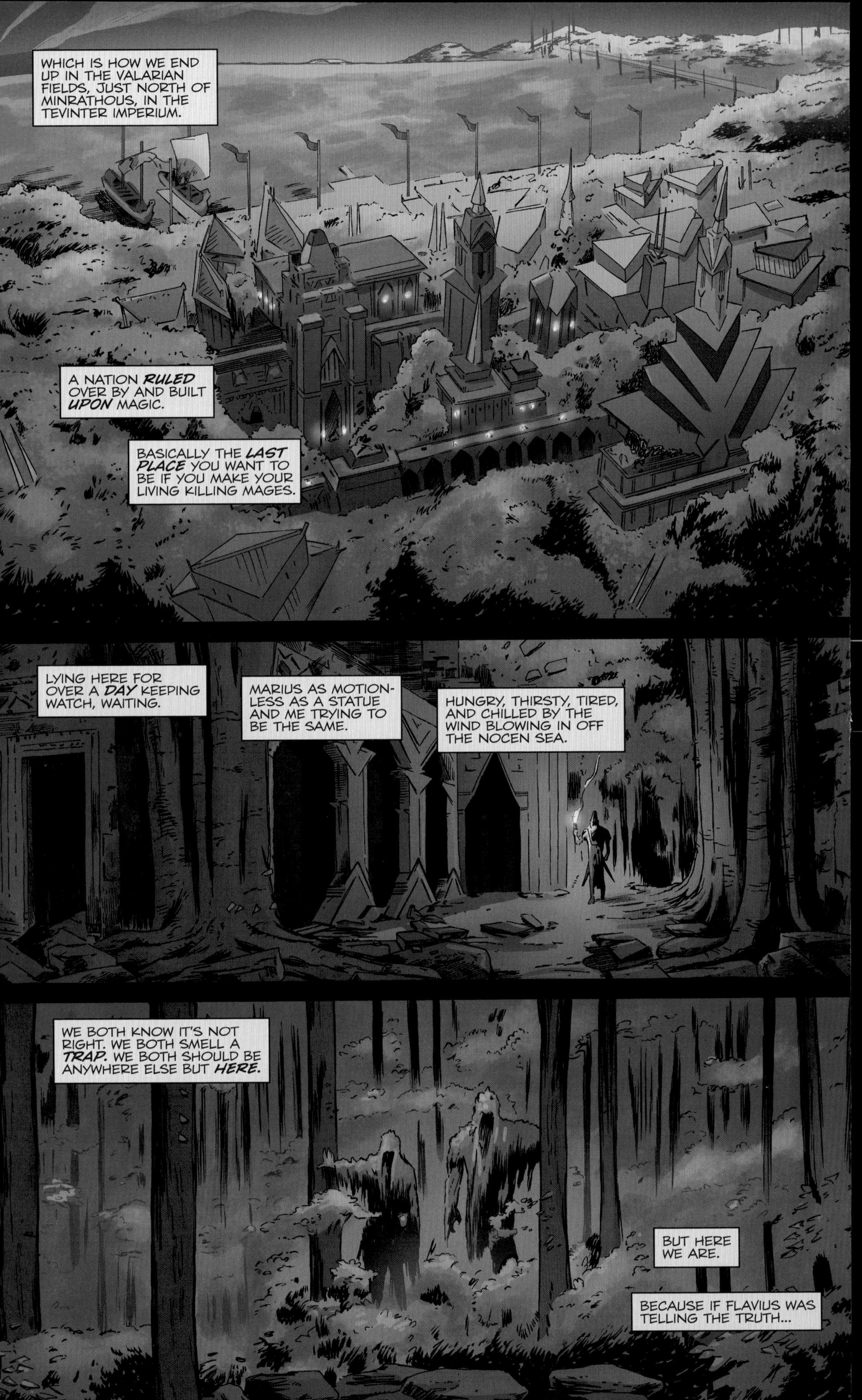
WHICH IS HOW WE END UP IN THE VALARIAN FIELDS, JUST NORTH OF MINRATHOUS, IN THE TEVINTER IMPERIUM.
A NATION RULED OVER BY AND BUILT UPON MAGIC.
BASICALLY THE LAST PLACE YOU WANT TO BE IF YOU MAKE YOUR LIVING KILLING MAGES.
LYING HERE FOR OVER A DAY KEEPING WATCH, WAITING.
MARIUS AS MOTIONLESS AS A STATUE AND ME TRYING TO BE THE SAME.
HUNGRY, THIRSTY, TIRED, AND CHILLED BY THE WIND BLOWING IN OFF THE NOCEN SEA.
WE BOTH KNOW IT'S NOT RIGHT. WE BOTH SMELL A TRAP. WE BOTH SHOULD BE ANYWHERE ELSE BUT HERE.
BUT HERE WE ARE.
BECAUSE IF FLAVIUS WAS TELLING THE TRUTH...

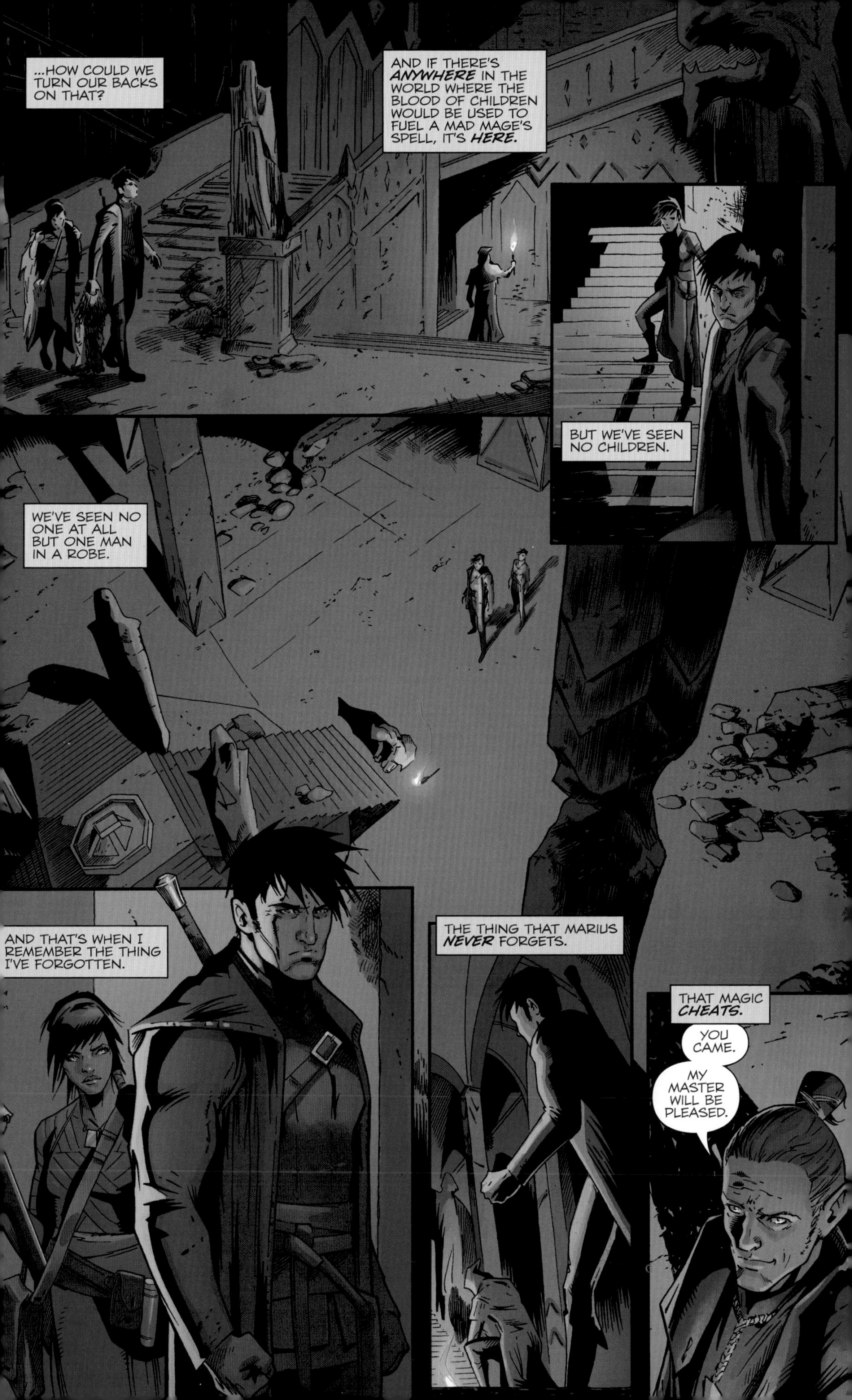

...HOW COULD WE TURN OUR BACKS ON THAT?
AND IF THERE'S *ANYWHERE* IN THE WORLD WHERE THE BLOOD OF CHILDREN WOULD BE USED TO FUEL A MAD MAGE'S SPELL, IT'S *HERE.*
BUT WE'VE SEEN NO CHILDREN.
WE'VE SEEN NO ONE AT ALL BUT ONE MAN IN A ROBE.
AND THAT'S WHEN I REMEMBER THE THING I'VE FORGOTTEN.
THE THING THAT MARIUS *NEVER* FORGETS.
THAT MAGIC *CHEATS.*
YOU CAME.
MY MASTER WILL BE PLEASED.

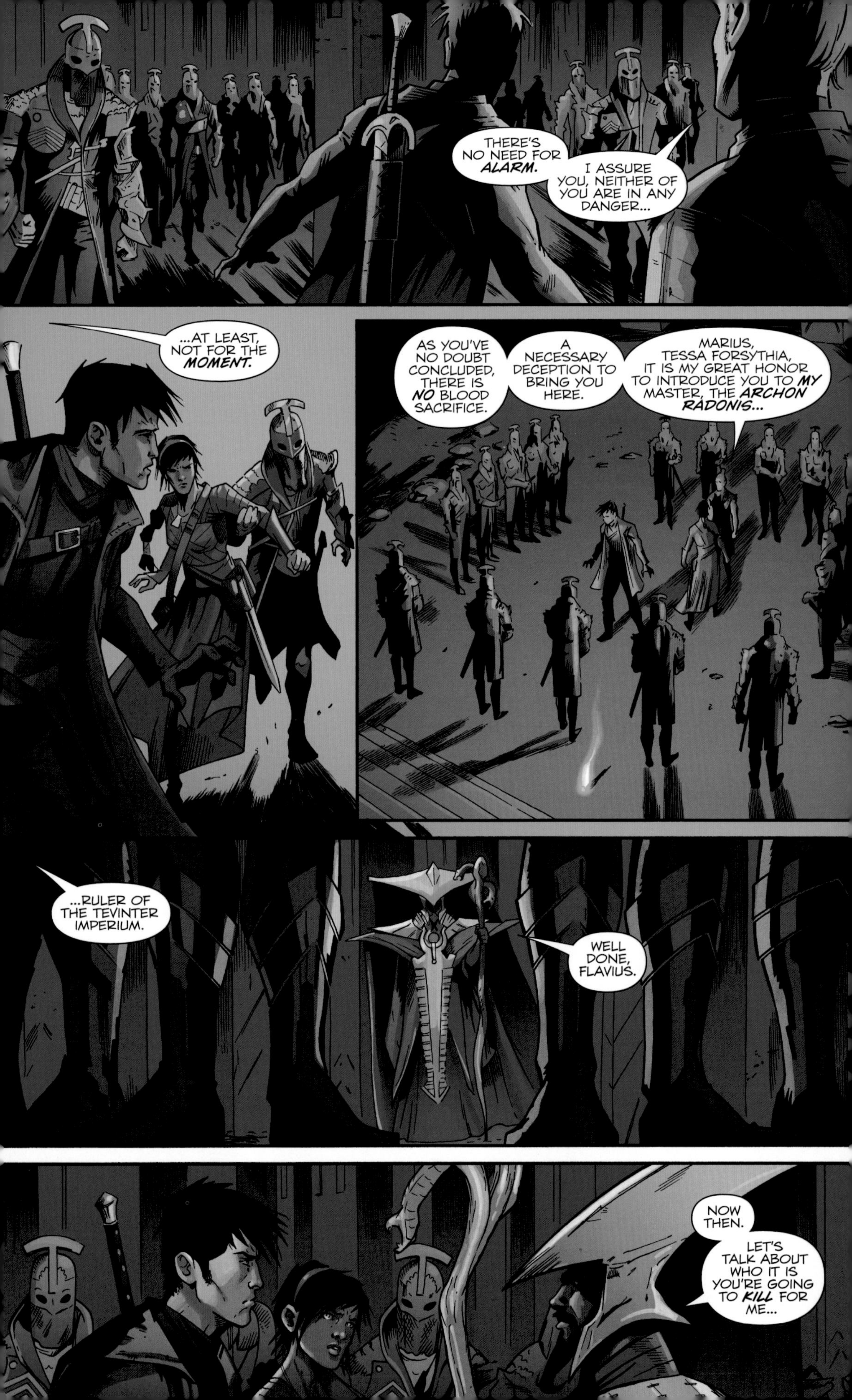
THERE'S NO NEED FOR ALARM.
I ASSURE YOU, NEITHER OF YOU ARE IN ANY DANGER...
...AT LEAST, NOT FOR THE MOMENT.
AS YOU'VE NO DOUBT CONCLUDED, THERE IS NO BLOOD SACRIFICE.
A NECESSARY DECEPTION TO BRING YOU HERE.
MARIUS, TESSA FORSYTHIA, IT IS MY GREAT HONOR TO INTRODUCE YOU TO MY MASTER, THE ARCHON RADONIS...
...RULER OF THE TEVINTER IMPERIUM.
WELL DONE, FLAVIUS.
NOW THEN.
LET'S TALK ABOUT WHO IT IS YOU'RE GOING TO KILL FOR ME...

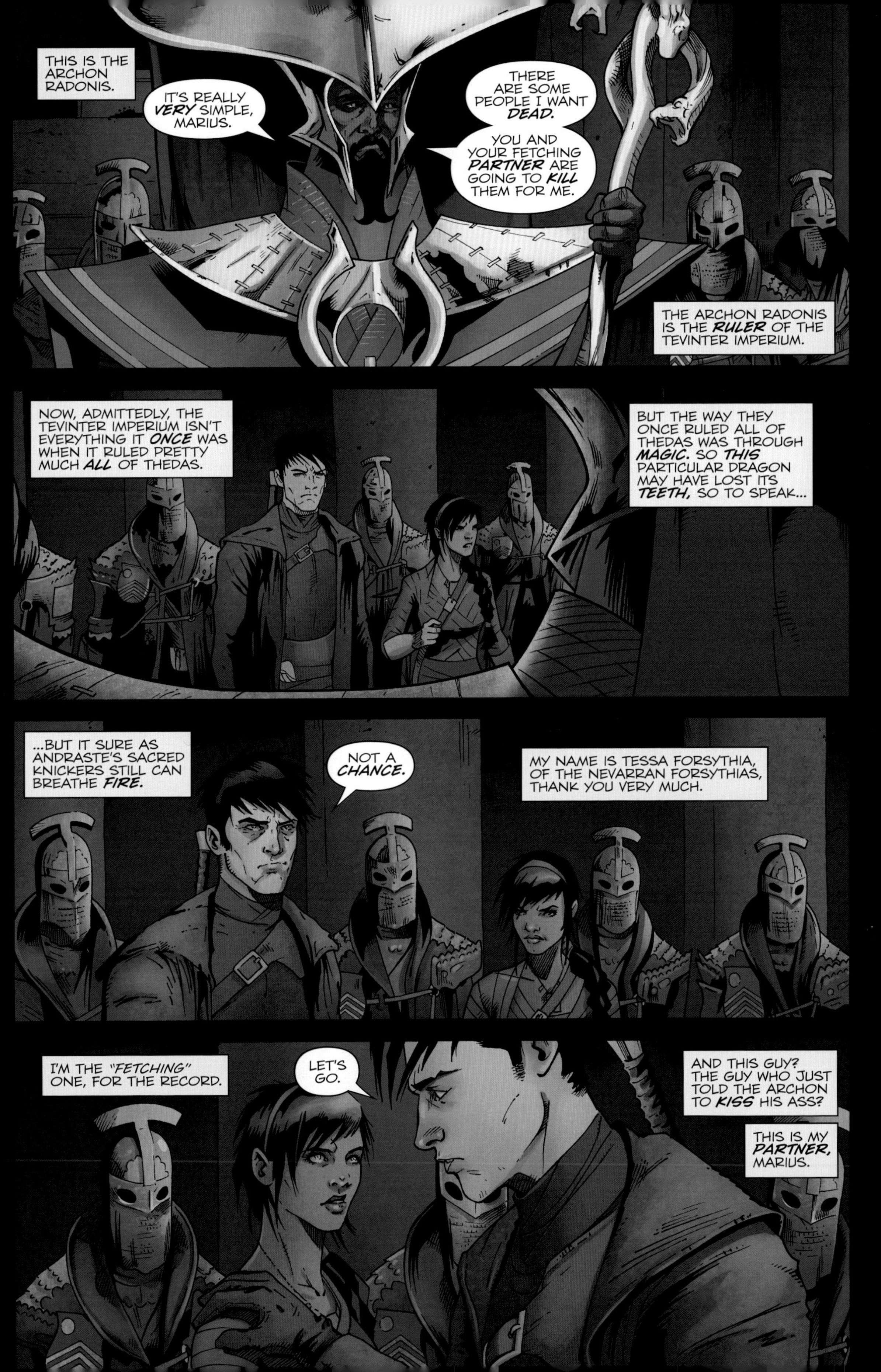
THIS IS THE ARCHON RADONIS.
IT'S REALLY VERY SIMPLE, MARIUS.
THERE ARE SOME PEOPLE I WANT DEAD.
YOU AND YOUR FETCHING PARTNER ARE GOING TO KILL THEM FOR ME.
THE ARCHON RADONIS IS THE RULER OF THE TEVINTER IMPERIUM.
NOW, ADMITTEDLY, THE TEVINTER IMPERIUM ISN'T EVERYTHING IT ONCE WAS WHEN IT RULED PRETTY MUCH ALL OF THEDAS.
BUT THE WAY THEY ONCE RULED ALL OF THEDAS WAS THROUGH MAGIC. SO THIS PARTICULAR DRAGON MAY HAVE LOST ITS TEETH, SO TO SPEAK...
...BUT IT SURE AS ANDRASTE'S SACRED KNICKERS STILL CAN BREATHE FIRE.
NOT A CHANCE.
MY NAME IS TESSA FORSYTHIA, OF THE NEVARRAN FORSYTHIAS, THANK YOU VERY MUCH.
I'M THE "FETCHING" ONE, FOR THE RECORD.
LET'S GO.
AND THIS GUY? THE GUY WHO JUST TOLD THE ARCHON TO KISS HIS ASS?
THIS IS MY PARTNER, MARIUS.

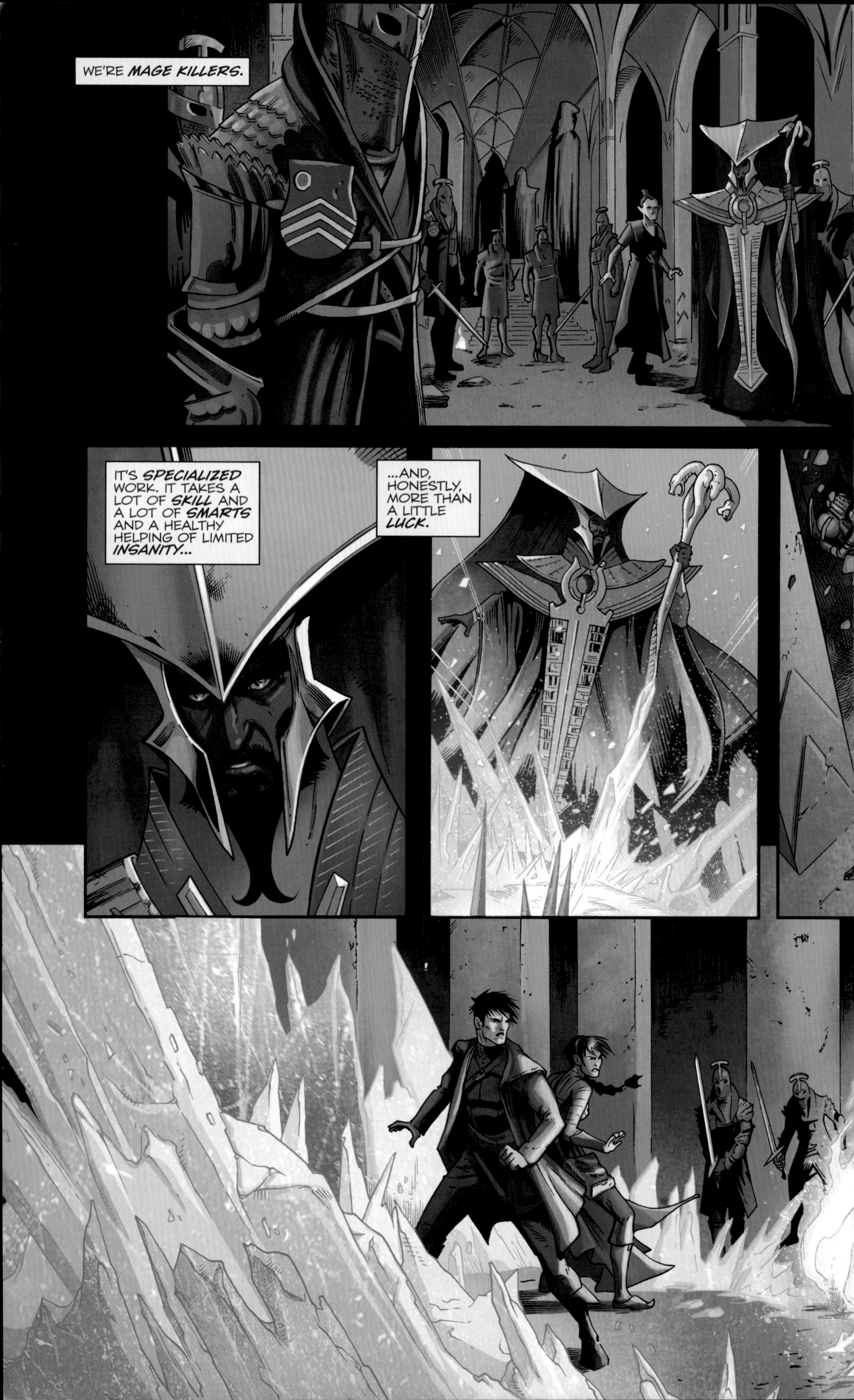
WE'RE MAGE KILLERS.
IT'S SPECIALIZED WORK. IT TAKES A LOT OF SKILL AND A LOT OF SMARTS AND A HEALTHY HELPING OF LIMITED INSANITY...
...AND, HONESTLY, MORE THAN A LITTLE LUCK.

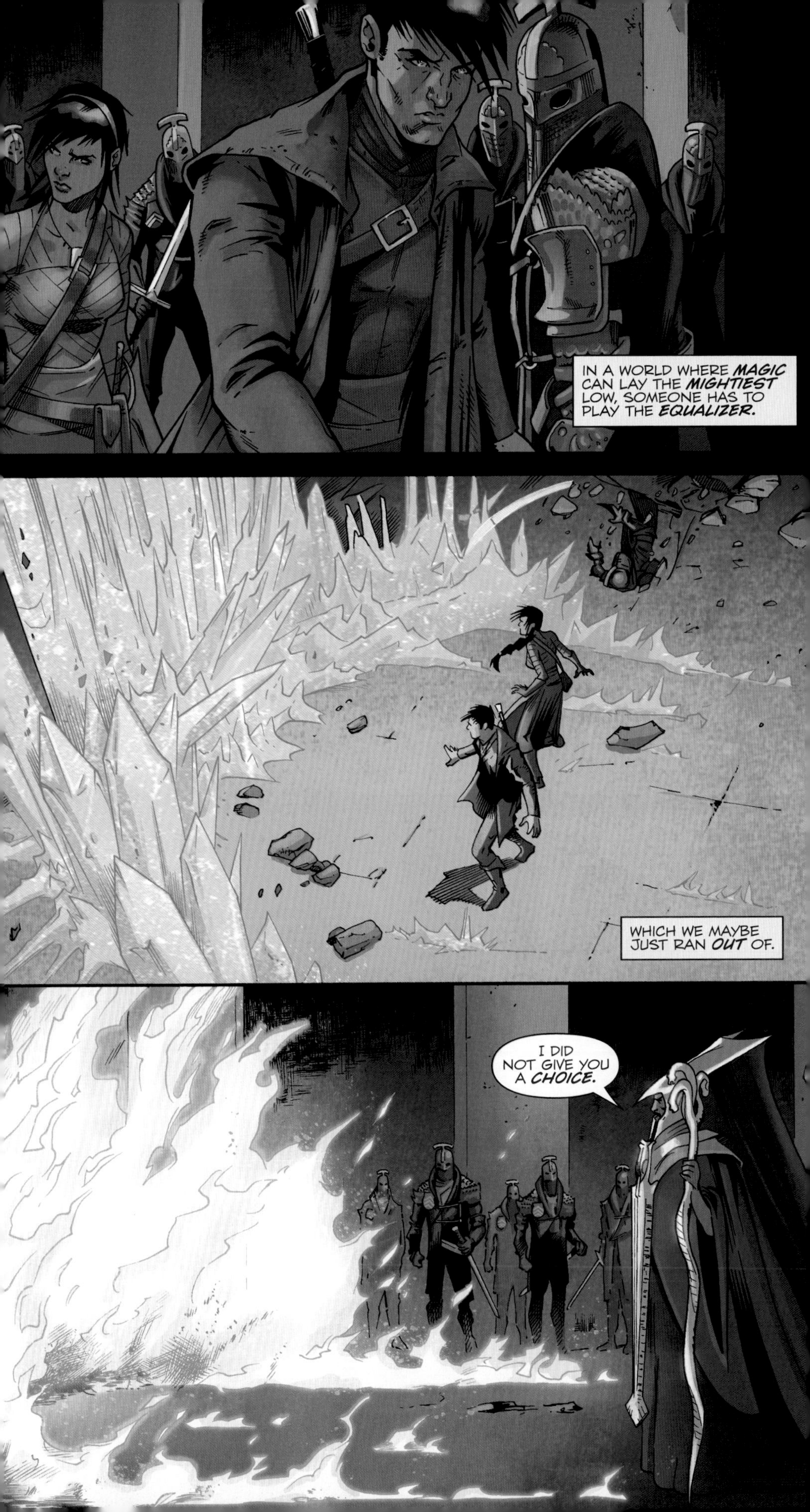
IN A WORLD WHERE MAGIC CAN LAY THE MIGHTIEST LOW, SOMEONE HAS TO PLAY THE EQUALIZER.
WHICH WE MAYBE JUST RAN OUT OF.
I DID NOT GIVE YOU A CHOICE.

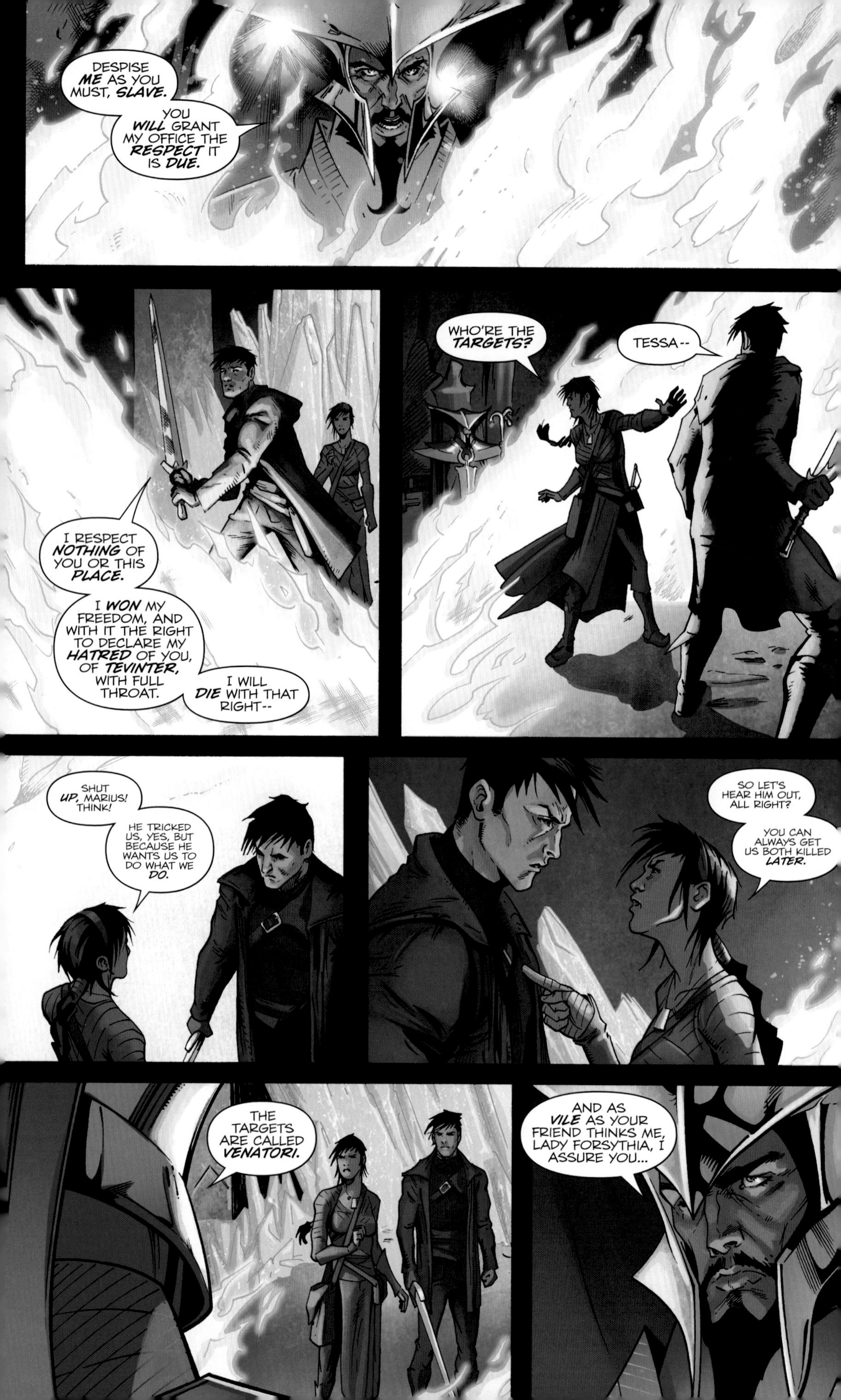

DESPISE ME AS YOU MUST, SLAVE.
YOU WILL GRANT MY OFFICE THE RESPECT IT IS DUE.
I RESPECT NOTHING OF YOU OR THIS PLACE.
I WON MY FREEDOM, AND WITH IT THE RIGHT TO DECLARE MY HATRED OF YOU, OF TEVINTER, WITH FULL THROAT.
I WILL DIE WITH THAT RIGHT--
WHO'RE THE TARGETS?
TESSA--
SHUT UP, MARIUS! THINK!
HE TRICKED US, YES, BUT BECAUSE HE WANTS US TO DO WHAT WE DO.
SO LET'S HEAR HIM OUT, ALL RIGHT?
YOU CAN ALWAYS GET US BOTH KILLED LATER.
THE TARGETS ARE CALLED VENATORI.
AND AS VILE AS YOUR FRIEND THINKS ME, LADY FORSYTHIA, I ASSURE YOU...

"...THE VENATORI ARE INFINITELY *WORSE*.

"THEY ARE A *CULT*, A SECRET SOCIETY LED BY SOME OF THE MOST POWERFUL MAGES IN ALL OF TEVINTER.

"POWER COVETS *POWER*, AND THUS THEY COVET MORE AND MORE.

"THEY SEEK TO RESTORE THE IMPERIUM OF *OLD*...

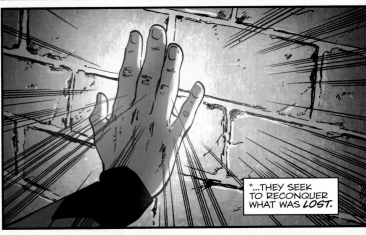

"...THEY SEEK TO RECONQUER WHAT WAS *LOST*.

"THINK ON THAT.

"THEN CONSIDER *THIS*:

"THEY WILL STOP AT NOTHING -- *NOTHING* -- TO ACHIEVE THAT GOAL."

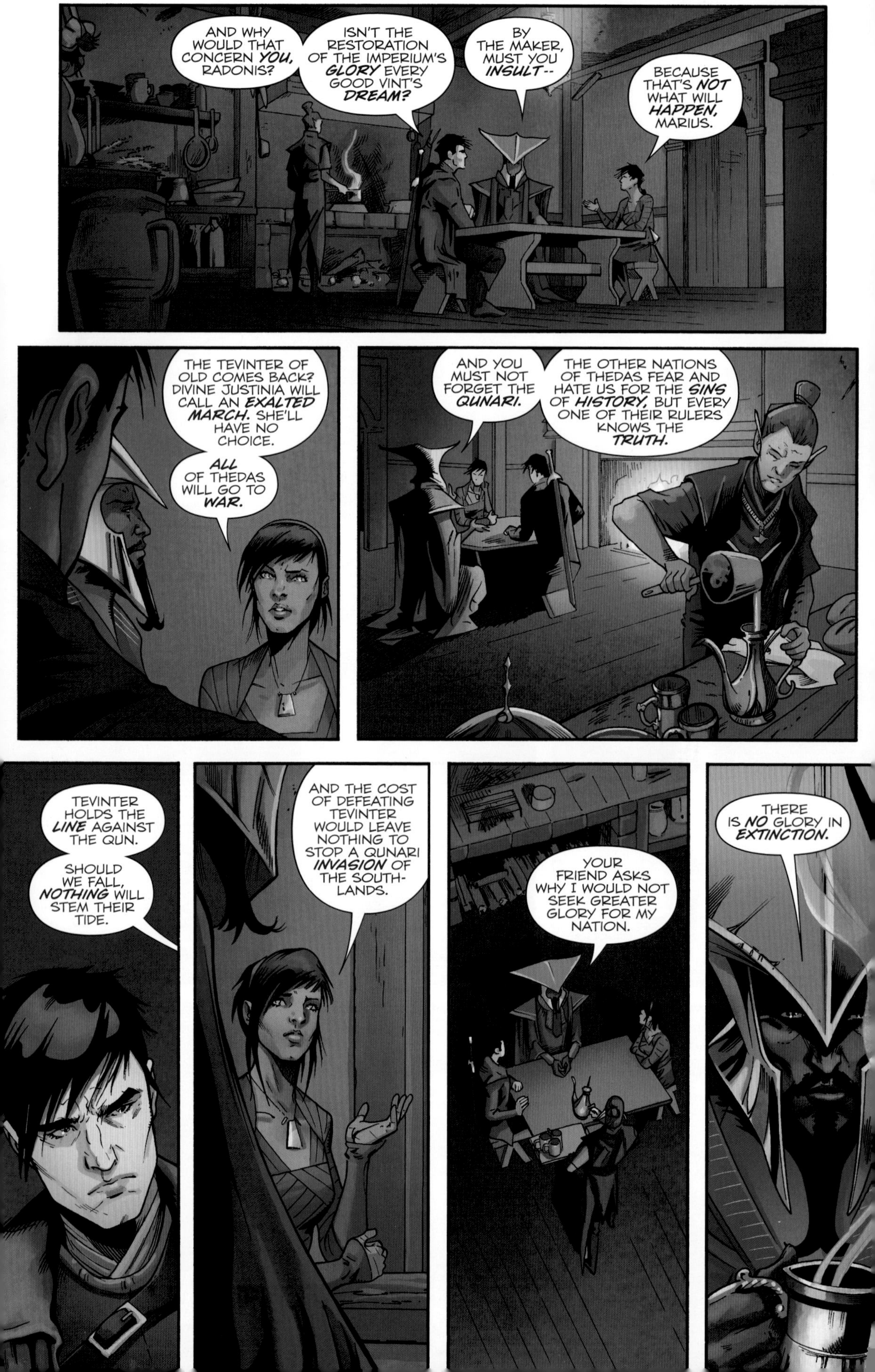
AND WHY WOULD THAT CONCERN *YOU,* RADONIS?
ISN'T THE RESTORATION OF THE IMPERIUM'S *GLORY* EVERY GOOD VINT'S *DREAM?*
BY THE MAKER, MUST YOU *INSULT*--
BECAUSE THAT'S *NOT* WHAT WILL *HAPPEN,* MARIUS.
THE TEVINTER OF OLD COMES BACK? DIVINE JUSTINIA WILL CALL AN *EXALTED MARCH*. SHE'LL HAVE NO CHOICE.
ALL OF THEDAS WILL GO TO *WAR*.
AND YOU MUST NOT FORGET THE *QUNARI*.
THE OTHER NATIONS OF THEDAS FEAR AND HATE US FOR THE *SINS* OF *HISTORY,* BUT EVERY ONE OF THEIR RULERS KNOWS THE *TRUTH*.
TEVINTER HOLDS THE *LINE* AGAINST THE QUN.
SHOULD WE FALL, *NOTHING* WILL STEM THEIR TIDE.
AND THE COST OF DEFEATING TEVINTER WOULD LEAVE NOTHING TO STOP A QUNARI *INVASION* OF THE SOUTH-LANDS.
YOUR FRIEND ASKS WHY I WOULD NOT SEEK GREATER GLORY FOR MY NATION.
THERE IS *NO* GLORY IN *EXTINCTION*.

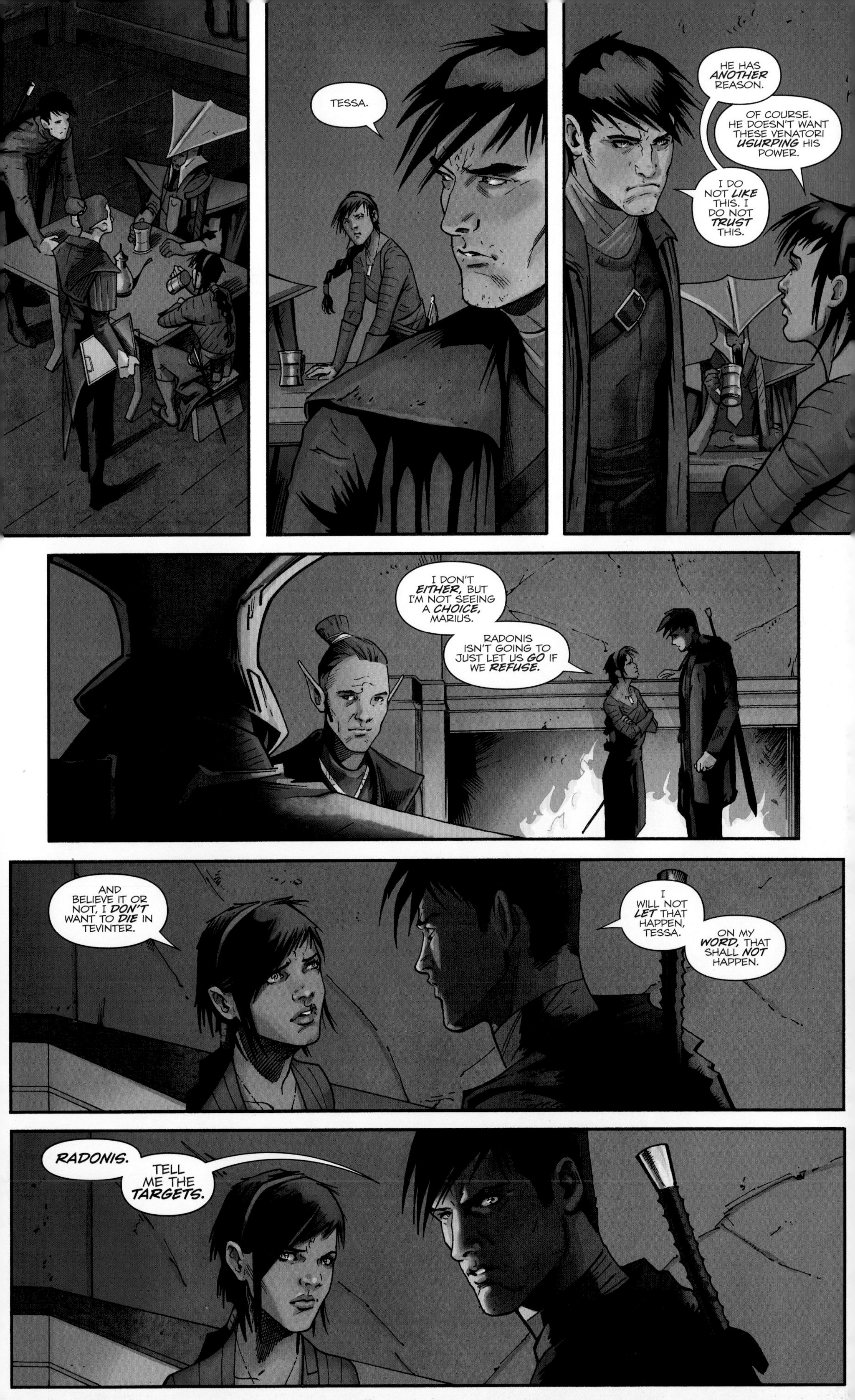
TESSA.
HE HAS ANOTHER REASON.
OF COURSE. HE DOESN'T WANT THESE VENATORI USURPING HIS POWER.
I DO NOT LIKE THIS. I DO NOT TRUST THIS.
I DON'T EITHER, BUT I'M NOT SEEING A CHOICE, MARIUS.
RADONIS ISN'T GOING TO JUST LET US GO IF WE REFUSE.
AND BELIEVE IT OR NOT, I DON'T WANT TO DIE IN TEVINTER.
I WILL NOT LET THAT HAPPEN, TESSA.
ON MY WORD, THAT SHALL NOT HAPPEN.
RADONIS.
TELL ME THE TARGETS.

HE GAVE US A LIST OF *FOUR NAMES*, MAGES RADONIS HAD IDENTIFIED AS LEADERS OF THE VENATORI, ALL OF THEM IN THE CAPITAL, MINRATHOUS.

HE WAS CERTAIN THERE WERE *OTHERS*, BUT THESE FOUR, THEY WERE THE ONES HE WANTED DEALT WITH *FIRST*.

AND IT WENT WITHOUT SAYING THAT THEY WERE *HARD* TARGETS, ALL OF THEM.

PEOPLE WHO WANT TO RESTORE THE *"GLORY OF THE IMPERIUM"* WEREN'T LIKELY TO BE *POOR*, FOR INSTANCE.

THEY WEREN'T LIKELY TO BE *EASY* TO GET *ALONE*.

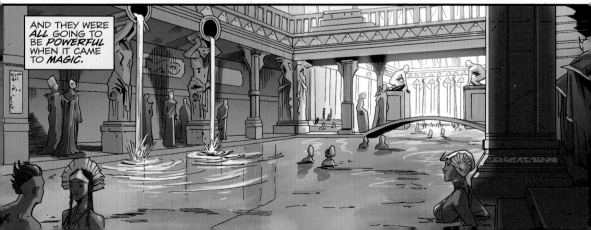

AND THEY WERE *ALL* GOING TO BE *POWERFUL* WHEN IT CAME TO *MAGIC*.

THE FIRST TARGET WAS NAMED HAVIAN SULARA.

ALL THE UPPER-CLASS FAMILIES IN TEVINTER OWN SLAVES, BUT HAVIAN WAS BUYING IN BULK.

RADONIS SUSPECTED HIM OF SHIPPING THEM OUT OF TEVINTER TO ORLAIS. HE DIDN'T KNOW WHY.

NUMBER TWO WAS CORINNIA CRALLIUS.

A WIDOW TWICE OVER, SHE HAD FIVE SEPARATE LOVERS THAT I COUNTED IN THE TWO WEEKS WE WATCHED HER.

NEVER SAW HER SMILE ONCE.

THE THIRD, PAULUS NIMIAN.

ANOTHER ALTUS -- THEY WERE ALL ALTUS, ALL UPPER-CLASS MAGES -- HE SPENT HOURS EVERY DAY IN THE GREAT LIBRARY.

EVERYONE WHO WORKED THERE WAS TERRIFIED OF HIM.

BUT NUMBER FOUR, SHE WAS THE ODD ONE.

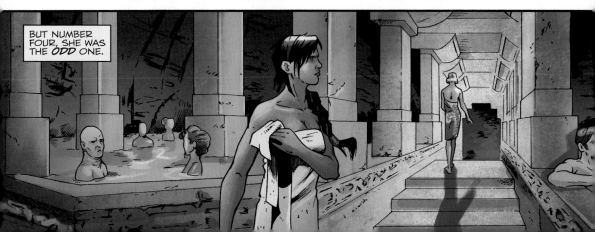

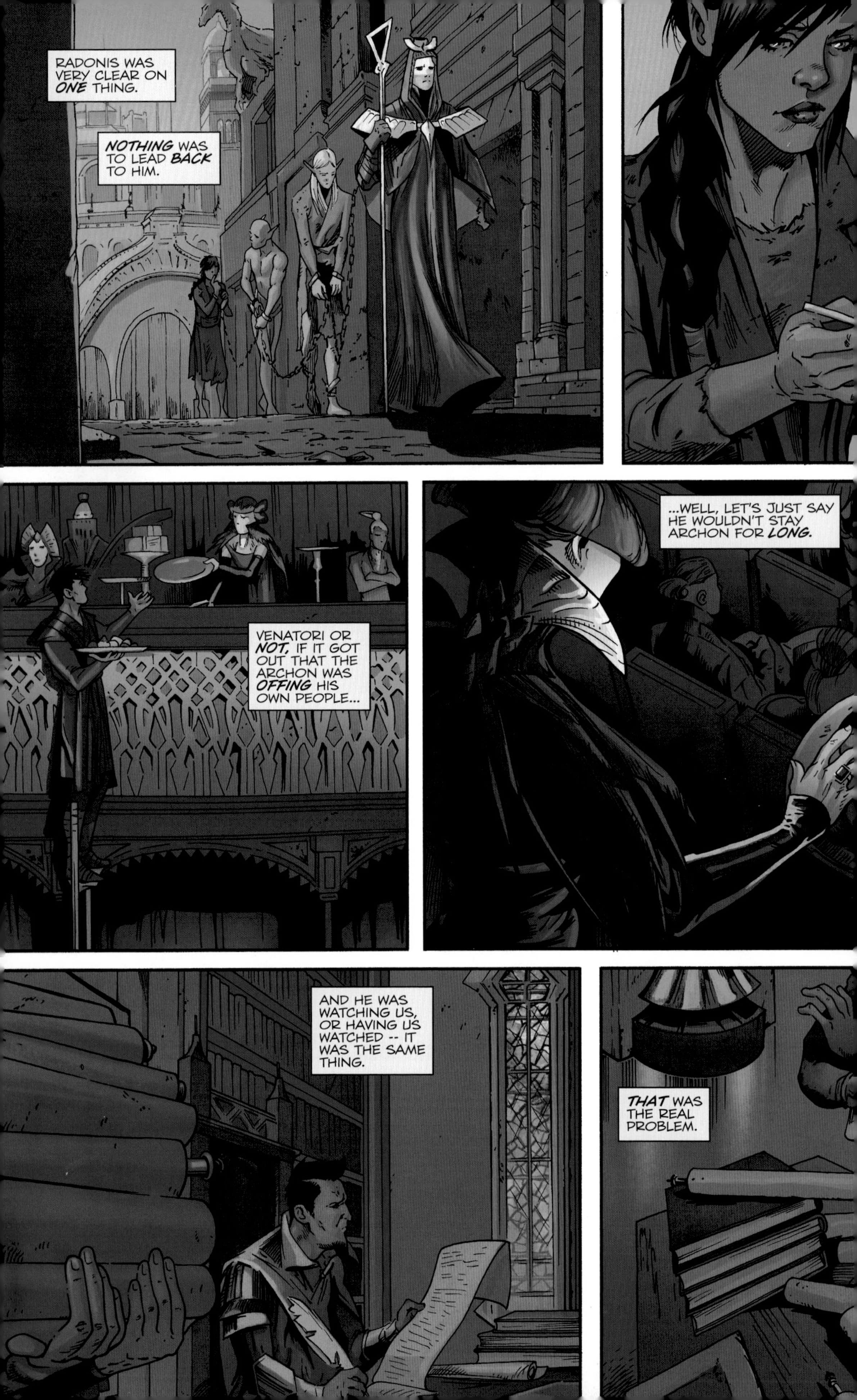
RADONIS WAS VERY CLEAR ON ONE THING.
NOTHING WAS TO LEAD BACK TO HIM.
VENATORI OR NOT, IF IT GOT OUT THAT THE ARCHON WAS OFFING HIS OWN PEOPLE...
...WELL, LET'S JUST SAY HE WOULDN'T STAY ARCHON FOR LONG.
AND HE WAS WATCHING US, OR HAVING US WATCHED -- IT WAS THE SAME THING.
THAT WAS THE REAL PROBLEM.

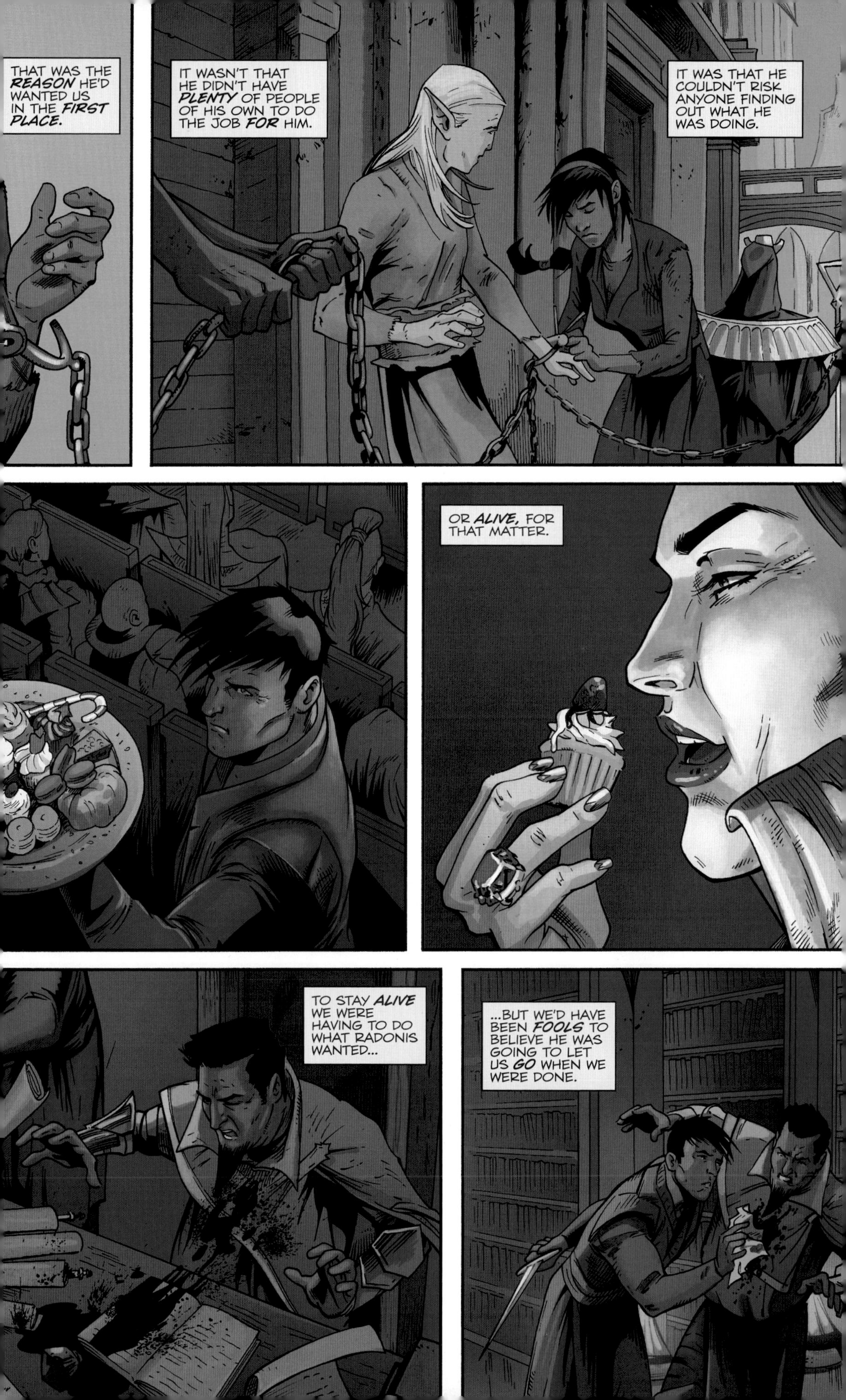
THAT WAS THE REASON HE'D WANTED US IN THE FIRST PLACE.
IT WASN'T THAT HE DIDN'T HAVE PLENTY OF PEOPLE OF HIS OWN TO DO THE JOB FOR HIM.
IT WAS THAT HE COULDN'T RISK ANYONE FINDING OUT WHAT HE WAS DOING.
OR ALIVE, FOR THAT MATTER.
TO STAY ALIVE WE WERE HAVING TO DO WHAT RADONIS WANTED...
...BUT WE'D HAVE BEEN FOOLS TO BELIEVE HE WAS GOING TO LET US GO WHEN WE WERE DONE.

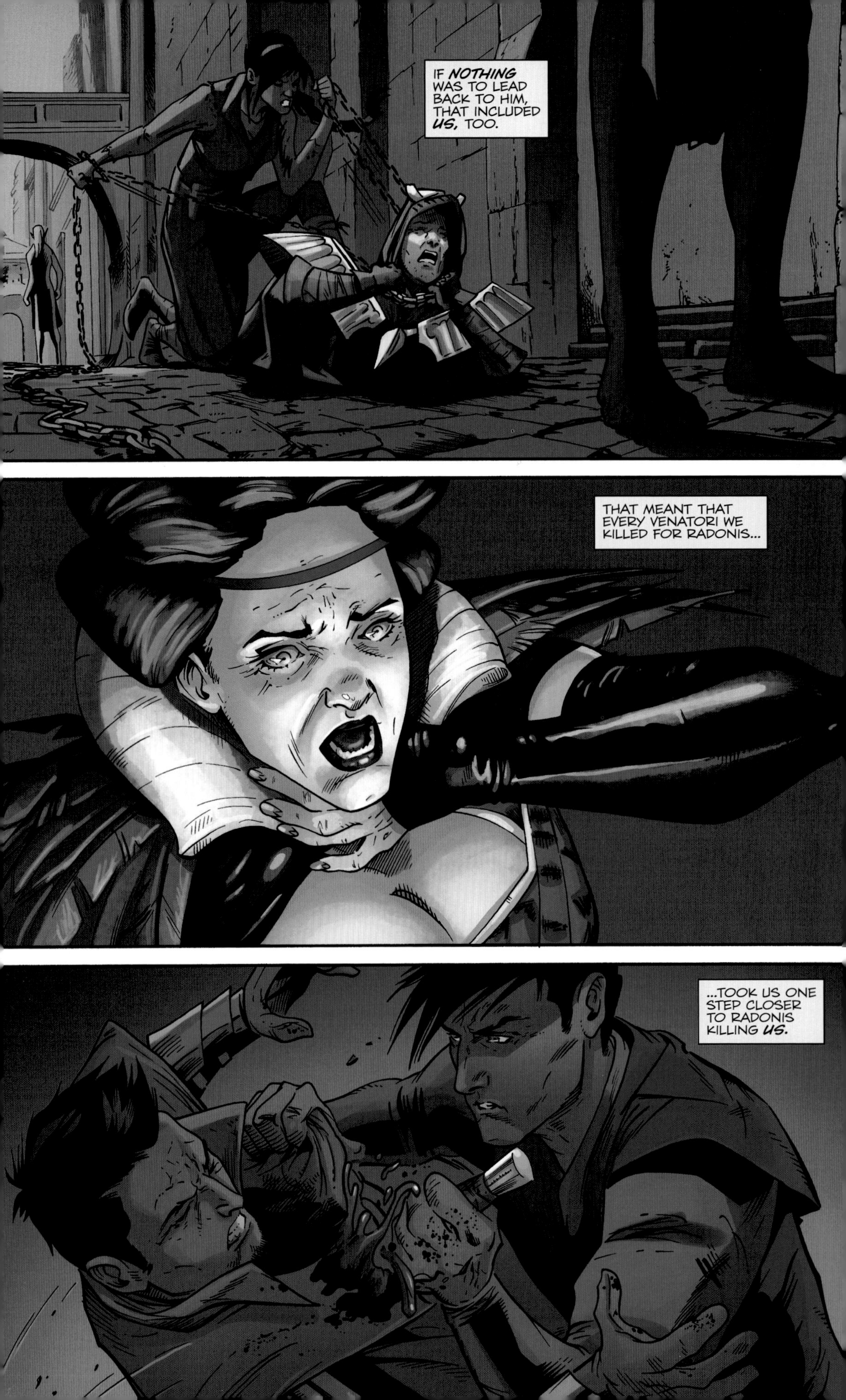
IF *NOTHING* WAS TO LEAD BACK TO HIM, THAT INCLUDED *US*, TOO.
THAT MEANT THAT EVERY VENATORI WE KILLED FOR RADONIS...
...TOOK US ONE STEP CLOSER TO RADONIS KILLING *US*.

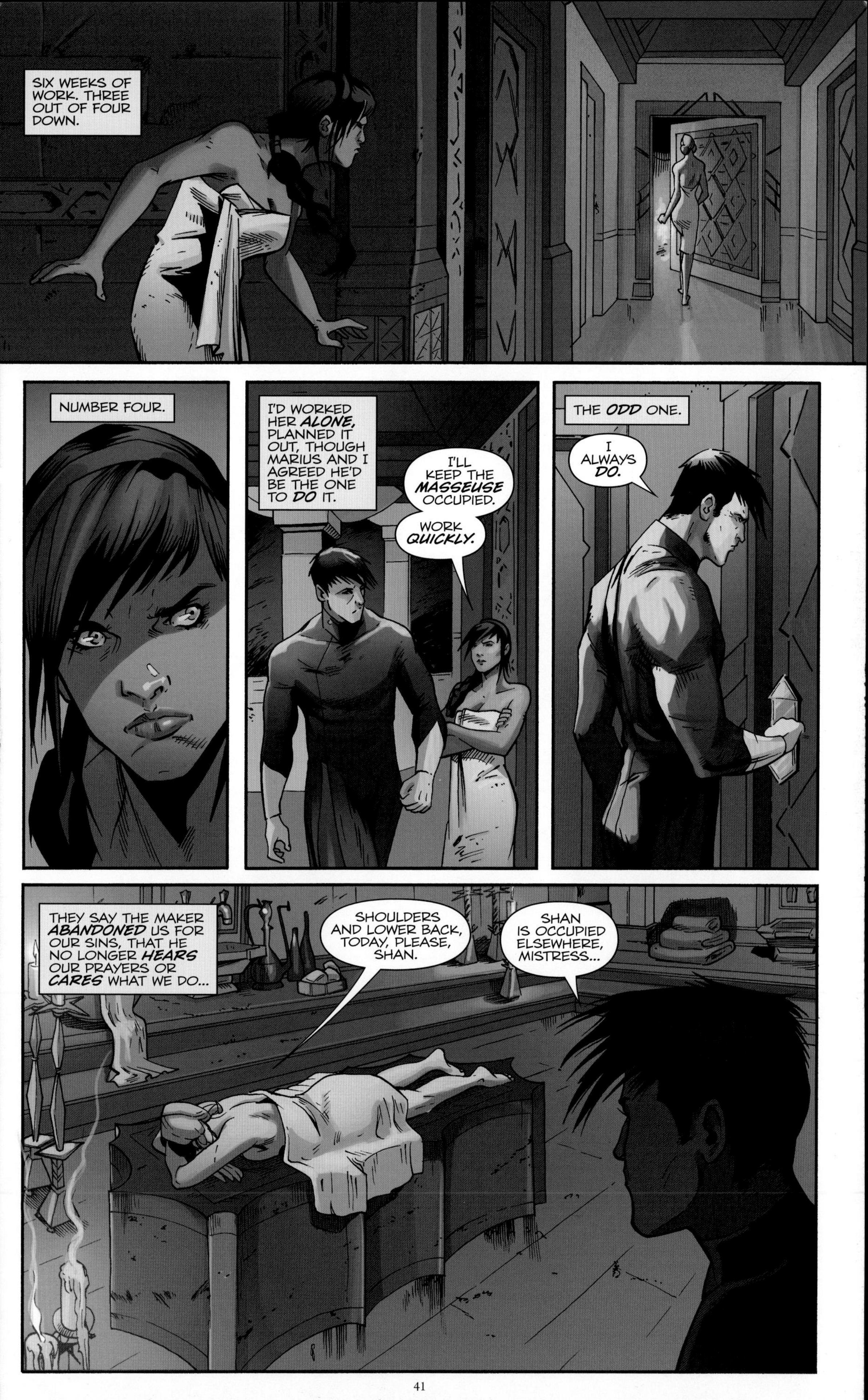

SIX WEEKS OF WORK. THREE OUT OF FOUR DOWN.
NUMBER FOUR.
I'D WORKED HER ALONE, PLANNED IT OUT, THOUGH MARIUS AND I AGREED HE'D BE THE ONE TO DO IT.
I'LL KEEP THE MASSEUSE OCCUPIED.
WORK QUICKLY.
THE ODD ONE.
I ALWAYS DO.
THEY SAY THE MAKER ABANDONED US FOR OUR SINS, THAT HE NO LONGER HEARS OUR PRAYERS OR CARES WHAT WE DO...
SHOULDERS AND LOWER BACK, TODAY, PLEASE, SHAN.
SHAN IS OCCUPIED ELSEWHERE, MISTRESS...

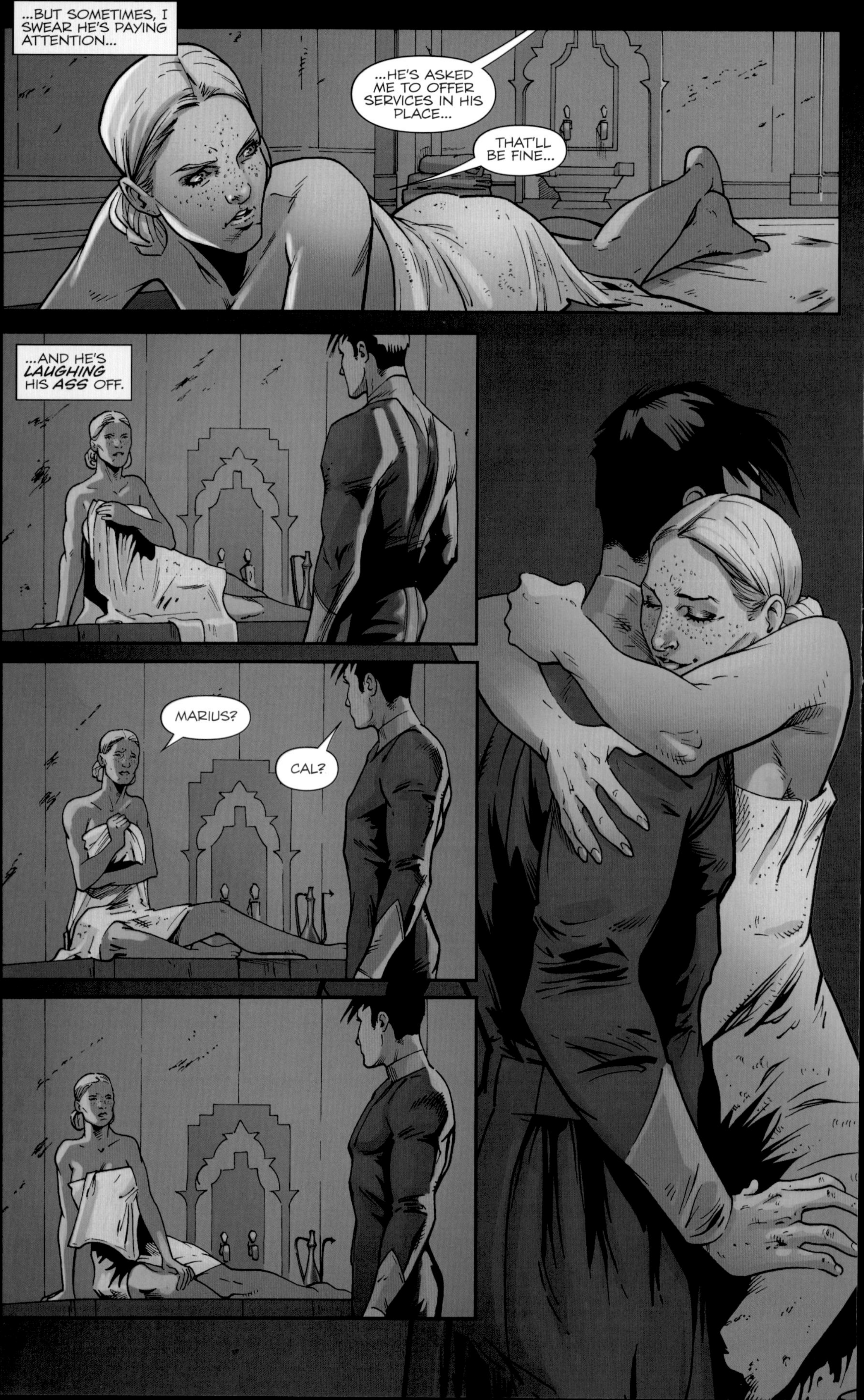
...BUT SOMETIMES, I SWEAR HE'S PAYING ATTENTION...
...HE'S ASKED ME TO OFFER SERVICES IN HIS PLACE...
THAT'LL BE FINE...
...AND HE'S *LAUGHING* HIS *ASS* OFF.
MARIUS?
CAL?

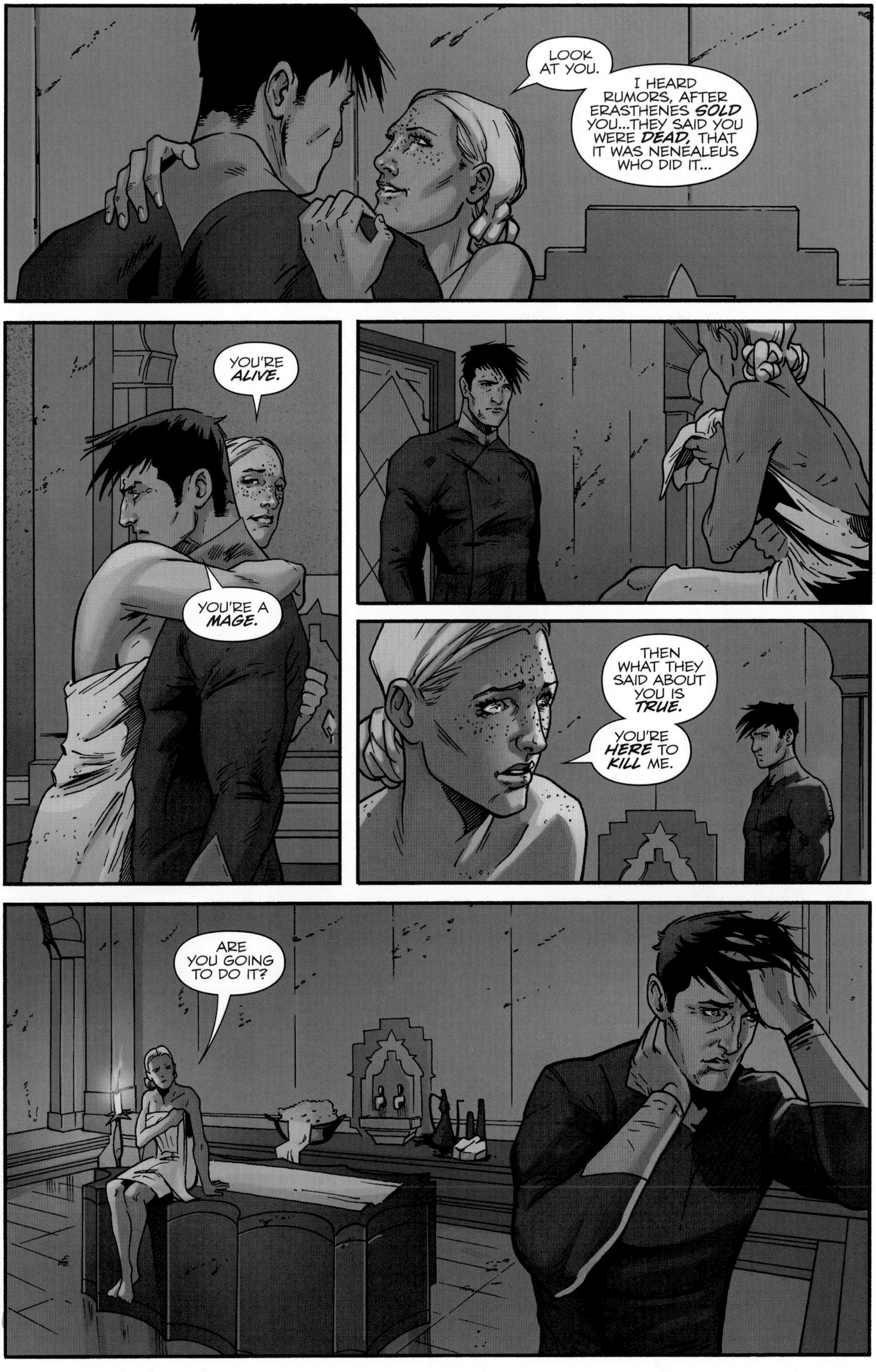
LOOK AT YOU.
I HEARD RUMORS, AFTER ERASTHENES SOLD YOU...THEY SAID YOU WERE DEAD, THAT IT WAS NENEALEUS WHO DID IT...
YOU'RE ALIVE.
YOU'RE A MAGE.
THEN WHAT THEY SAID ABOUT YOU IS TRUE.
YOU'RE HERE TO KILL ME.
ARE YOU GOING TO DO IT?

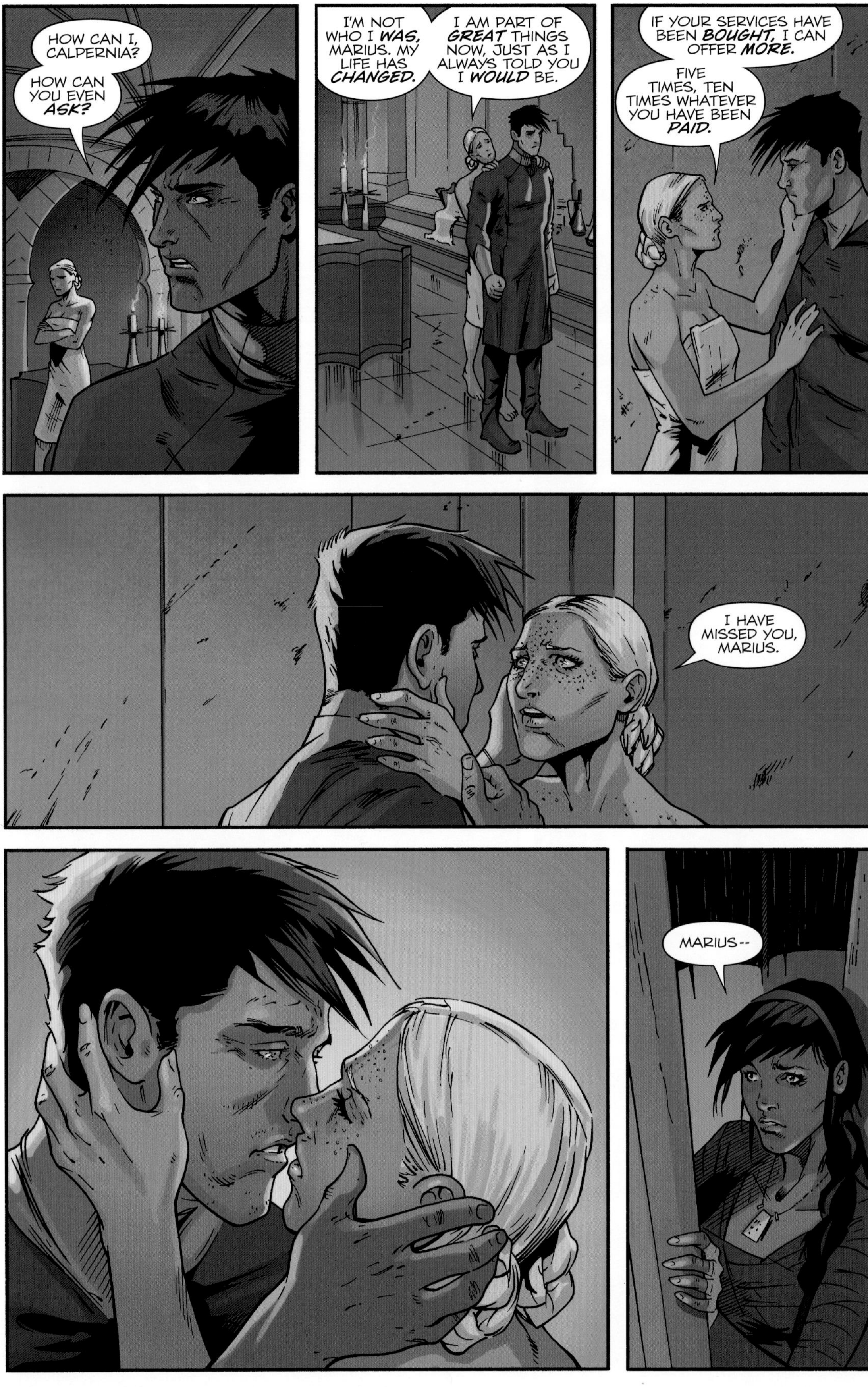
HOW CAN I, CALPERNIA?
HOW CAN YOU EVEN ASK?
I'M NOT WHO I WAS, MARIUS. MY LIFE HAS CHANGED.
I AM PART OF GREAT THINGS NOW, JUST AS I ALWAYS TOLD YOU I WOULD BE.
IF YOUR SERVICES HAVE BEEN BOUGHT, I CAN OFFER MORE.
FIVE TIMES, TEN TIMES WHATEVER YOU HAVE BEEN PAID.
I HAVE MISSED YOU, MARIUS.
MARIUS--

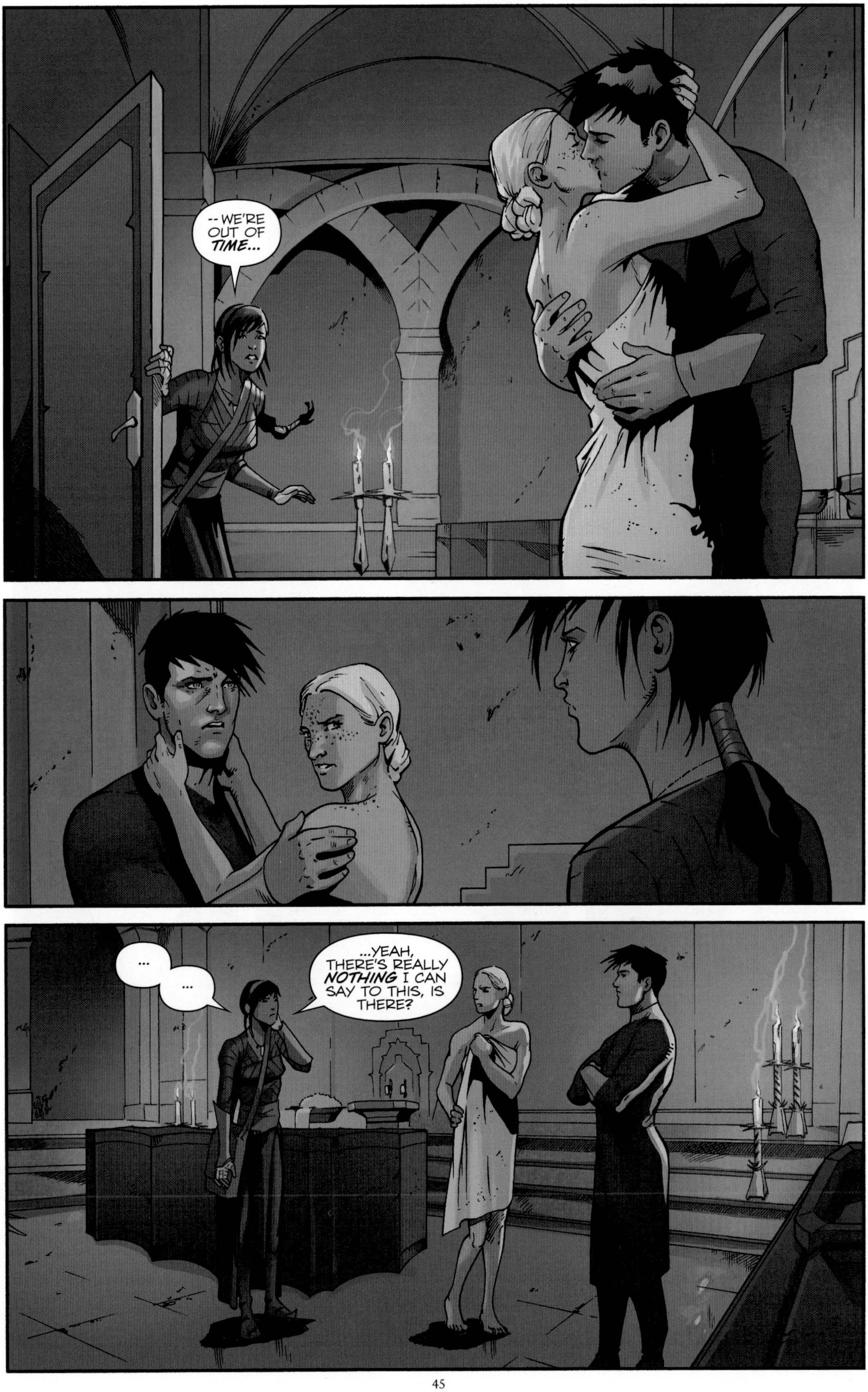
--WE'RE OUT OF *TIME*...
...
...
...YEAH, THERE'S REALLY ***NOTHING*** I CAN SAY TO THIS, IS THERE?

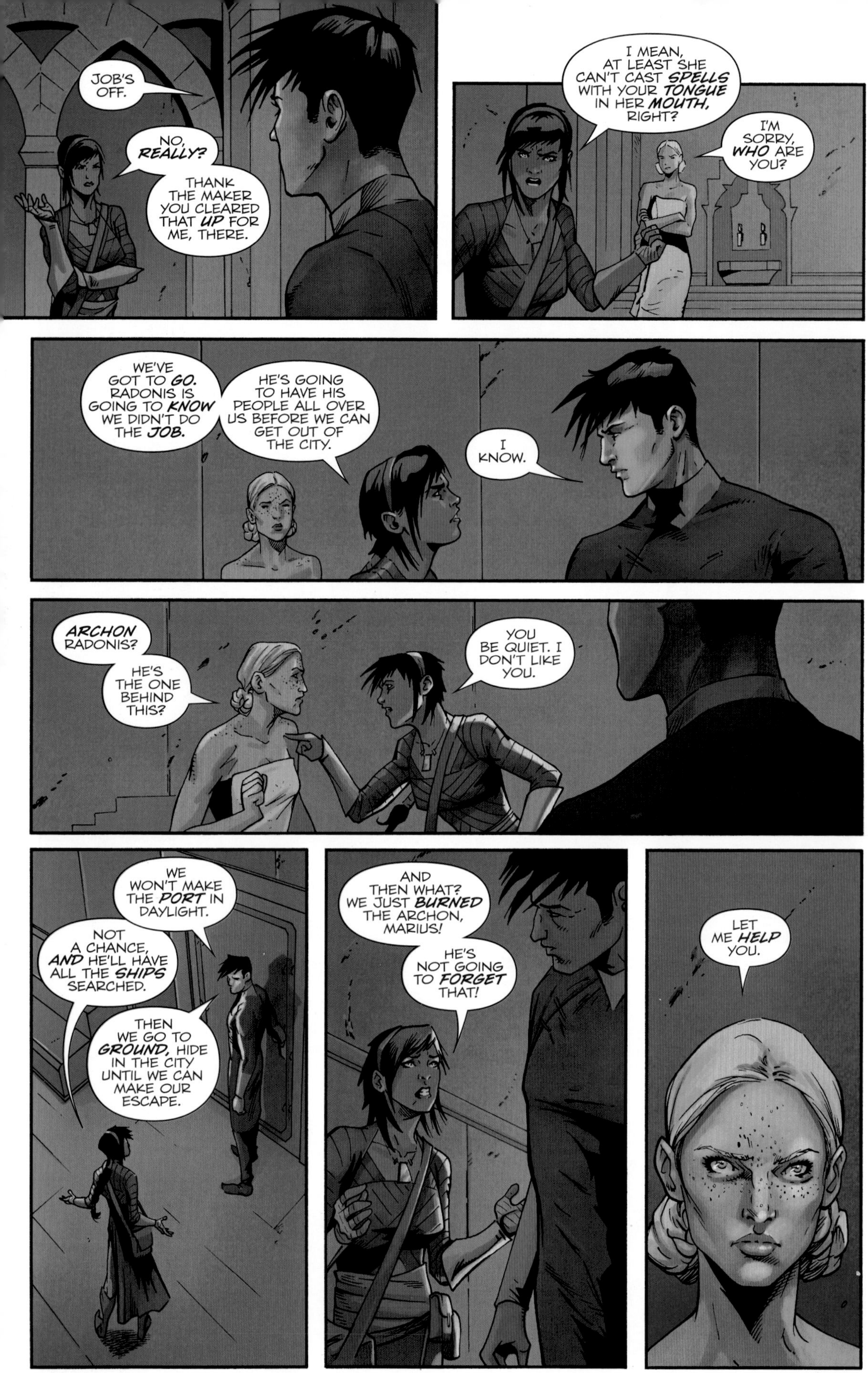

JOB'S OFF.
NO, REALLY?
THANK THE MAKER YOU CLEARED THAT UP FOR ME, THERE.
I MEAN, AT LEAST SHE CAN'T CAST SPELLS WITH YOUR TONGUE IN HER MOUTH, RIGHT?
I'M SORRY, WHO ARE YOU?
WE'VE GOT TO GO. RADONIS IS GOING TO KNOW WE DIDN'T DO THE JOB.
HE'S GOING TO HAVE HIS PEOPLE ALL OVER US BEFORE WE CAN GET OUT OF THE CITY.
I KNOW.
ARCHON RADONIS?
HE'S THE ONE BEHIND THIS?
YOU BE QUIET. I DON'T LIKE YOU.
WE WON'T MAKE THE PORT IN DAYLIGHT.
NOT A CHANCE, AND HE'LL HAVE ALL THE SHIPS SEARCHED.
THEN WE GO TO GROUND, HIDE IN THE CITY UNTIL WE CAN MAKE OUR ESCAPE.
AND THEN WHAT? WE JUST BURNED THE ARCHON, MARIUS!
HE'S NOT GOING TO FORGET THAT!
LET ME HELP YOU.

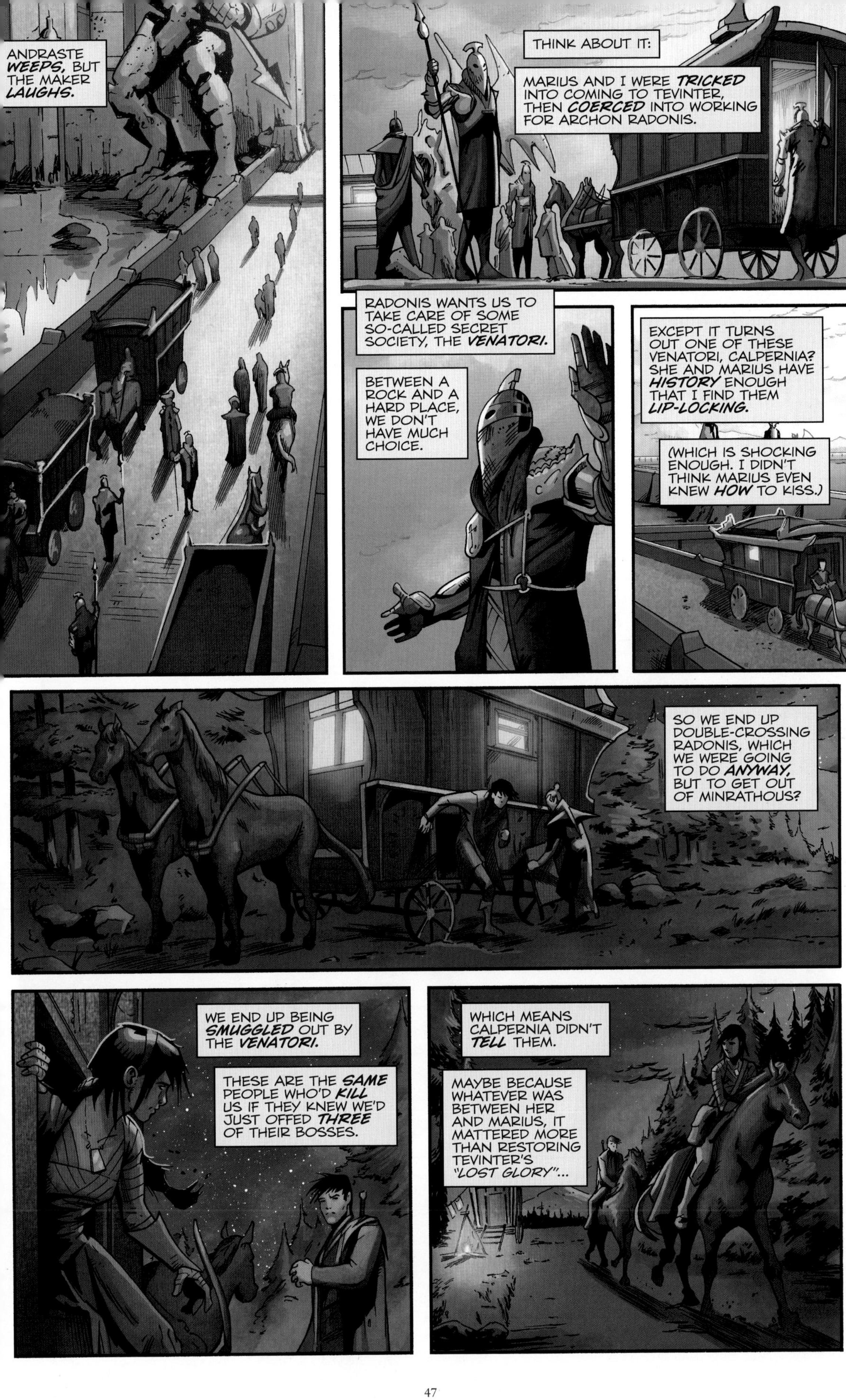
ANDRASTE WEEPS, BUT THE MAKER LAUGHS.
THINK ABOUT IT:
MARIUS AND I WERE TRICKED INTO COMING TO TEVINTER, THEN COERCED INTO WORKING FOR ARCHON RADONIS.
RADONIS WANTS US TO TAKE CARE OF SOME SO-CALLED SECRET SOCIETY, THE VENATORI.
BETWEEN A ROCK AND A HARD PLACE, WE DON'T HAVE MUCH CHOICE.
EXCEPT IT TURNS OUT ONE OF THESE VENATORI, CALPERNIA? SHE AND MARIUS HAVE HISTORY ENOUGH THAT I FIND THEM LIP-LOCKING.
(WHICH IS SHOCKING ENOUGH. I DIDN'T THINK MARIUS EVEN KNEW HOW TO KISS.)
SO WE END UP DOUBLE-CROSSING RADONIS, WHICH WE WERE GOING TO DO ANYWAY, BUT TO GET OUT OF MINRATHOUS?
WE END UP BEING SMUGGLED OUT BY THE VENATORI.
THESE ARE THE SAME PEOPLE WHO'D KILL US IF THEY KNEW WE'D JUST OFFED THREE OF THEIR BOSSES.
WHICH MEANS CALPERNIA DIDN'T TELL THEM.
MAYBE BECAUSE WHATEVER WAS BETWEEN HER AND MARIUS, IT MATTERED MORE THAN RESTORING TEVINTER'S "LOST GLORY"...

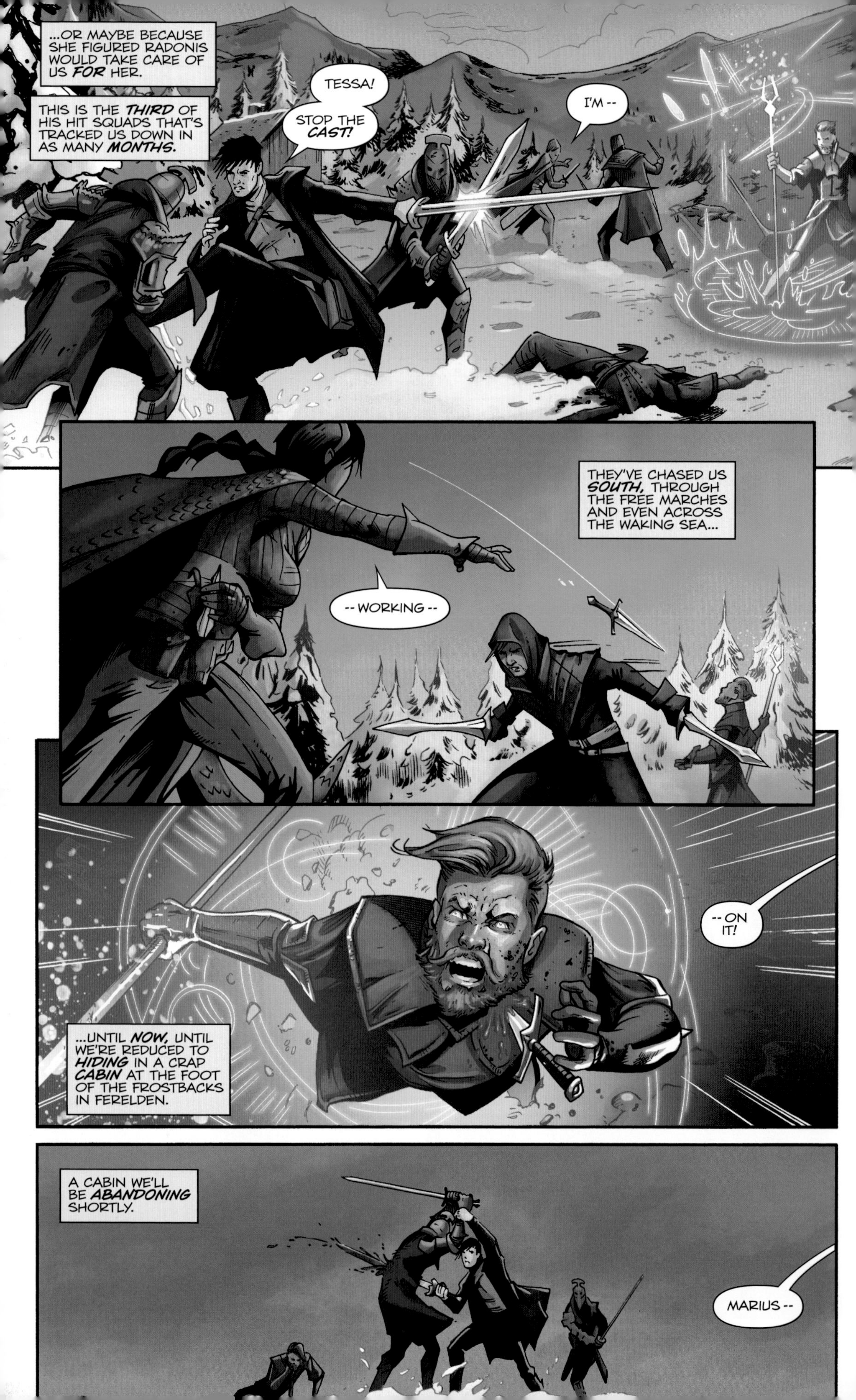
...OR MAYBE BECAUSE SHE FIGURED RADONIS WOULD TAKE CARE OF US FOR HER.
THIS IS THE THIRD OF HIS HIT SQUADS THAT'S TRACKED US DOWN IN AS MANY MONTHS.
TESSA!
STOP THE CAST!
I'M --
THEY'VE CHASED US SOUTH, THROUGH THE FREE MARCHES AND EVEN ACROSS THE WAKING SEA...
-- WORKING --
...UNTIL NOW, UNTIL WE'RE REDUCED TO HIDING IN A CRAP CABIN AT THE FOOT OF THE FROSTBACKS IN FERELDEN.
-- ON IT!
A CABIN WE'LL BE ABANDONING SHORTLY.
MARIUS --

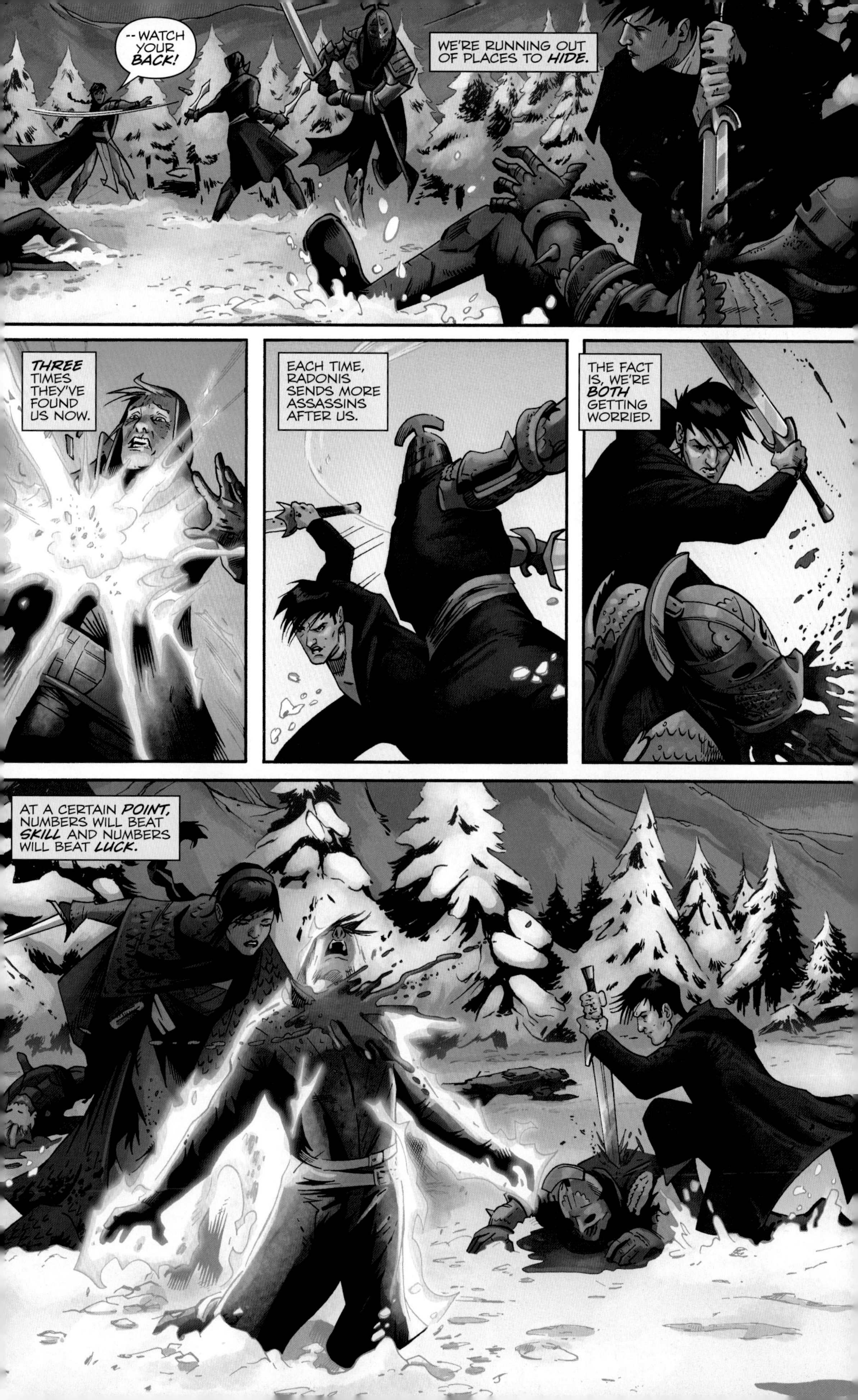
--WATCH YOUR BACK!
WE'RE RUNNING OUT OF PLACES TO HIDE.
THREE TIMES THEY'VE FOUND US NOW.
EACH TIME, RADONIS SENDS MORE ASSASSINS AFTER US.
THE FACT IS, WE'RE BOTH GETTING WORRIED.
AT A CERTAIN POINT, NUMBERS WILL BEAT SKILL AND NUMBERS WILL BEAT LUCK.

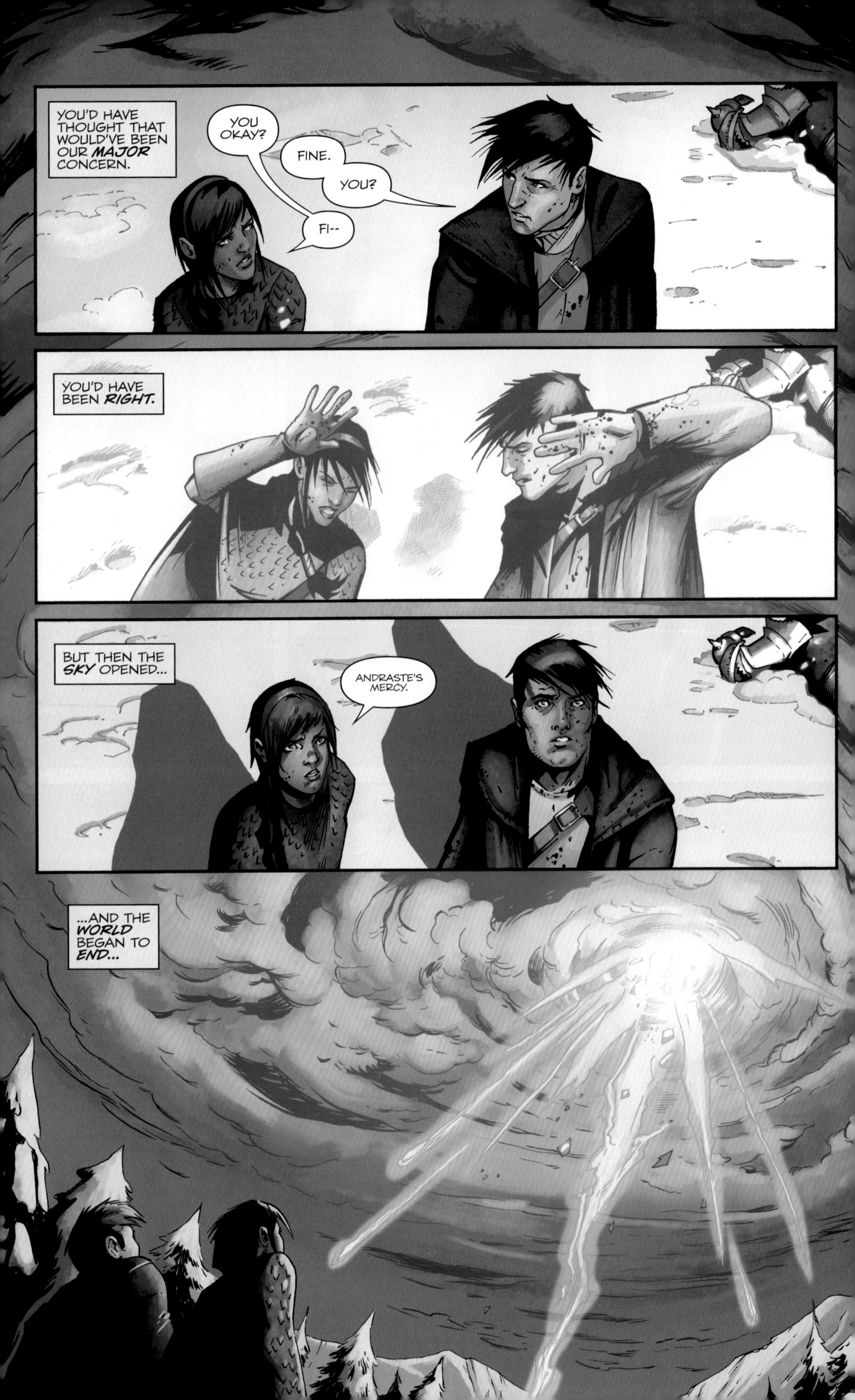

YOU'D HAVE THOUGHT THAT WOULD'VE BEEN OUR MAJOR CONCERN.
YOU OKAY?
FINE.
YOU?
FI--
YOU'D HAVE BEEN RIGHT.
BUT THEN THE SKY OPENED...
ANDRASTE'S MERCY.
...AND THE WORLD BEGAN TO END...

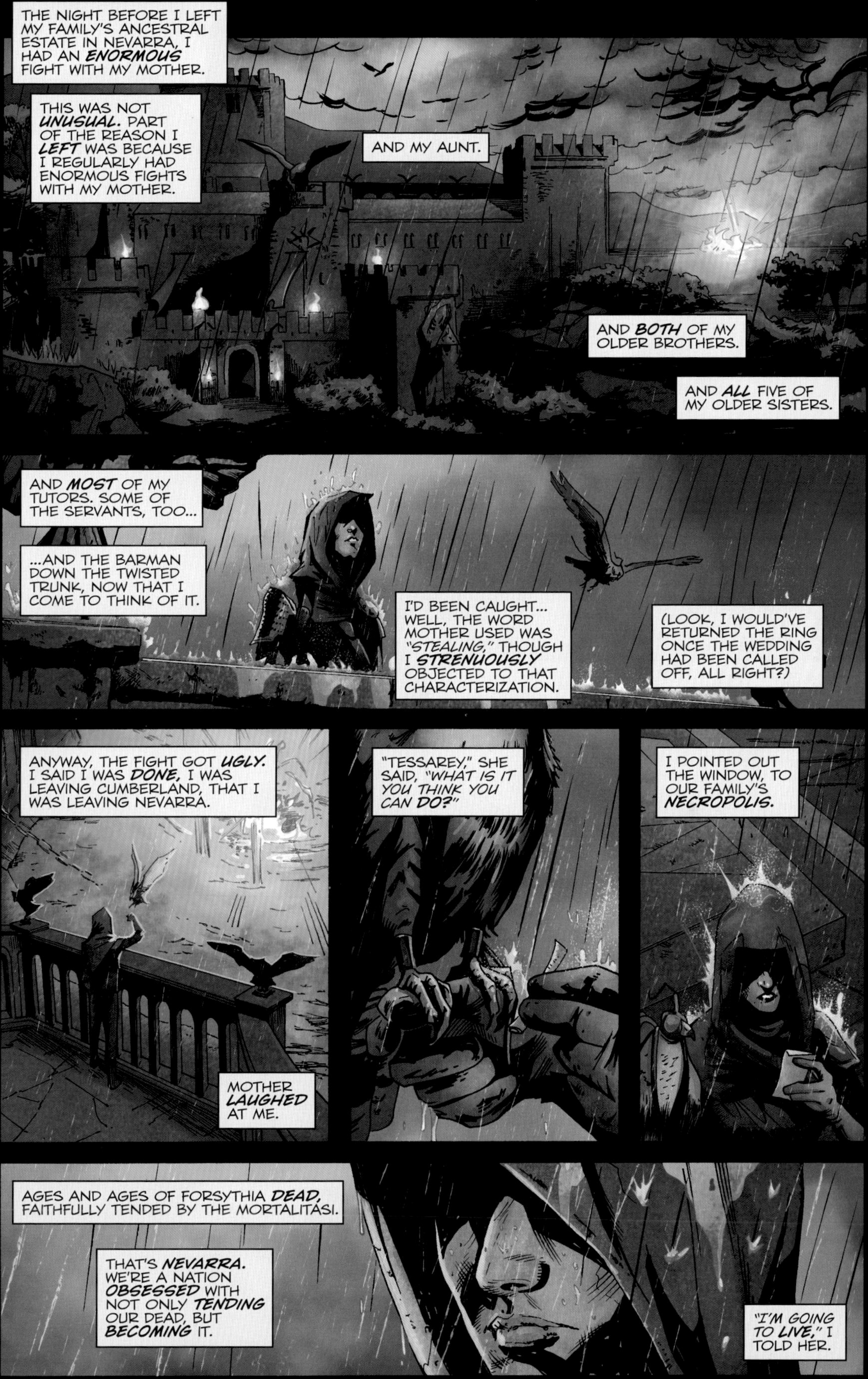

THE NIGHT BEFORE I LEFT MY FAMILY'S ANCESTRAL ESTATE IN NEVARRA, I HAD AN ENORMOUS FIGHT WITH MY MOTHER.
THIS WAS NOT UNUSUAL. PART OF THE REASON I LEFT WAS BECAUSE I REGULARLY HAD ENORMOUS FIGHTS WITH MY MOTHER.
AND MY AUNT.
AND BOTH OF MY OLDER BROTHERS.
AND ALL FIVE OF MY OLDER SISTERS.
AND MOST OF MY TUTORS. SOME OF THE SERVANTS, TOO...
...AND THE BARMAN DOWN THE TWISTED TRUNK, NOW THAT I COME TO THINK OF IT.
I'D BEEN CAUGHT... WELL, THE WORD MOTHER USED WAS "STEALING," THOUGH I STRENUOUSLY OBJECTED TO THAT CHARACTERIZATION.
(LOOK, I WOULD'VE RETURNED THE RING ONCE THE WEDDING HAD BEEN CALLED OFF, ALL RIGHT?)
ANYWAY, THE FIGHT GOT UGLY. I SAID I WAS DONE, I WAS LEAVING CUMBERLAND, THAT I WAS LEAVING NEVARRA.
MOTHER LAUGHED AT ME.
"TESSAREY," SHE SAID, "WHAT IS IT YOU THINK YOU CAN DO?"
I POINTED OUT THE WINDOW, TO OUR FAMILY'S NECROPOLIS.
AGES AND AGES OF FORSYTHIA DEAD, FAITHFULLY TENDED BY THE MORTALITASI.
THAT'S NEVARRA. WE'RE A NATION OBSESSED WITH NOT ONLY TENDING OUR DEAD, BUT BECOMING IT.
"I'M GOING TO LIVE," I TOLD HER.

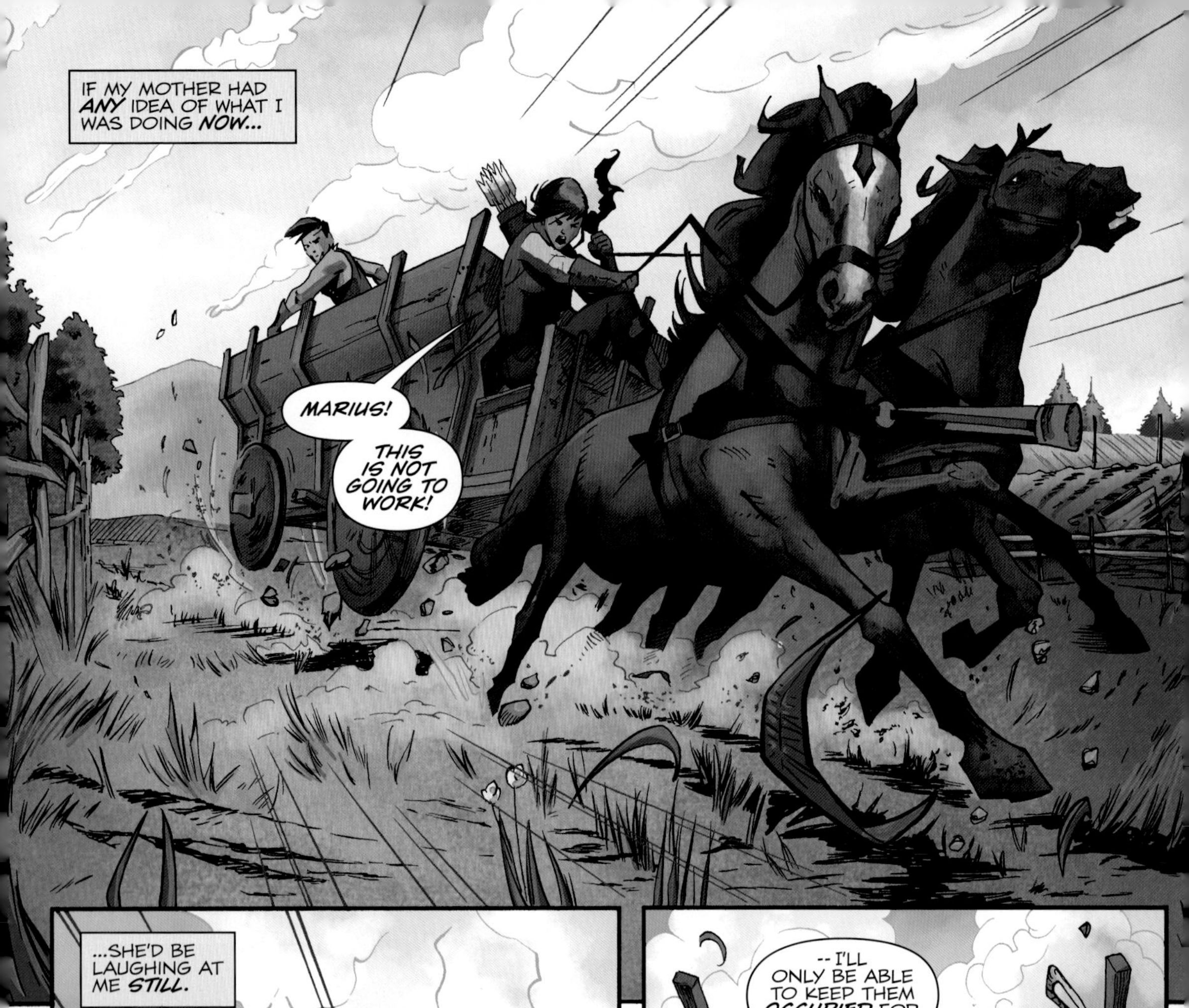
IF MY MOTHER HAD ANY IDEA OF WHAT I WAS DOING NOW...
MARIUS!
THIS IS NOT GOING TO WORK!

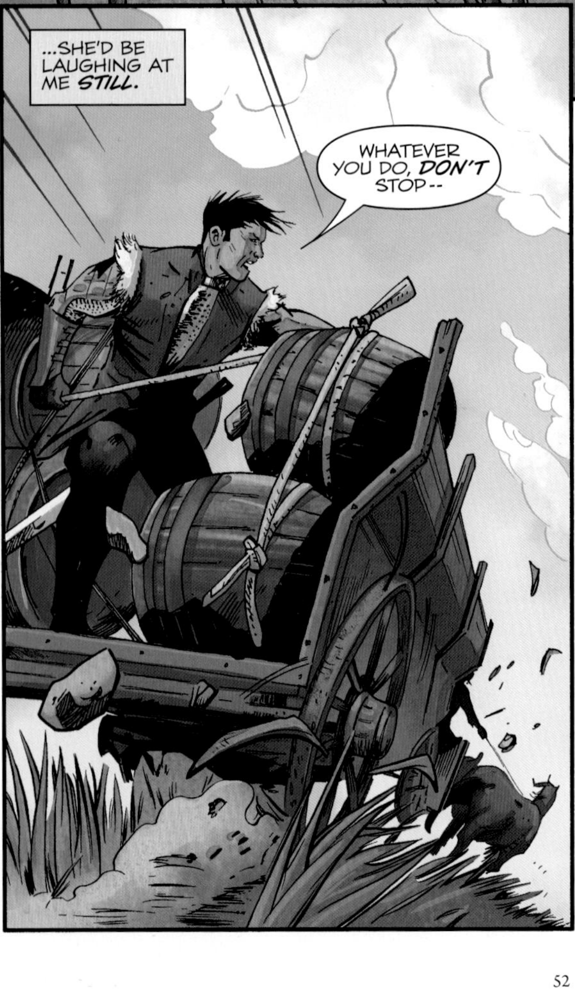
...SHE'D BE LAUGHING AT ME STILL.
WHATEVER YOU DO, DON'T STOP--

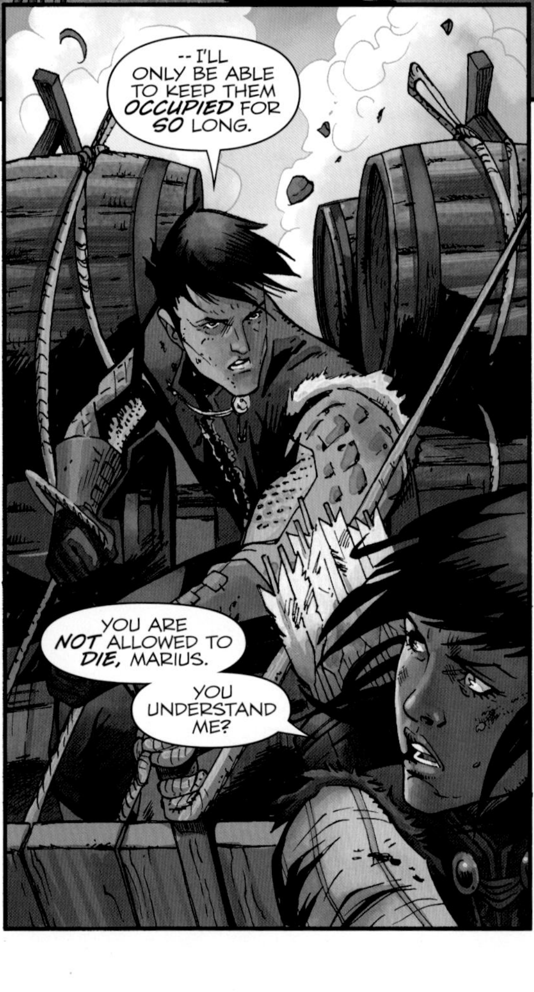
--I'LL ONLY BE ABLE TO KEEP THEM OCCUPIED FOR SO LONG.
YOU ARE NOT ALLOWED TO DIE, MARIUS.
YOU UNDERSTAND ME?

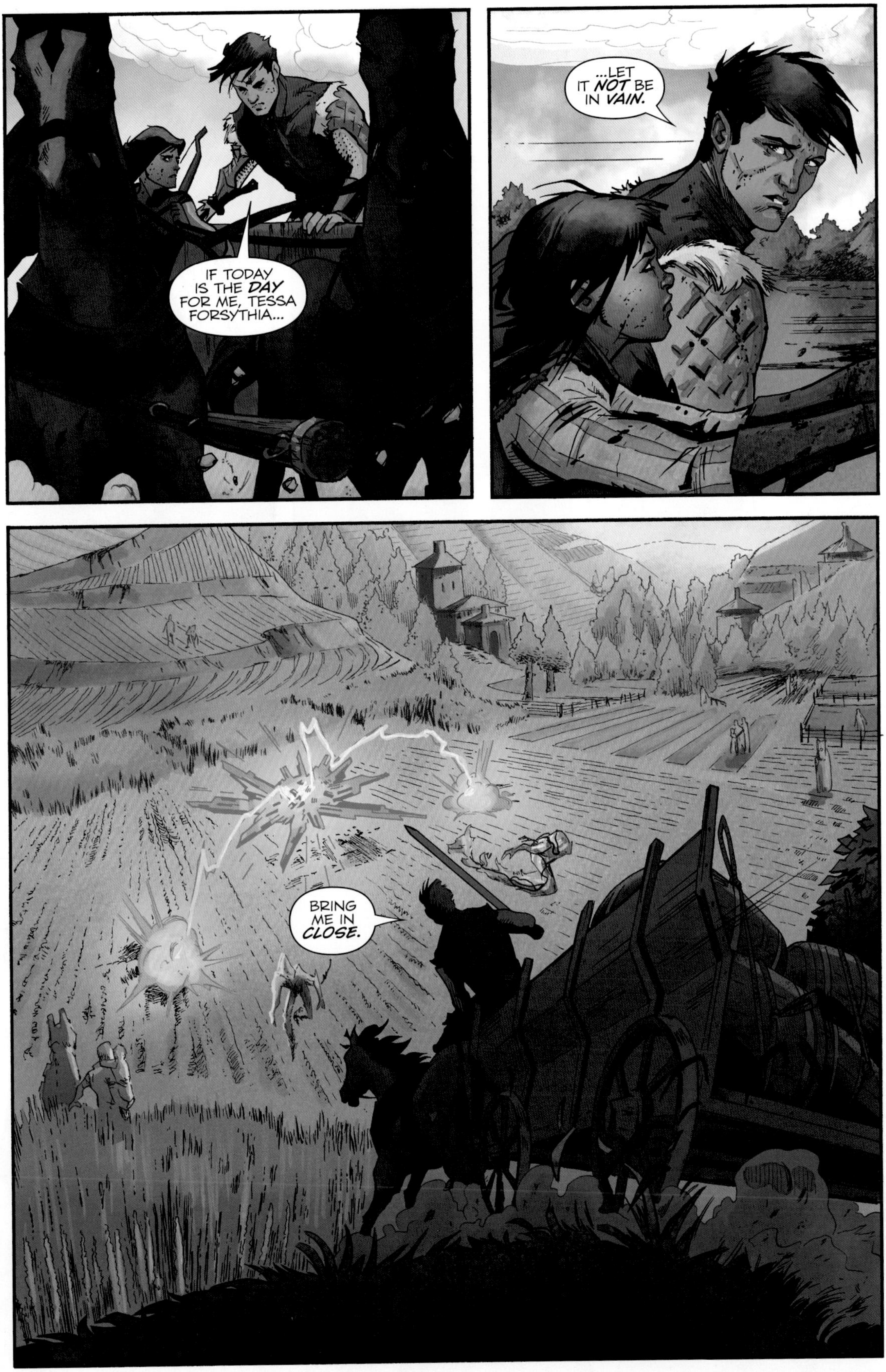
IF TODAY IS THE DAY FOR ME, TESSA FORSYTHIA...
...LET IT NOT BE IN VAIN.
BRING ME IN CLOSE.

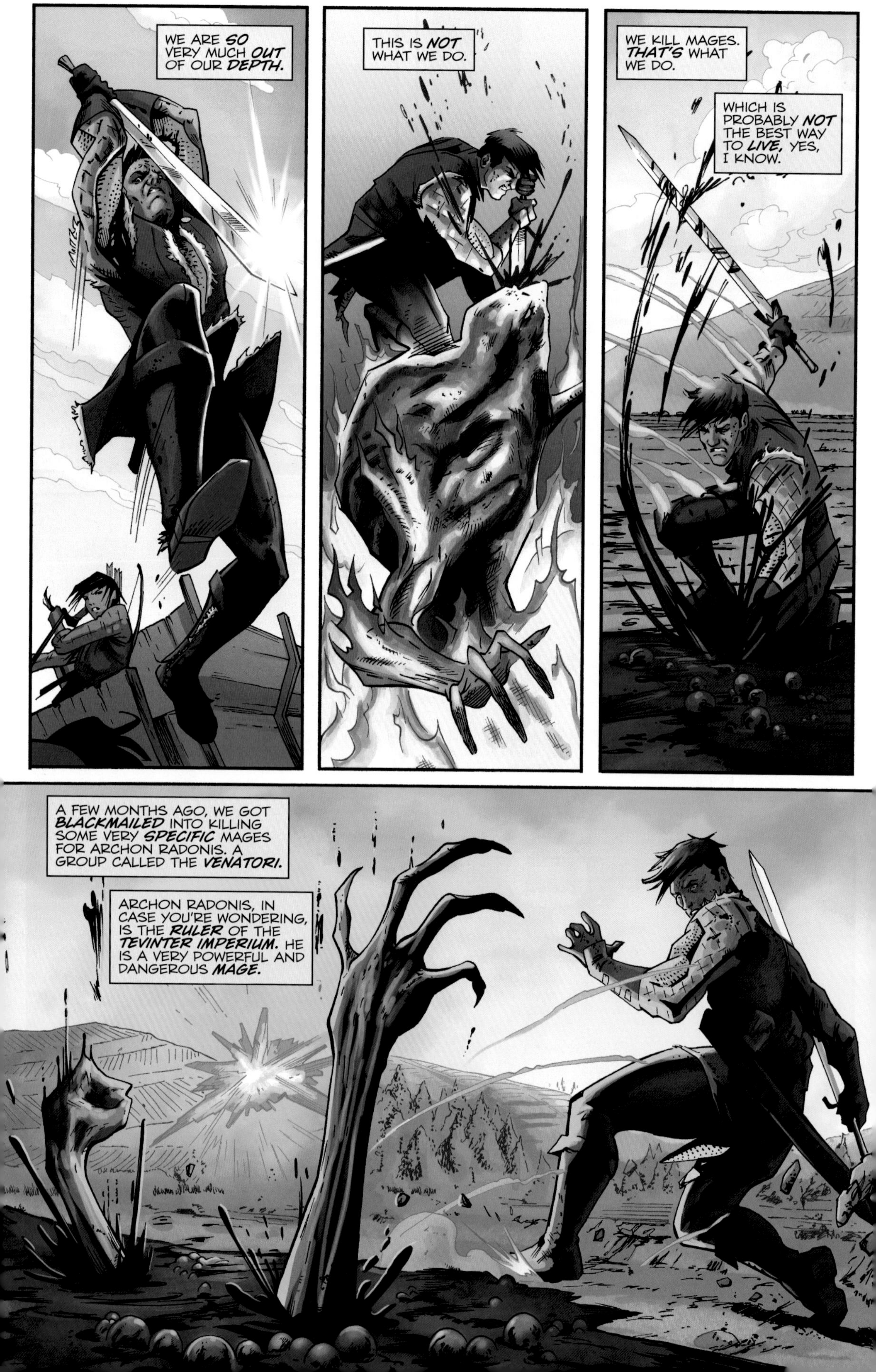
WE ARE SO VERY MUCH OUT OF OUR DEPTH.
THIS IS NOT WHAT WE DO.
WE KILL MAGES. THAT'S WHAT WE DO.
WHICH IS PROBABLY NOT THE BEST WAY TO LIVE, YES, I KNOW.
A FEW MONTHS AGO, WE GOT BLACKMAILED INTO KILLING SOME VERY SPECIFIC MAGES FOR ARCHON RADONIS. A GROUP CALLED THE VENATORI.
ARCHON RADONIS, IN CASE YOU'RE WONDERING, IS THE RULER OF THE TEVINTER IMPERIUM. HE IS A VERY POWERFUL AND DANGEROUS MAGE.

WE DOUBLE-CROSSED HIM AND LEFT THE JOB *UNFINISHED*.

NEEDLESS TO SAY, ARCHON RADONIS DIDN'T *LIKE* THAT. HE'S BEEN TRYING TO KILL US EVER *SINCE*.

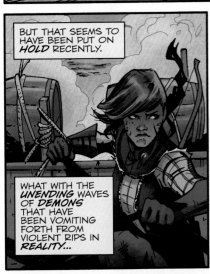

BUT THAT SEEMS TO HAVE BEEN PUT ON *HOLD* RECENTLY.

WHAT WITH THE *UNENDING* WAVES OF *DEMONS* THAT HAVE BEEN VOMITING FORTH FROM VIOLENT RIPS IN *REALITY*...

...FROM *TEARS* IN THE *VEIL* SEPARATING OUR WORLD FROM THE FADE...

...TEARS THAT *NOBODY* KNOWS HOW TO *CLOSE*.

WHAT WE ARE FIGHTING NOW IS THE *END* OF THE *WORLD*.

AND WE'RE *LOSING*.

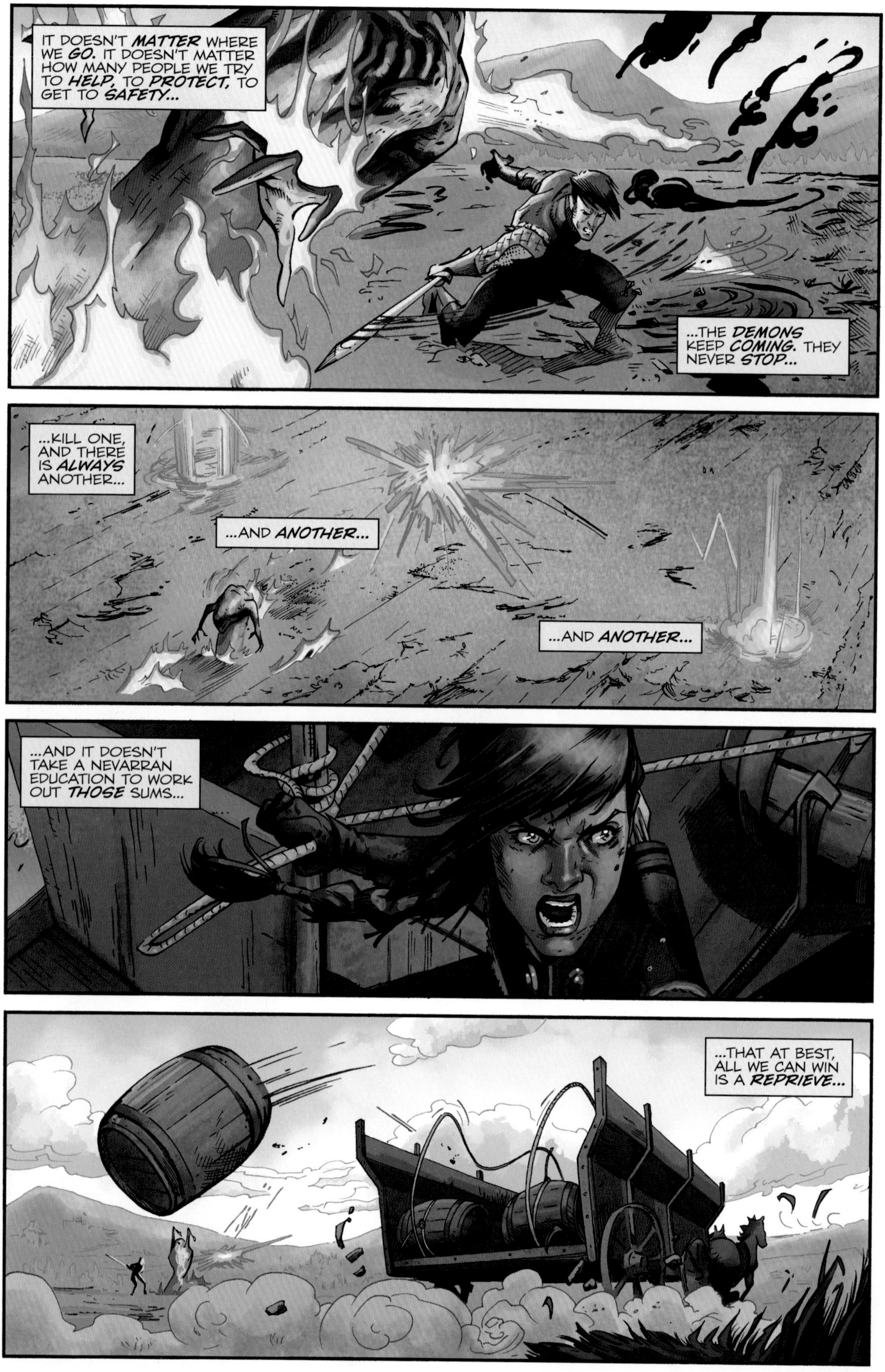
IT DOESN'T MATTER WHERE WE GO. IT DOESN'T MATTER HOW MANY PEOPLE WE TRY TO HELP, TO PROTECT, TO GET TO SAFETY...
...THE DEMONS KEEP COMING. THEY NEVER STOP...
...KILL ONE, AND THERE IS ALWAYS ANOTHER...
...AND ANOTHER...
...AND ANOTHER...
...AND IT DOESN'T TAKE A NEVARRAN EDUCATION TO WORK OUT THOSE SUMS...
...THAT AT BEST, ALL WE CAN WIN IS A REPRIEVE...

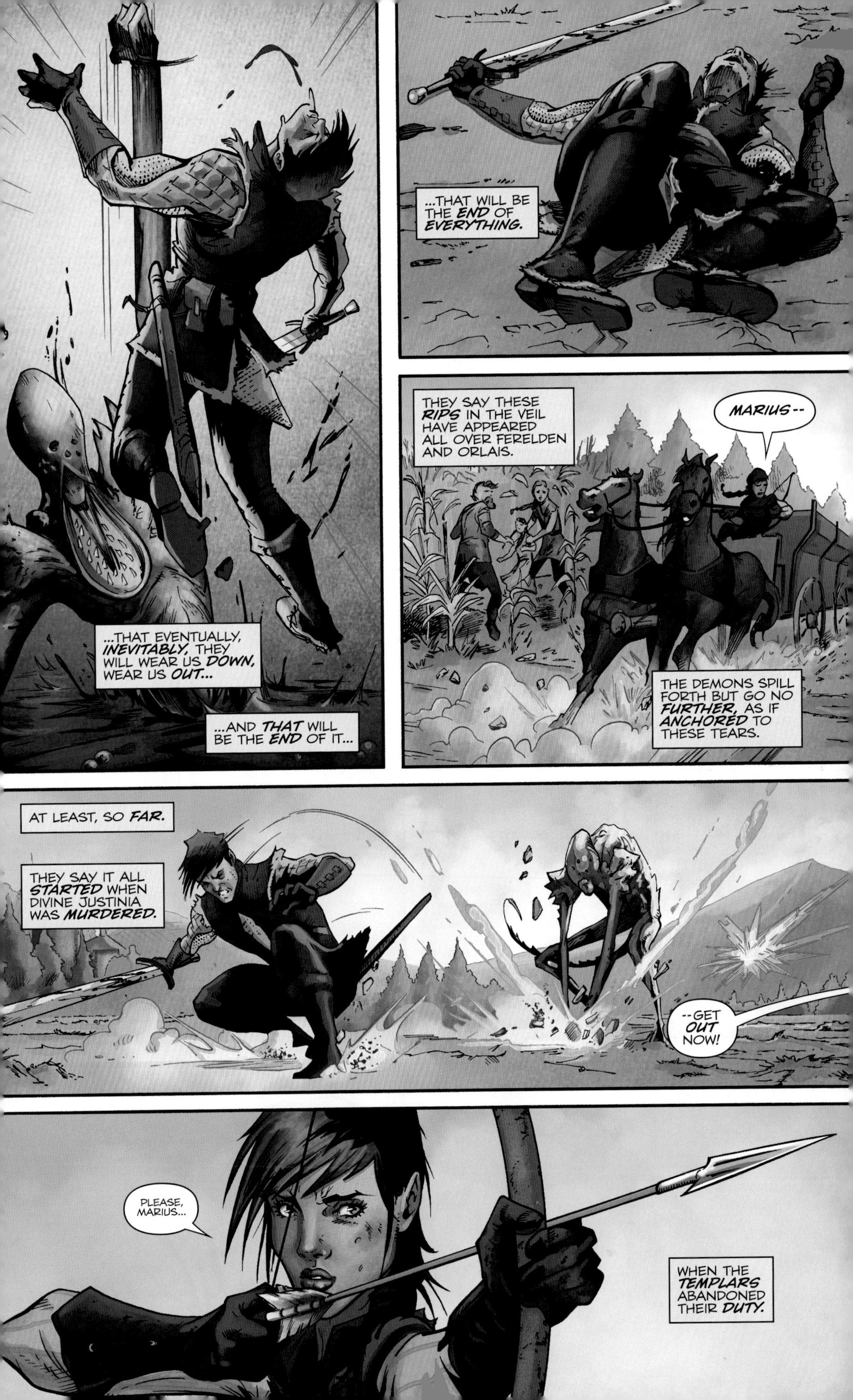
...THAT EVENTUALLY, INEVITABLY, THEY WILL WEAR US DOWN, WEAR US OUT...
...AND THAT WILL BE THE END OF IT...
...THAT WILL BE THE END OF EVERYTHING.
THEY SAY THESE RIPS IN THE VEIL HAVE APPEARED ALL OVER FERELDEN AND ORLAIS.
MARIUS --
THE DEMONS SPILL FORTH BUT GO NO FURTHER, AS IF ANCHORED TO THESE TEARS.
AT LEAST, SO FAR.
THEY SAY IT ALL STARTED WHEN DIVINE JUSTINIA WAS MURDERED.
--GET OUT NOW!
PLEASE, MARIUS...
WHEN THE TEMPLARS ABANDONED THEIR DUTY.

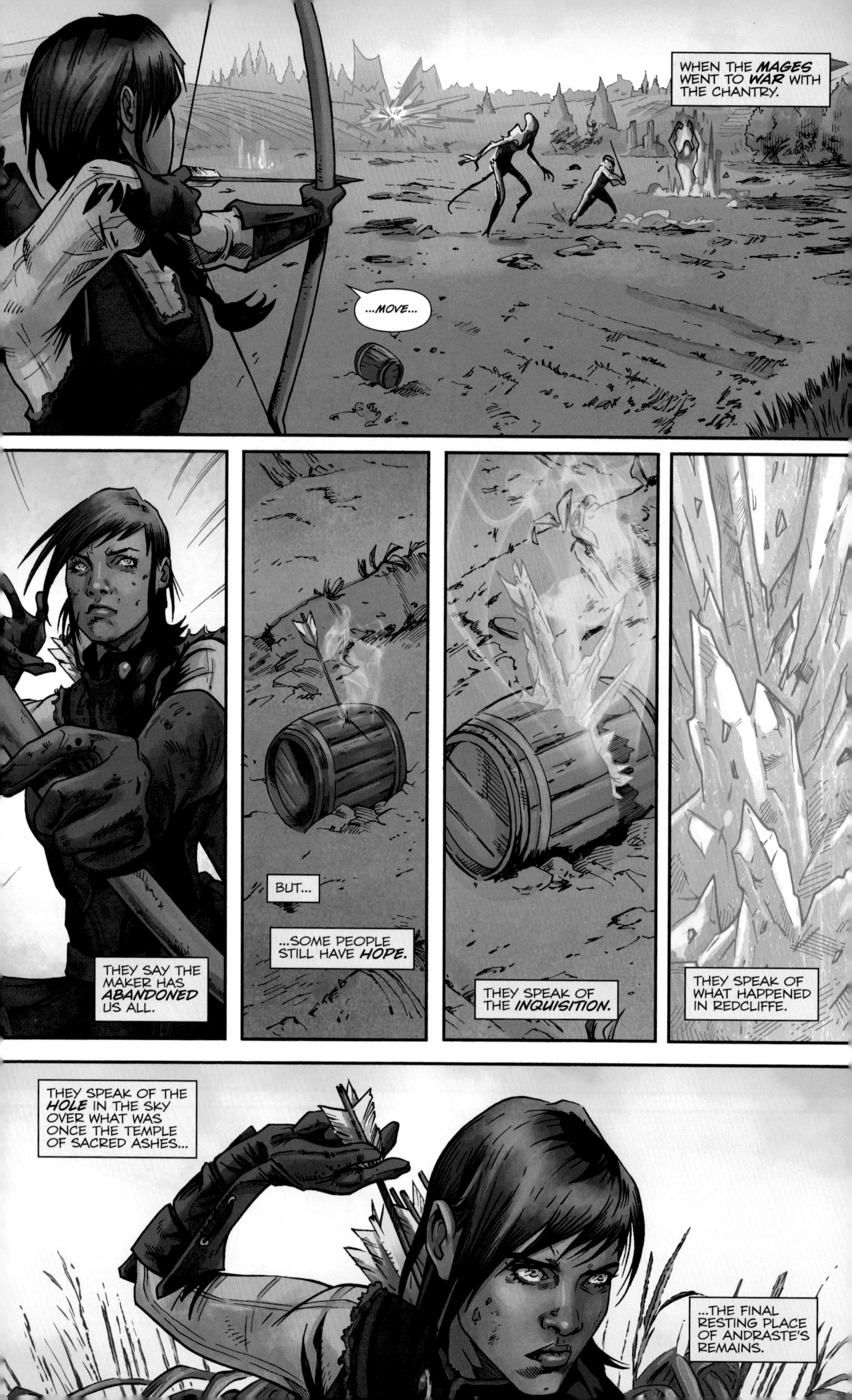
WHEN THE MAGES WENT TO WAR WITH THE CHANTRY.
...MOVE...
THEY SAY THE MAKER HAS ABANDONED US ALL.
BUT...
...SOME PEOPLE STILL HAVE HOPE.
THEY SPEAK OF THE INQUISITION.
THEY SPEAK OF WHAT HAPPENED IN REDCLIFFE.
THEY SPEAK OF THE HOLE IN THE SKY OVER WHAT WAS ONCE THE TEMPLE OF SACRED ASHES...
...THE FINAL RESTING PLACE OF ANDRASTE'S REMAINS.

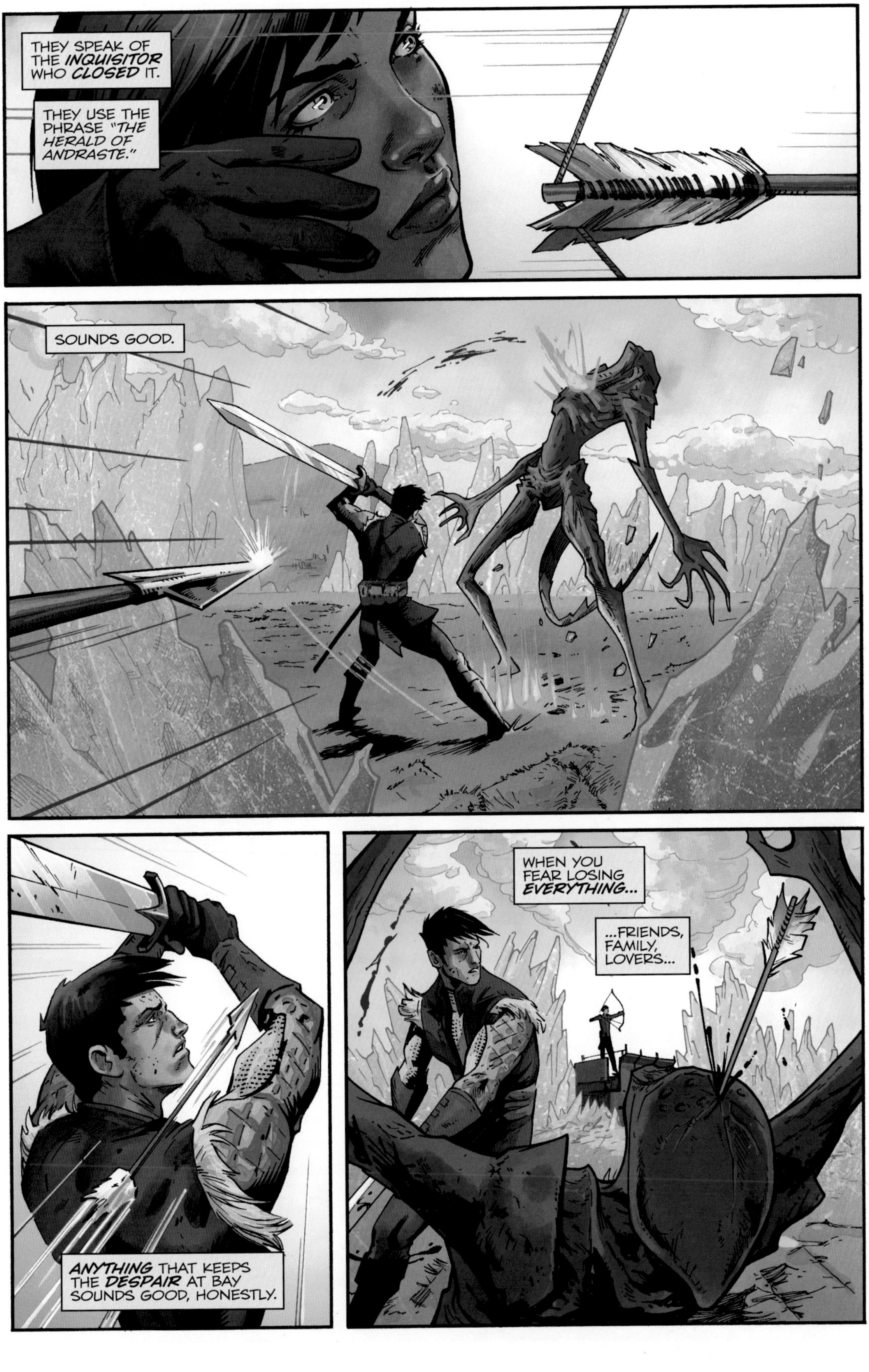
THEY SPEAK OF THE *INQUISITOR* WHO *CLOSED* IT.
THEY USE THE PHRASE *"THE HERALD OF ANDRASTE."*
SOUNDS GOOD.
ANYTHING THAT KEEPS THE *DESPAIR* AT BAY SOUNDS GOOD, HONESTLY.
WHEN YOU FEAR LOSING *EVERYTHING...*
...FRIENDS, FAMILY, LOVERS...

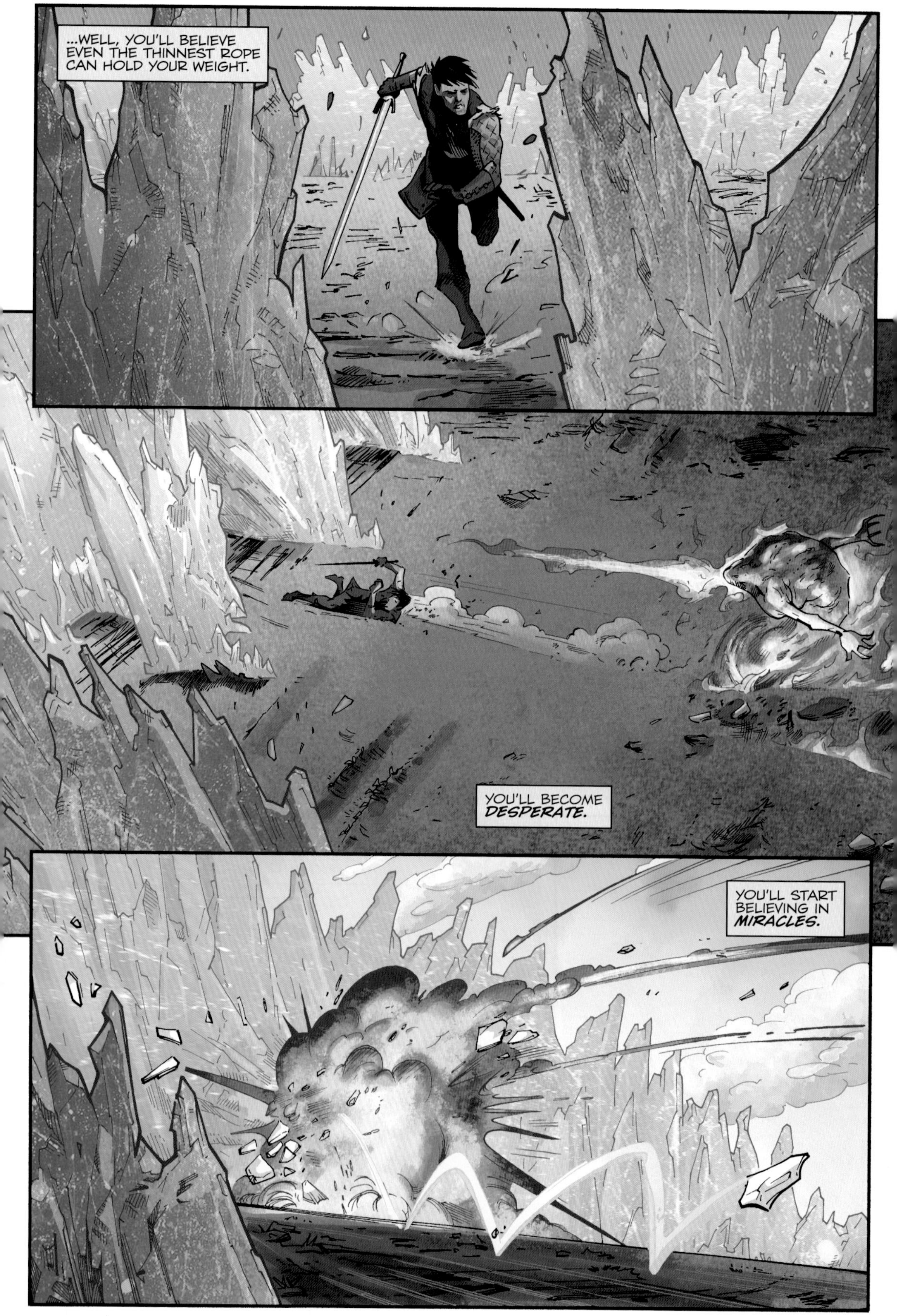
...WELL, YOU'LL BELIEVE EVEN THE THINNEST ROPE CAN HOLD YOUR WEIGHT.
YOU'LL BECOME DESPERATE.
YOU'LL START BELIEVING IN MIRACLES.

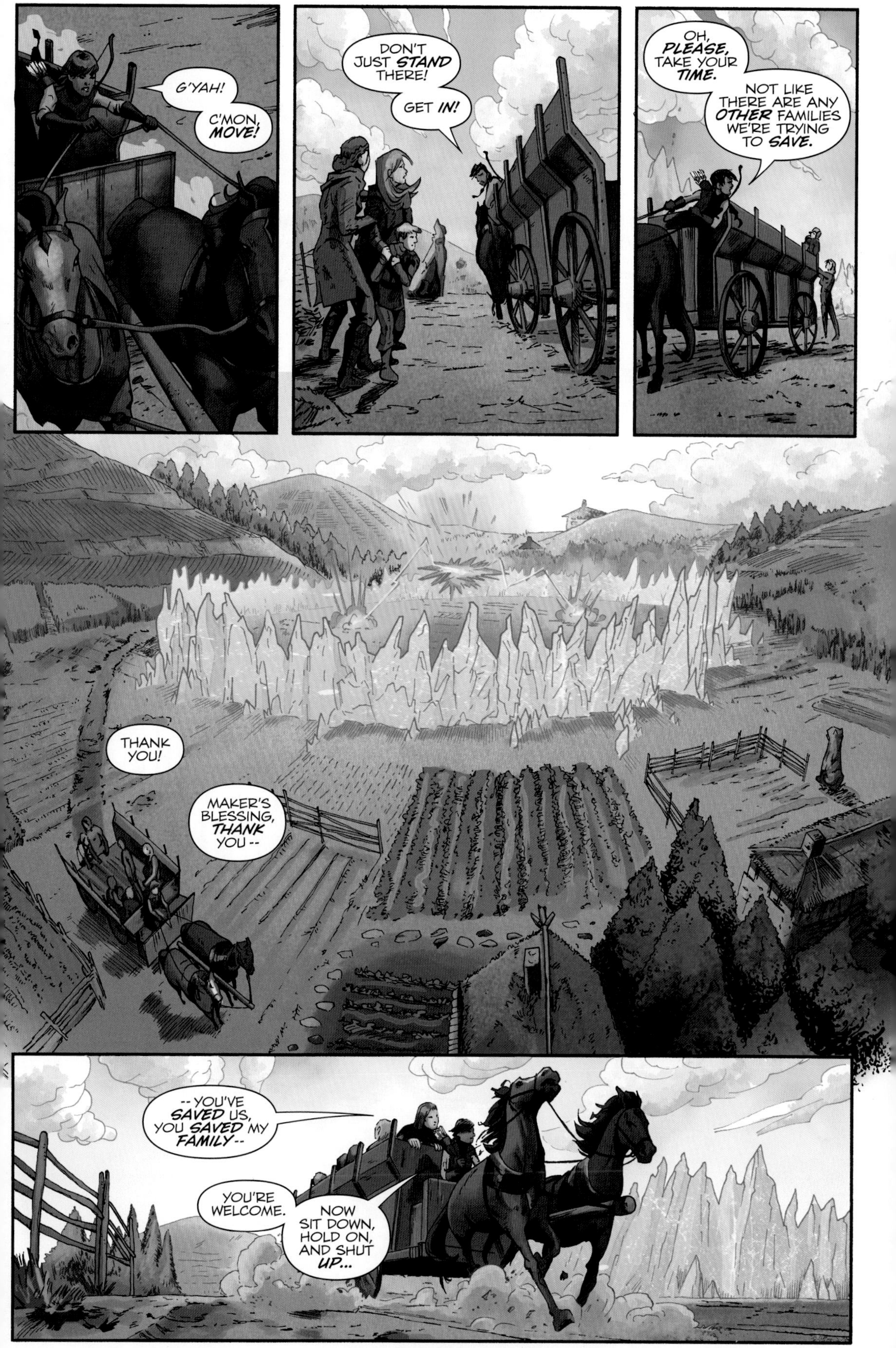
G'YAH!
C'MON, MOVE!
DON'T JUST STAND THERE!
GET IN!
OH, PLEASE, TAKE YOUR TIME.
NOT LIKE THERE ARE ANY OTHER FAMILIES WE'RE TRYING TO SAVE.
THANK YOU!
MAKER'S BLESSING, THANK YOU --
-- YOU'VE SAVED US, YOU SAVED MY FAMILY --
YOU'RE WELCOME.
NOW SIT DOWN, HOLD ON, AND SHUT UP...

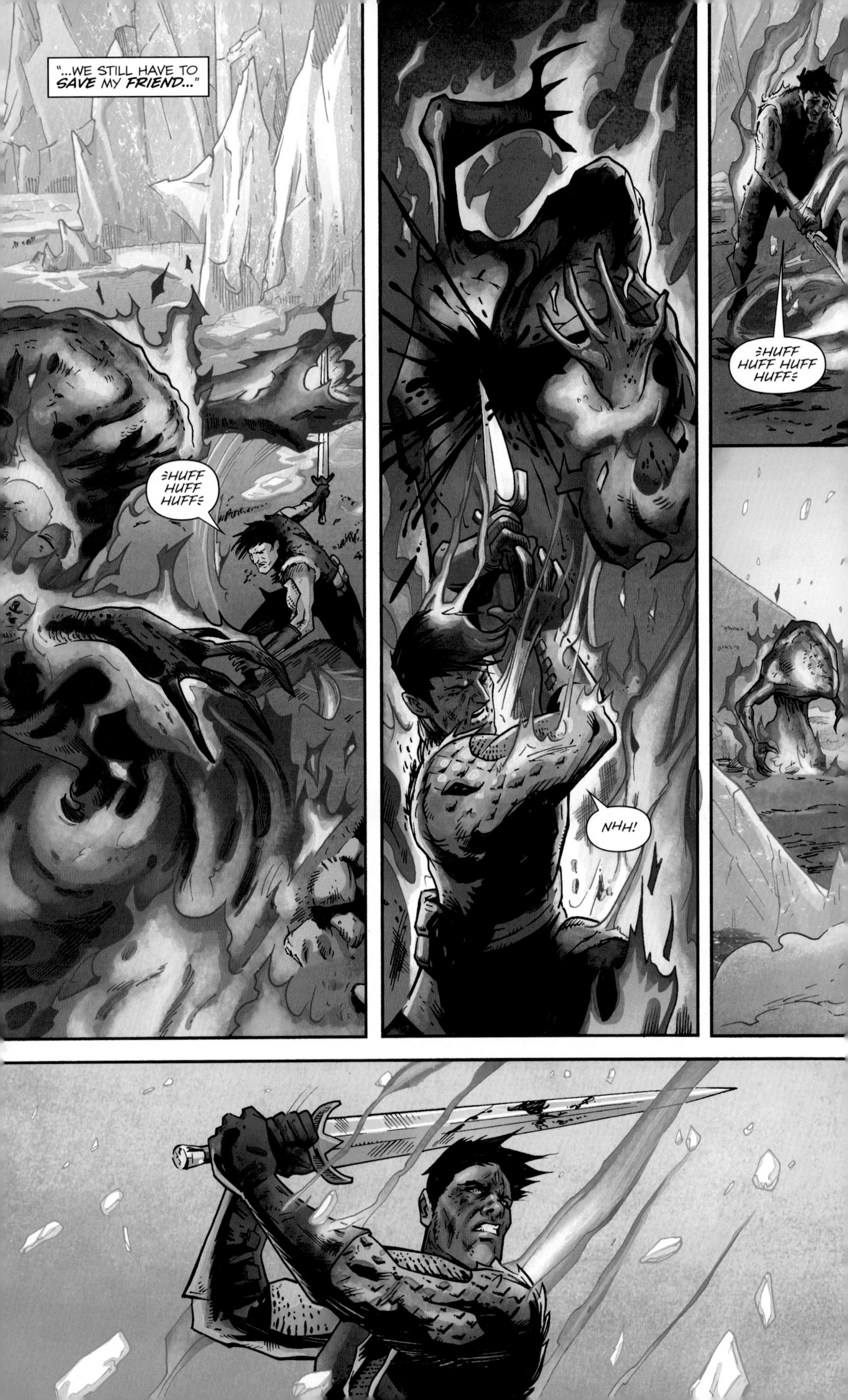
"...WE STILL HAVE TO SAVE MY FRIEND..."
HUFF HUFF HUFF
NHH!
HUFF HUFF HUFF HUFF

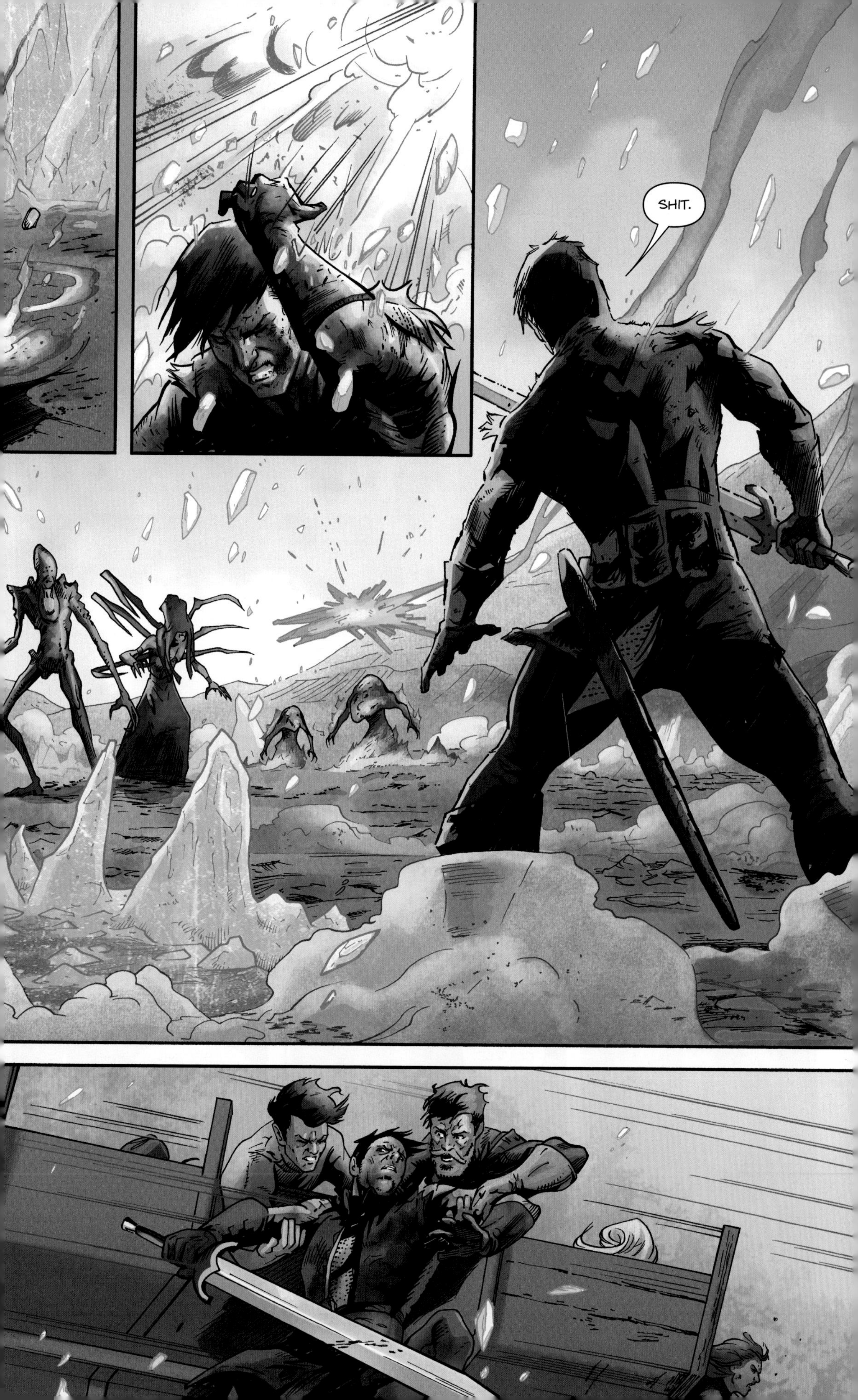
SHIT.

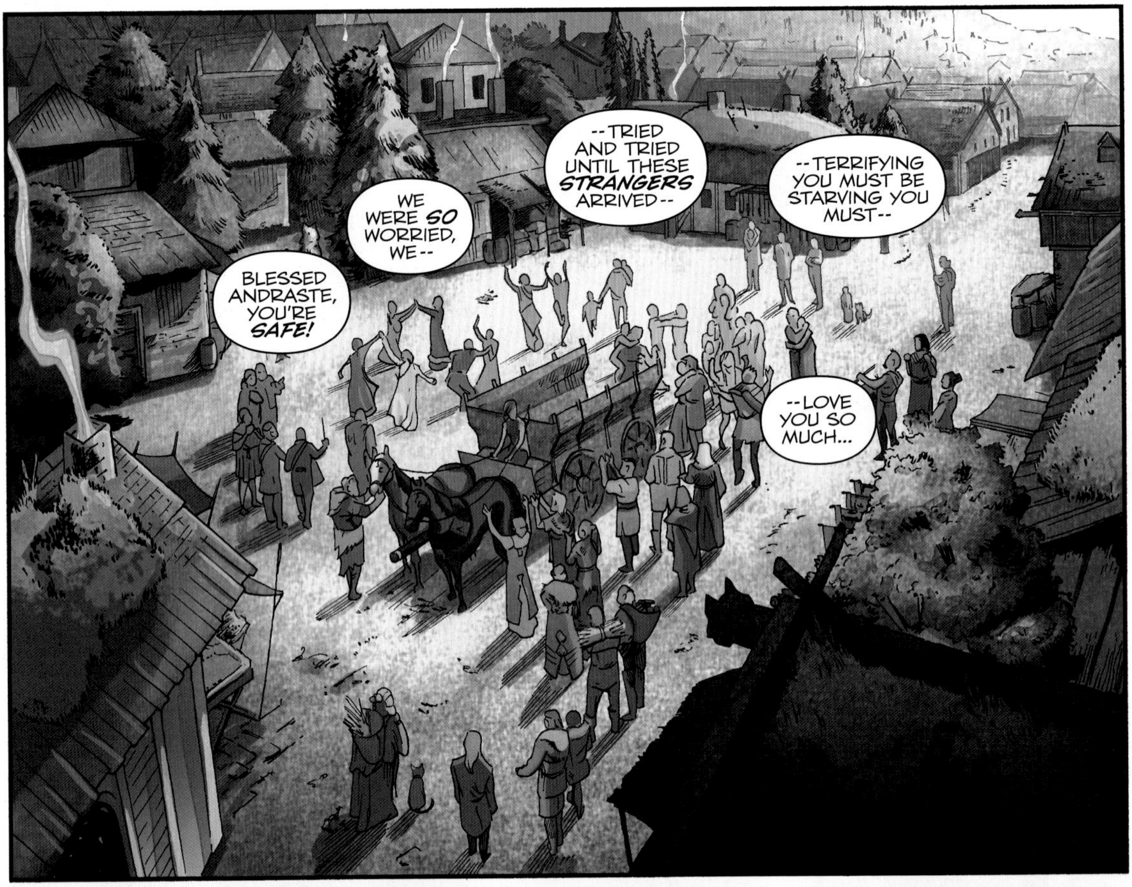
BLESSED ANDRASTE, YOU'RE SAFE!
WE WERE SO WORRIED, WE--
--TRIED AND TRIED UNTIL THESE STRANGERS ARRIVED--
--TERRIFYING YOU MUST BE STARVING YOU MUST--
--LOVE YOU SO MUCH...

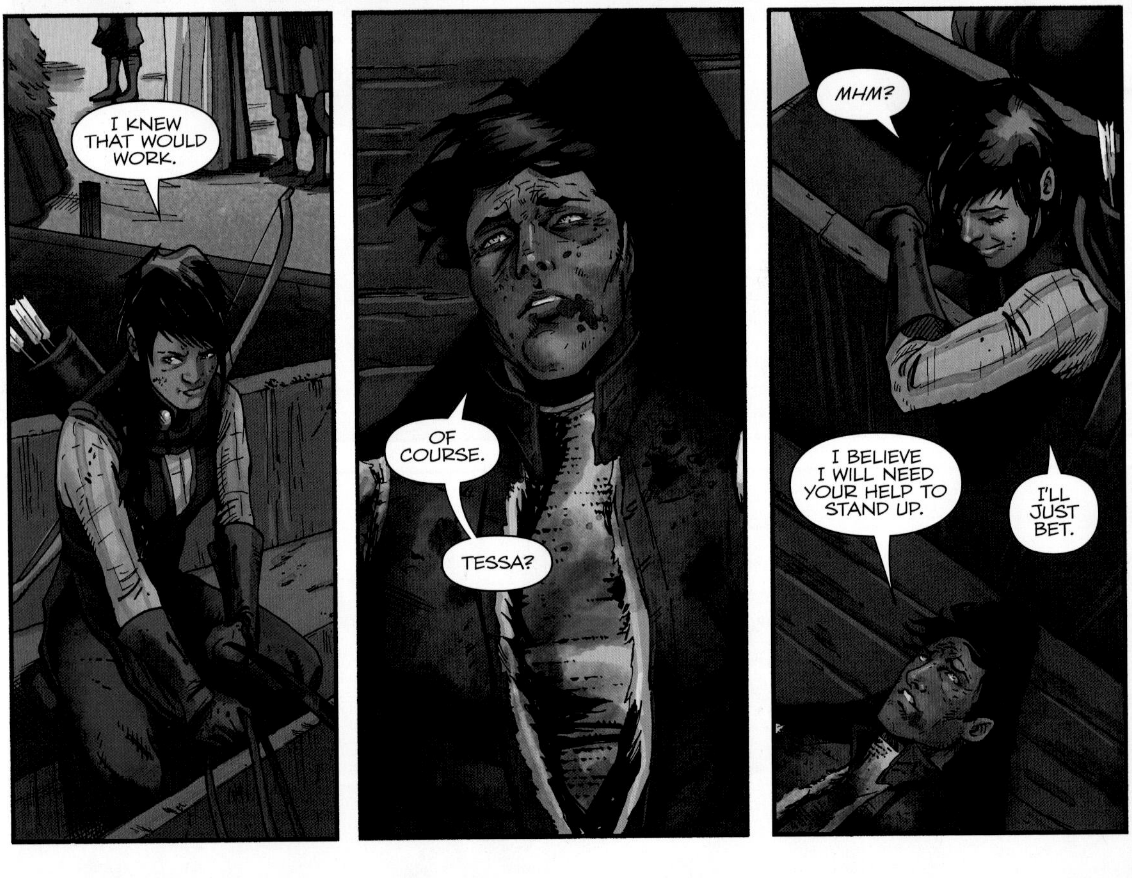
I KNEW THAT WOULD WORK.
OF COURSE.
TESSA?
MHM?
I BELIEVE I WILL NEED YOUR HELP TO STAND UP.
I'LL JUST BET.

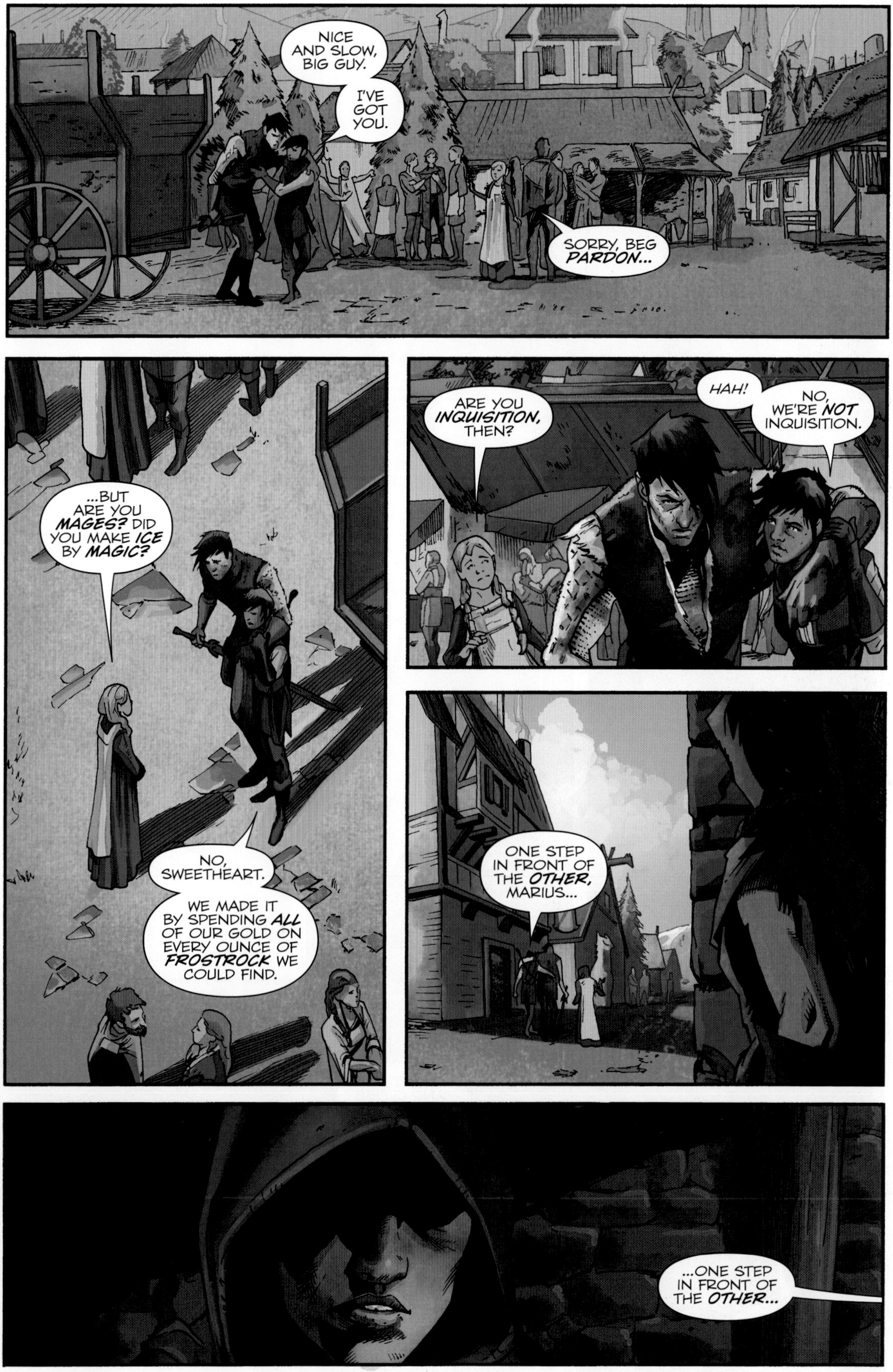
NICE AND SLOW, BIG GUY.
I'VE GOT YOU.
SORRY, BEG PARDON...
...BUT ARE YOU MAGES? DID YOU MAKE ICE BY MAGIC?
NO, SWEETHEART.
WE MADE IT BY SPENDING ALL OF OUR GOLD ON EVERY OUNCE OF FROSTROCK WE COULD FIND.
ARE YOU INQUISITION, THEN?
HAH!
NO, WE'RE NOT INQUISITION.
ONE STEP IN FRONT OF THE OTHER, MARIUS...
...ONE STEP IN FRONT OF THE OTHER...

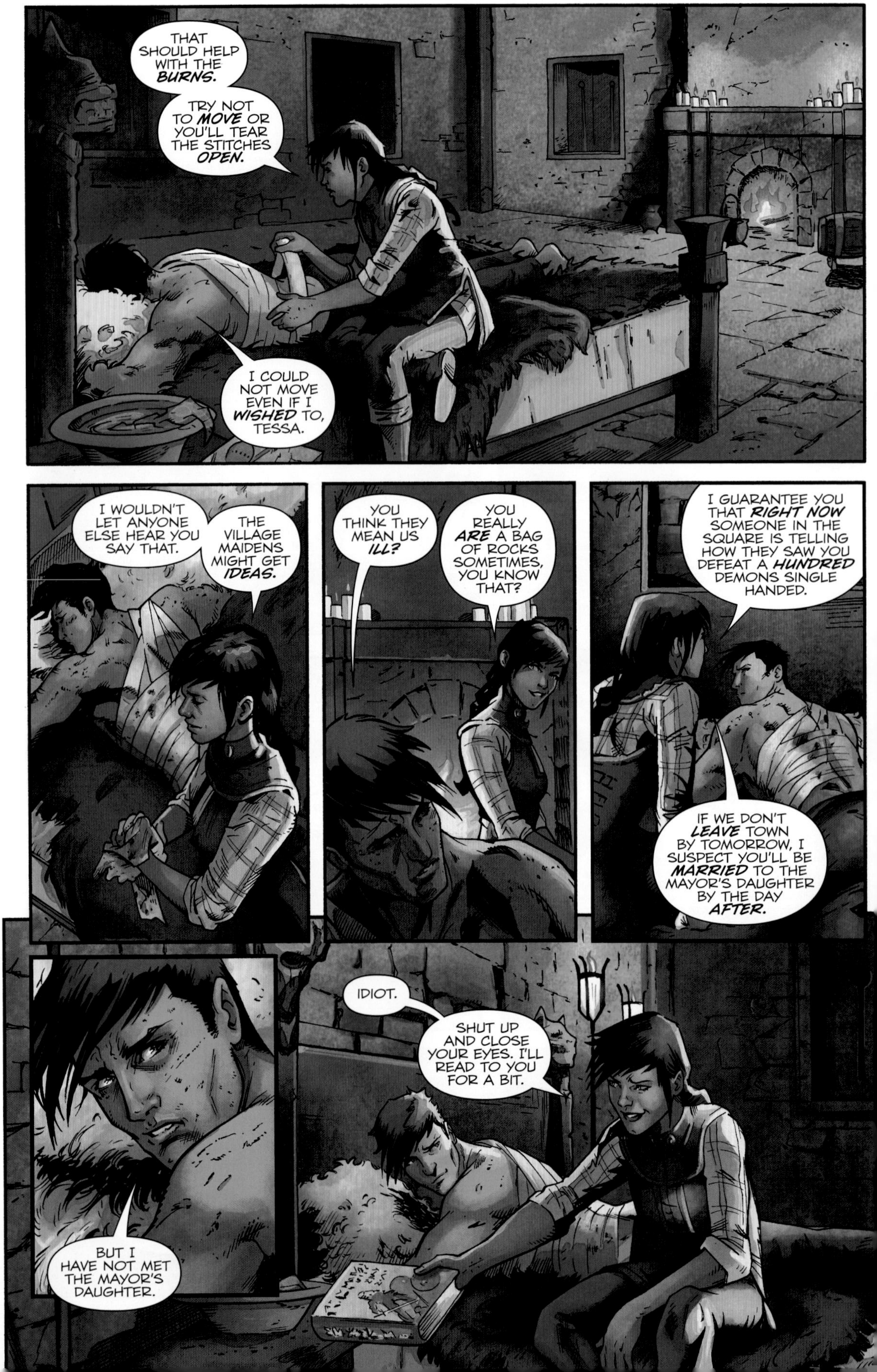
THAT SHOULD HELP WITH THE BURNS.
TRY NOT TO MOVE OR YOU'LL TEAR THE STITCHES OPEN.
I COULD NOT MOVE EVEN IF I WISHED TO, TESSA.
I WOULDN'T LET ANYONE ELSE HEAR YOU SAY THAT.
THE VILLAGE MAIDENS MIGHT GET IDEAS.
YOU THINK THEY MEAN US ILL?
YOU REALLY ARE A BAG OF ROCKS SOMETIMES, YOU KNOW THAT?
I GUARANTEE YOU THAT RIGHT NOW SOMEONE IN THE SQUARE IS TELLING HOW THEY SAW YOU DEFEAT A HUNDRED DEMONS SINGLE HANDED.
IF WE DON'T LEAVE TOWN BY TOMORROW, I SUSPECT YOU'LL BE MARRIED TO THE MAYOR'S DAUGHTER BY THE DAY AFTER.
BUT I HAVE NOT MET THE MAYOR'S DAUGHTER.
IDIOT.
SHUT UP AND CLOSE YOUR EYES. I'LL READ TO YOU FOR A BIT.

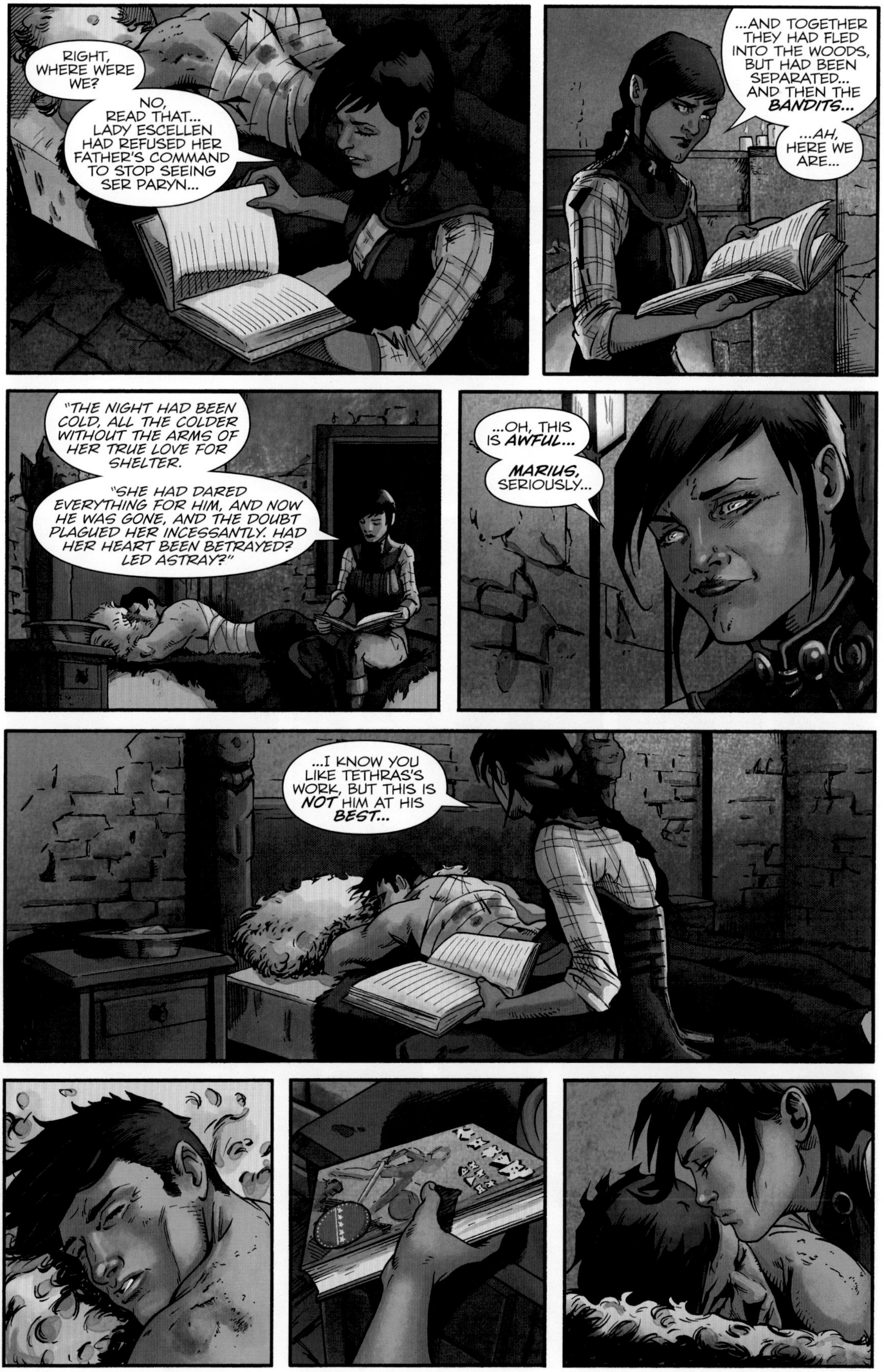
RIGHT, WHERE WE'RE WE?
NO, READ THAT... LADY ESCELLEN HAD REFUSED HER FATHER'S COMMAND TO STOP SEEING SER PARYN...
...AND TOGETHER THEY HAD FLED INTO THE WOODS, BUT HAD BEEN SEPARATED... AND THEN THE BANDITS...
...AH, HERE WE ARE...
"THE NIGHT HAD BEEN COLD, ALL THE COLDER WITHOUT THE ARMS OF HER TRUE LOVE FOR SHELTER.
"SHE HAD DARED EVERYTHING FOR HIM, AND NOW HE WAS GONE, AND THE DOUBT PLAGUED HER INCESSANTLY. HAD HER HEART BEEN BETRAYED? LED ASTRAY?"
...OH, THIS IS AWFUL...
MARIUS, SERIOUSLY...
...I KNOW YOU LIKE TETHRAS'S WORK, BUT THIS IS NOT HIM AT HIS BEST...

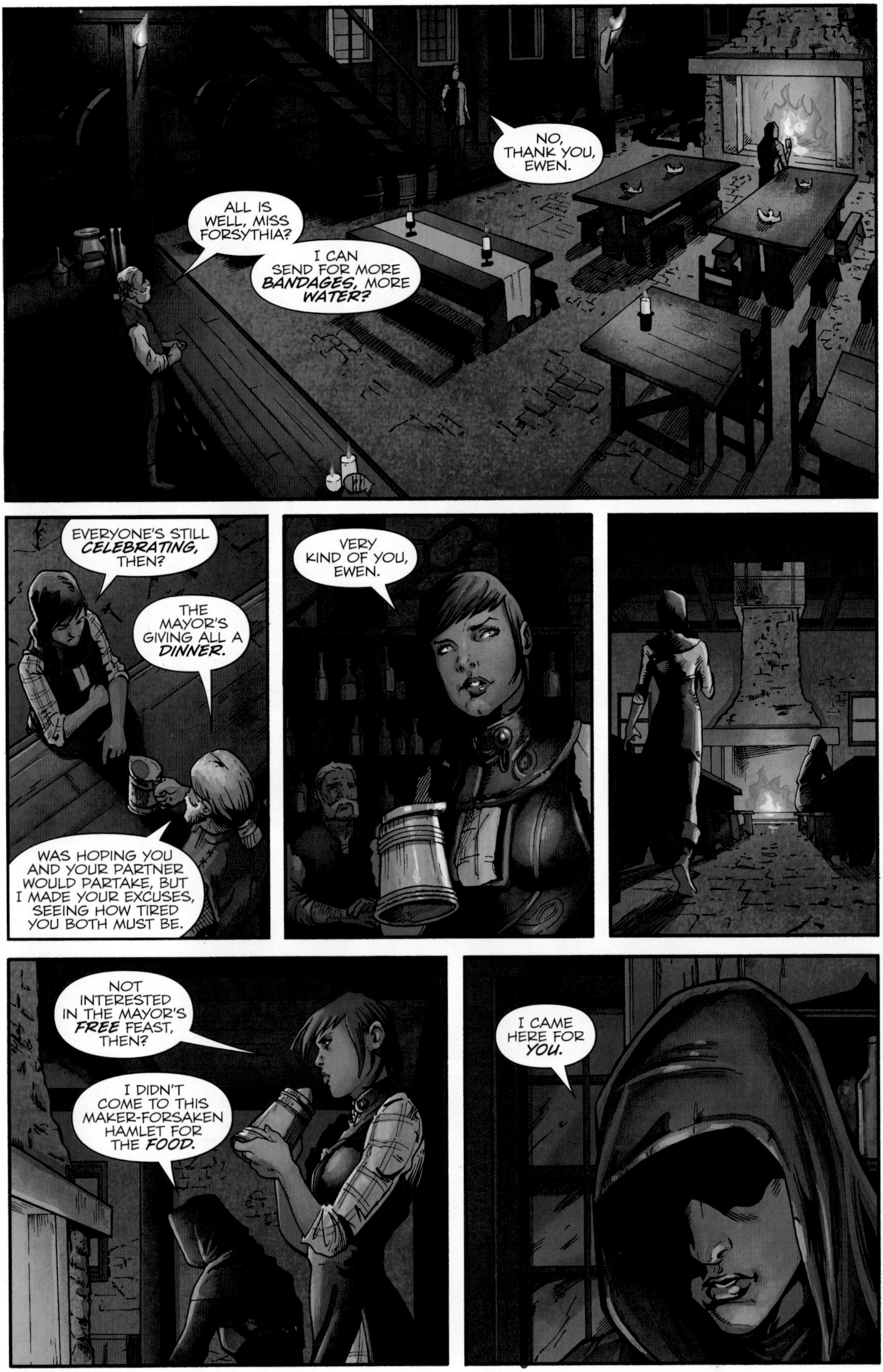
NO, THANK YOU, EWEN.
ALL IS WELL, MISS FORSYTHIA?
I CAN SEND FOR MORE BANDAGES, MORE WATER?
EVERYONE'S STILL CELEBRATING, THEN?
THE MAYOR'S GIVING ALL A DINNER.
WAS HOPING YOU AND YOUR PARTNER WOULD PARTAKE, BUT I MADE YOUR EXCUSES, SEEING HOW TIRED YOU BOTH MUST BE.
VERY KIND OF YOU, EWEN.
NOT INTERESTED IN THE MAYOR'S FREE FEAST, THEN?
I DIDN'T COME TO THIS MAKER-FORSAKEN HAMLET FOR THE FOOD.
I CAME HERE FOR YOU.

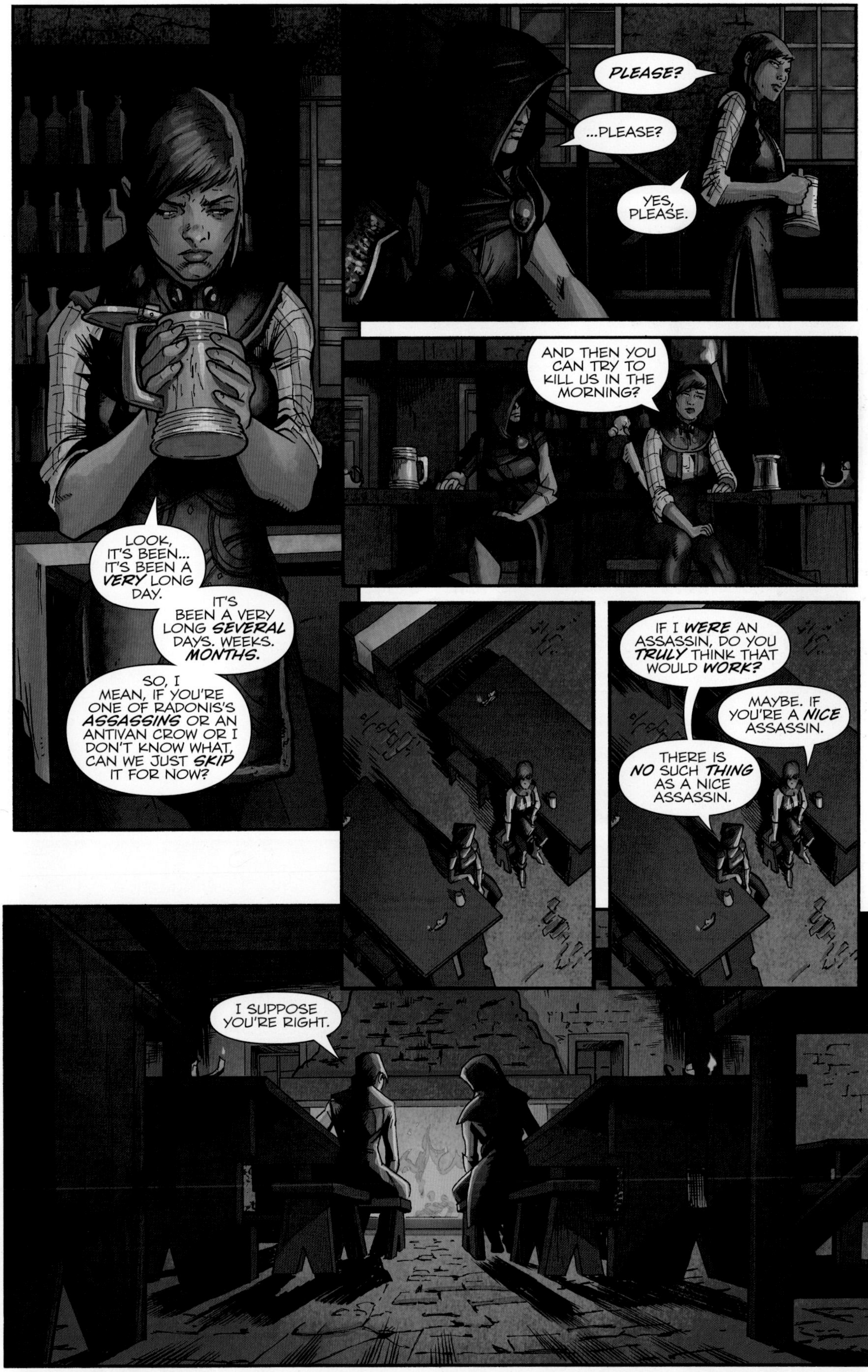
PLEASE?
...PLEASE?
YES, PLEASE.
LOOK, IT'S BEEN... IT'S BEEN A VERY LONG DAY.
IT'S BEEN A VERY LONG SEVERAL DAYS. WEEKS. MONTHS.
SO, I MEAN, IF YOU'RE ONE OF RADONIS'S ASSASSINS OR AN ANTIVAN CROW OR I DON'T KNOW WHAT, CAN WE JUST SKIP IT FOR NOW?
AND THEN YOU CAN TRY TO KILL US IN THE MORNING?
IF I WERE AN ASSASSIN, DO YOU TRULY THINK THAT WOULD WORK?
MAYBE. IF YOU'RE A NICE ASSASSIN.
THERE IS NO SUCH THING AS A NICE ASSASSIN.
I SUPPOSE YOU'RE RIGHT.

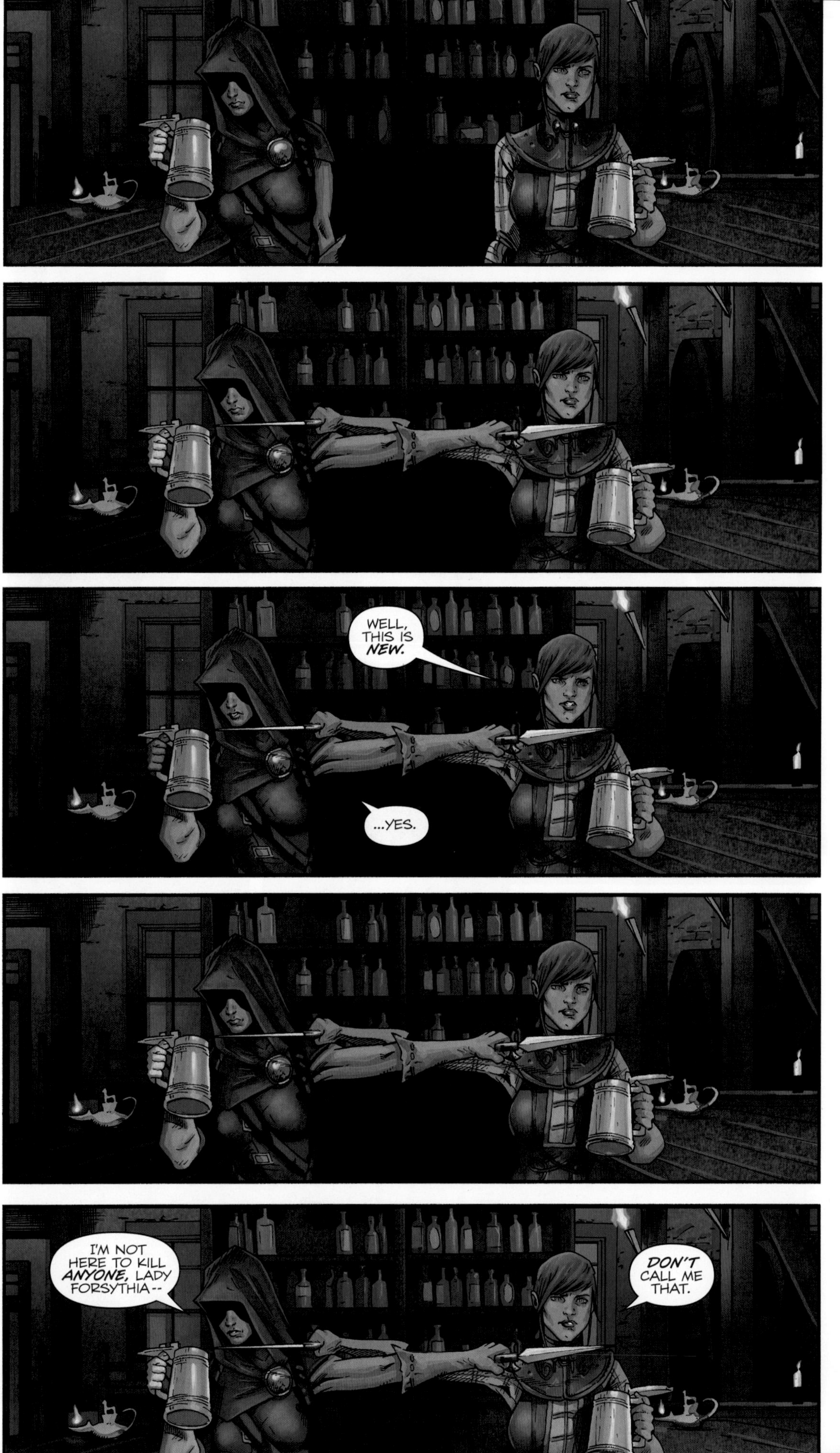
WELL, THIS IS NEW.
...YES.
I'M NOT HERE TO KILL ANYONE, LADY FORSYTHIA--
DON'T CALL ME THAT.

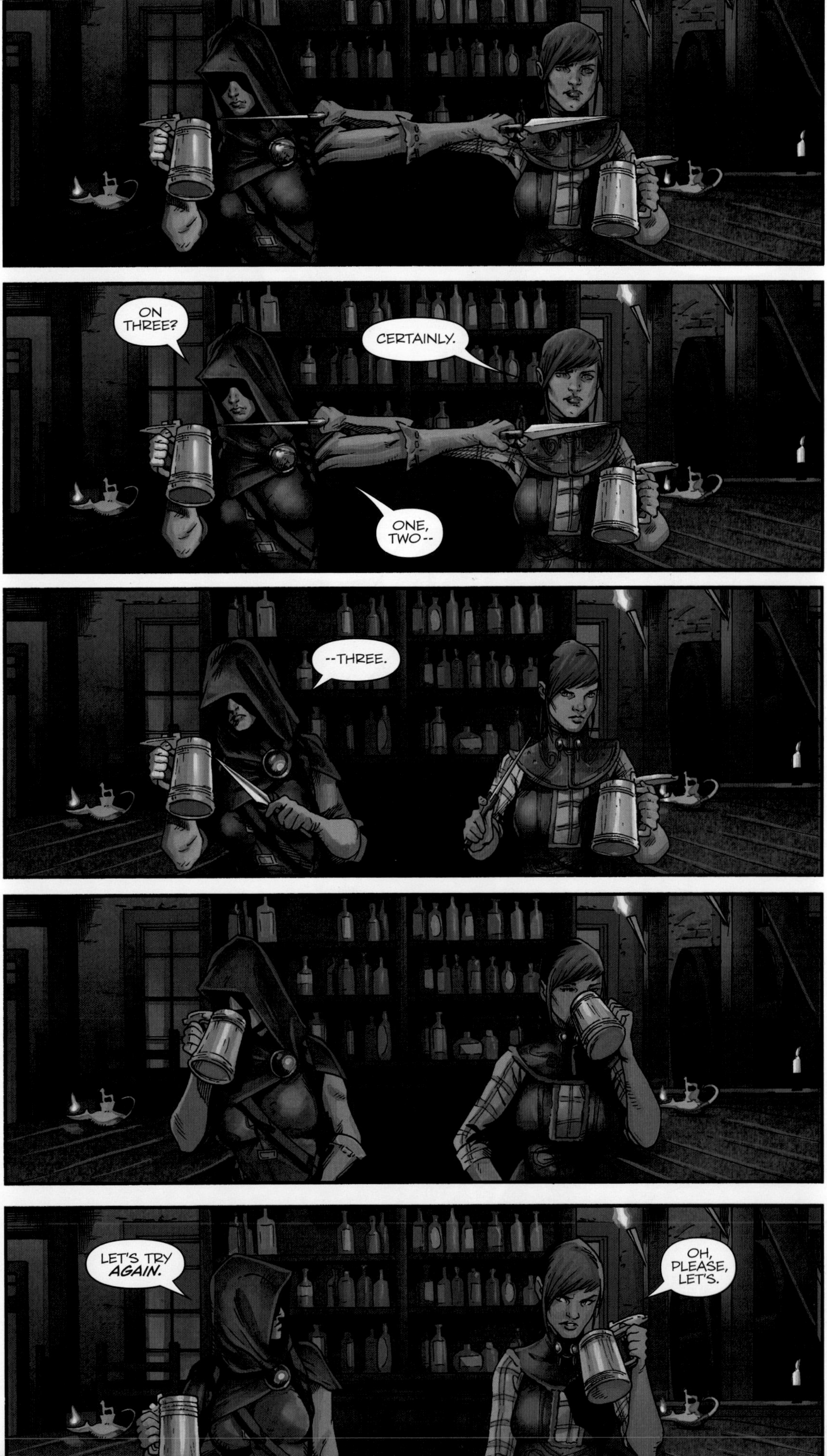
ON THREE?
CERTAINLY.
ONE, TWO--
--THREE.
LET'S TRY *AGAIN.*
OH, PLEASE, LET'S.

I'M NOT HERE FOR A BOUNTY, NOR TO FULFILL A *CONTRACT.*

I AM NOT AN ASSASSIN, AT LEAST, *NOT* AT *THIS* MOMENT.

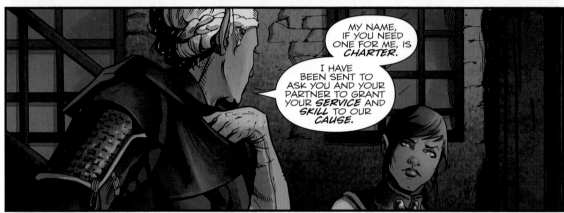

MY NAME, IF YOU NEED ONE FOR ME, IS *CHARTER.*

I HAVE BEEN SENT TO ASK YOU AND YOUR PARTNER TO GRANT YOUR *SERVICE* AND *SKILL* TO OUR *CAUSE.*

AND WHAT CAUSE WOULD *THAT* BE?

THE INQUISITION.

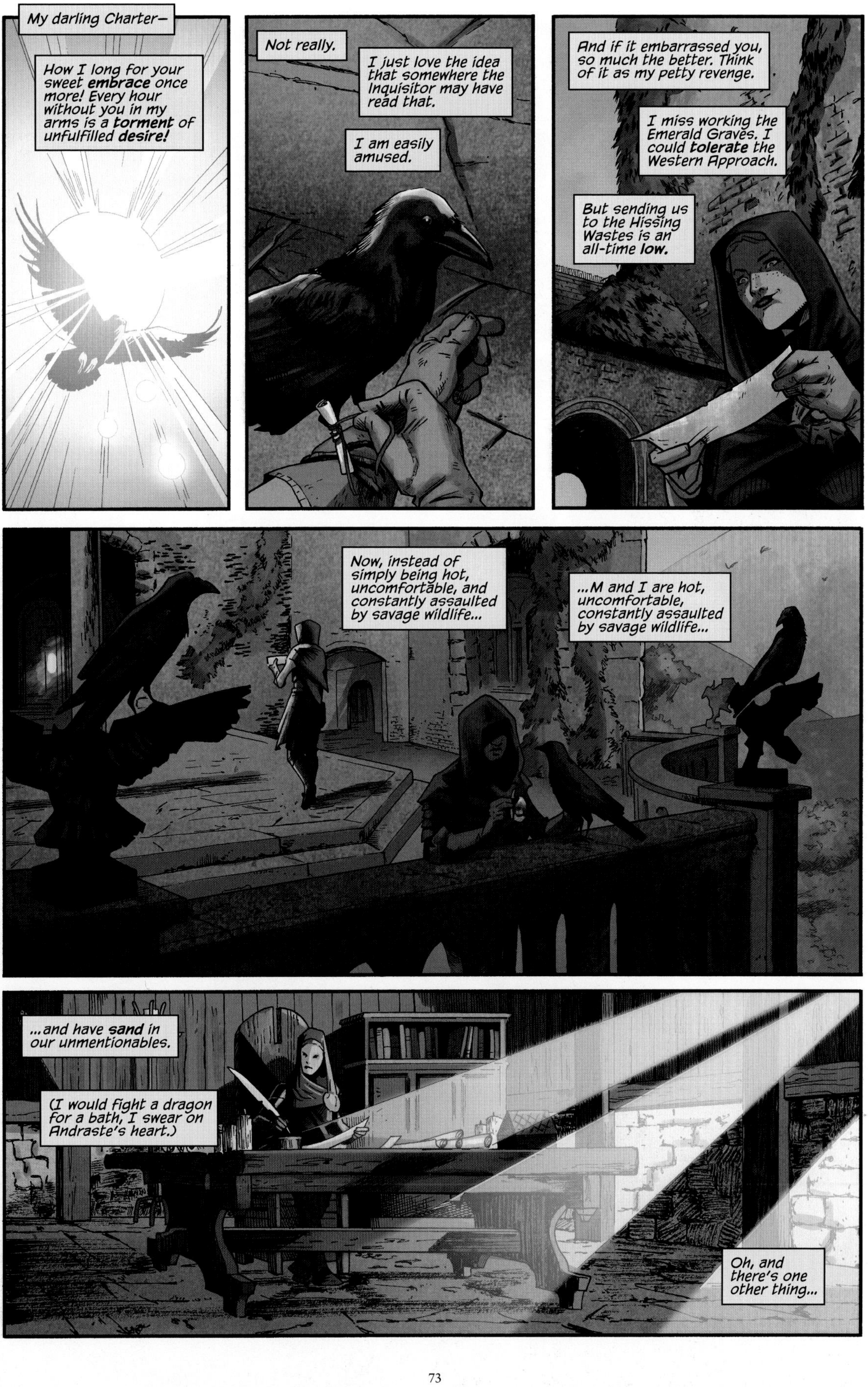
My darling Charter—
How I long for your sweet **embrace** once more! Every hour without you in my arms is a **torment** of unfulfilled **desire!**
Not really.
I just love the idea that somewhere the Inquisitor may have read that.
I am easily amused.
And if it embarrassed you, so much the better. Think of it as my petty revenge.
I miss working the Emerald Graves. I could **tolerate** the Western Approach.
But sending us to the Hissing Wastes is an all-time **low.**
Now, instead of simply being hot, uncomfortable, and constantly assaulted by savage wildlife...
...M and I are hot, uncomfortable, constantly assaulted by savage wildlife...
...and have **sand** in our unmentionables.
(I would fight a dragon for a bath, I swear on Andraste's heart.)
Oh, and there's one other thing...

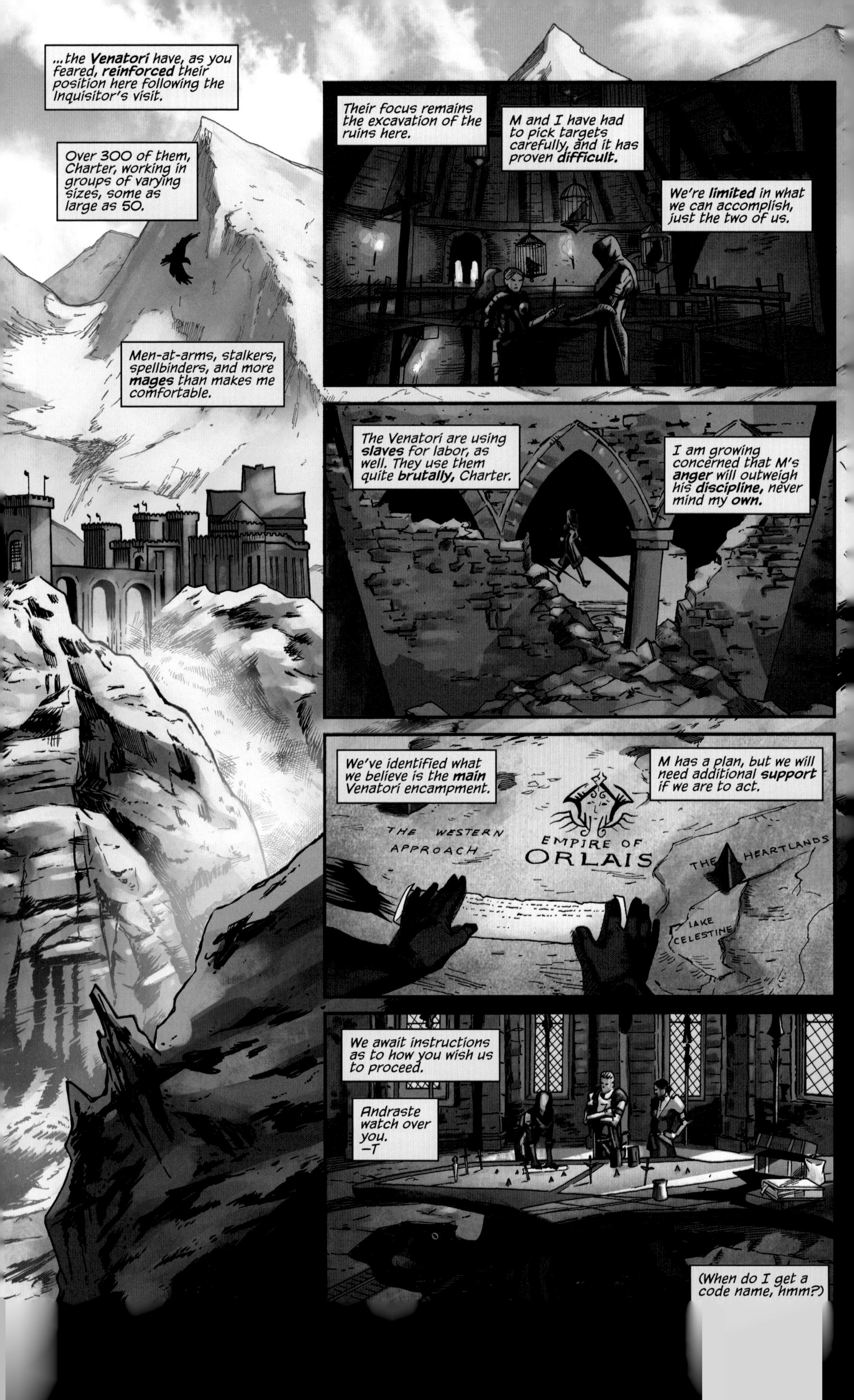
...the Venatori have, as you feared, reinforced their position here following the Inquisitor's visit.
Over 300 of them, Charter, working in groups of varying sizes, some as large as 50.
Men-at-arms, stalkers, spellbinders, and more mages than makes me comfortable.
Their focus remains the excavation of the ruins here.
M and I have had to pick targets carefully, and it has proven difficult.
We're limited in what we can accomplish, just the two of us.
The Venatori are using slaves for labor, as well. They use them quite brutally, Charter.
I am growing concerned that M's anger will outweigh his discipline, never mind my own.
We've identified what we believe is the main Venatori encampment.
M has a plan, but we will need additional support if we are to act.
THE WESTERN APPROACH
EMPIRE OF ORLAIS
THE HEARTLANDS
LAKE CELESTINE
We await instructions as to how you wish us to proceed.
Andraste watch over you.
—T
(When do I get a code name, hmm?)

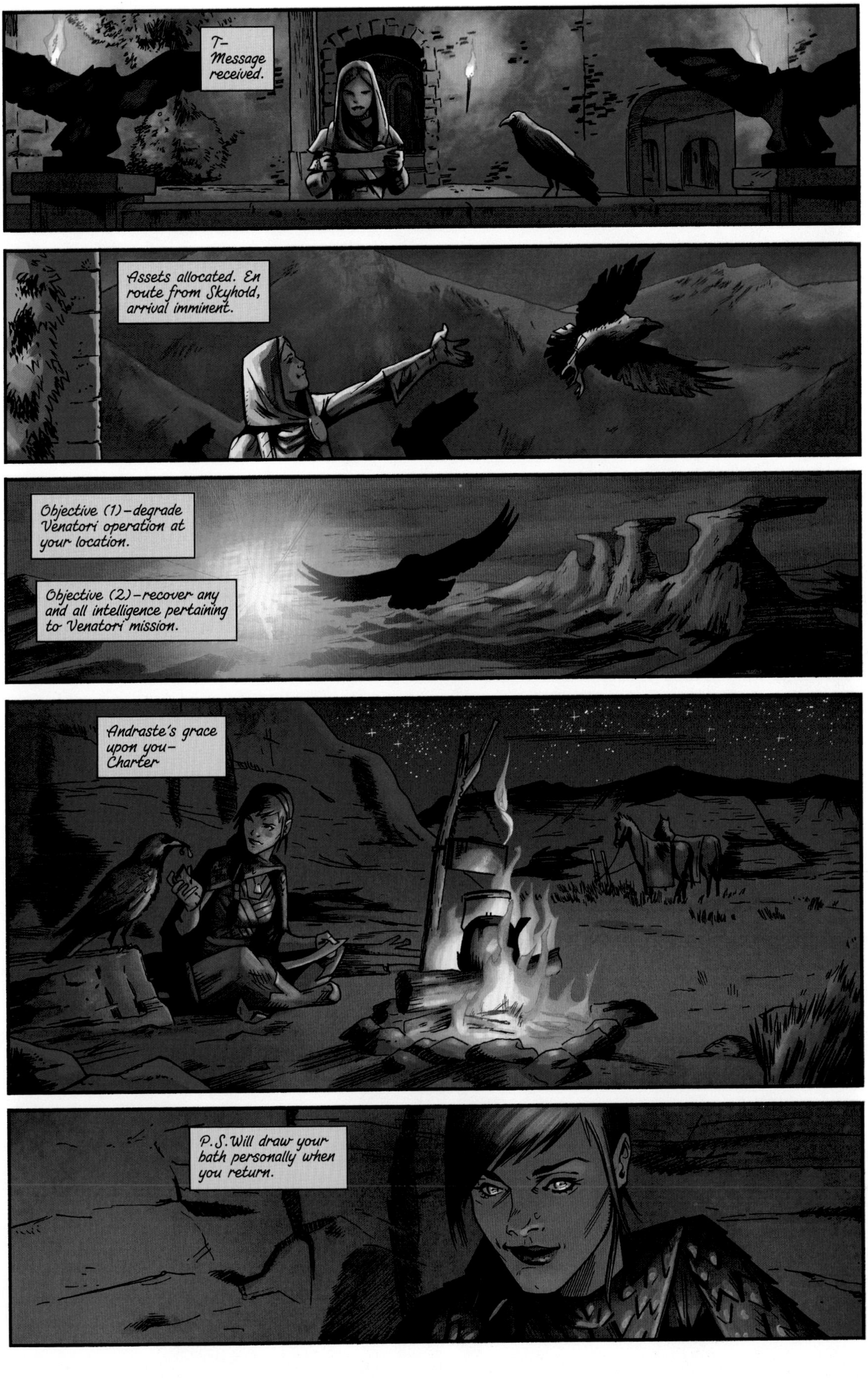
T-
Message
received.
Assets allocated. En route from Skyhold, arrival imminent.
Objective (1)—degrade Venatori operation at your location.
Objective (2)—recover any and all intelligence pertaining to Venatori mission.
Andraste's grace upon you—
Charter
P.S. Will draw your bath personally when you return.

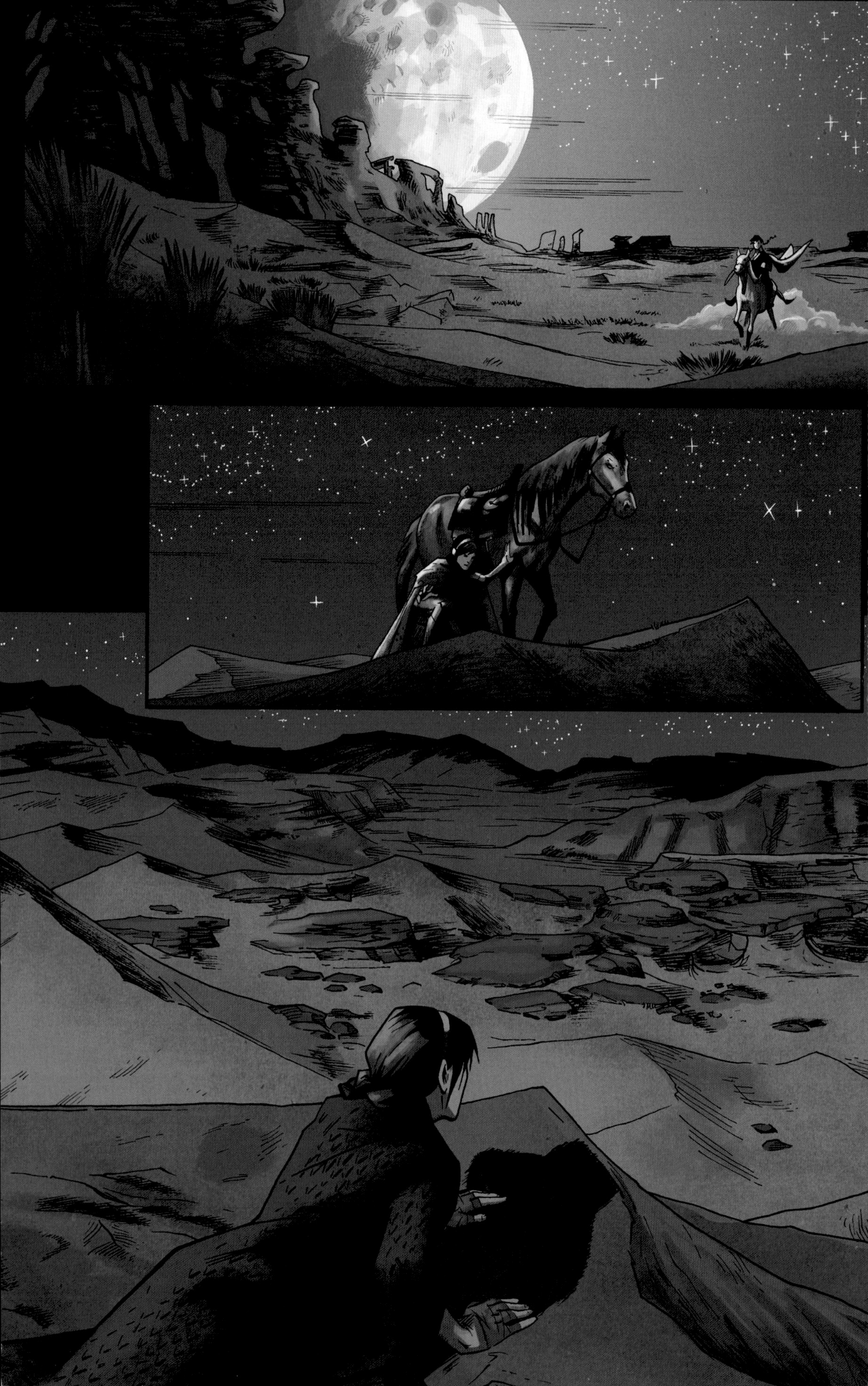

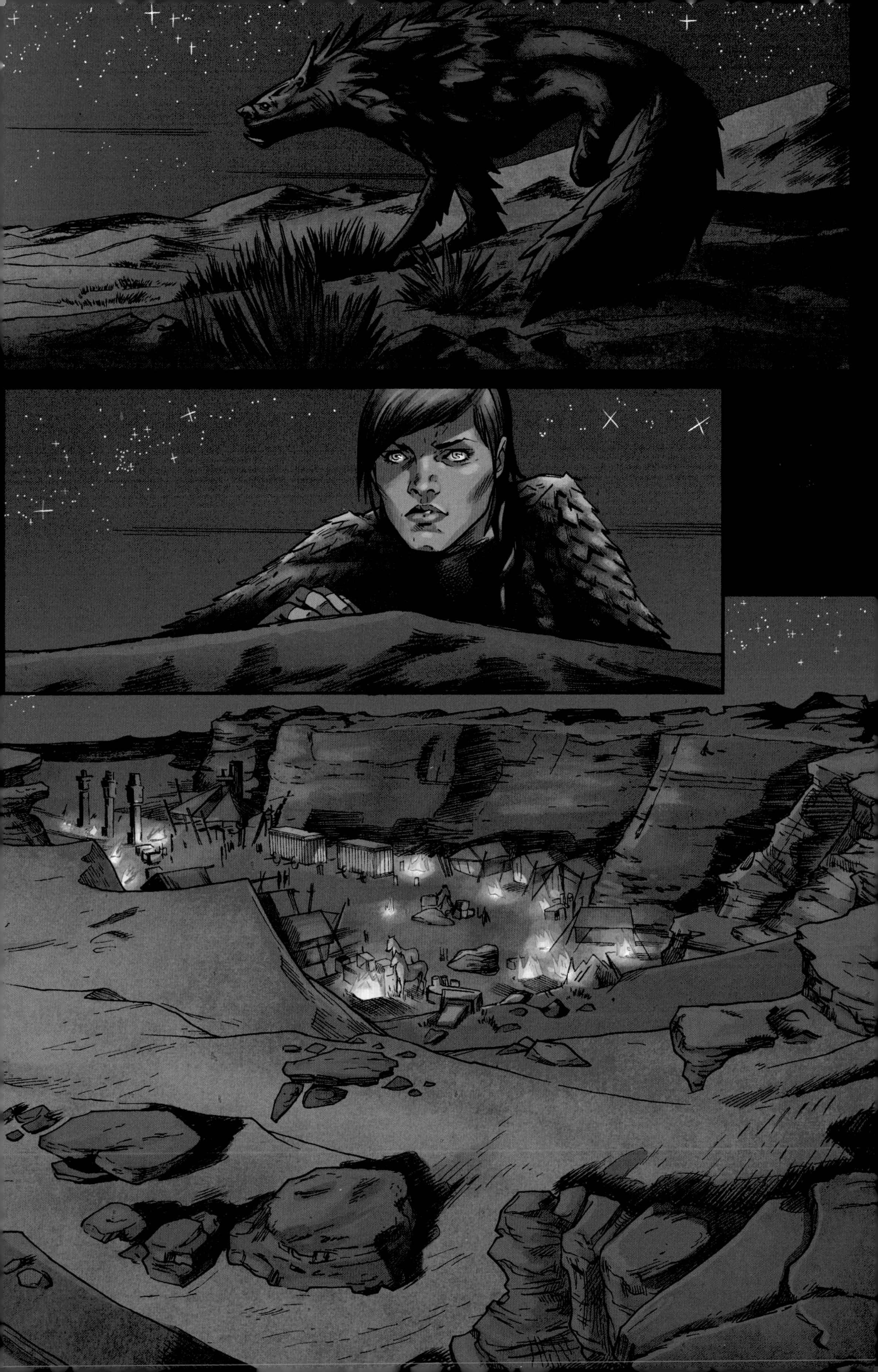

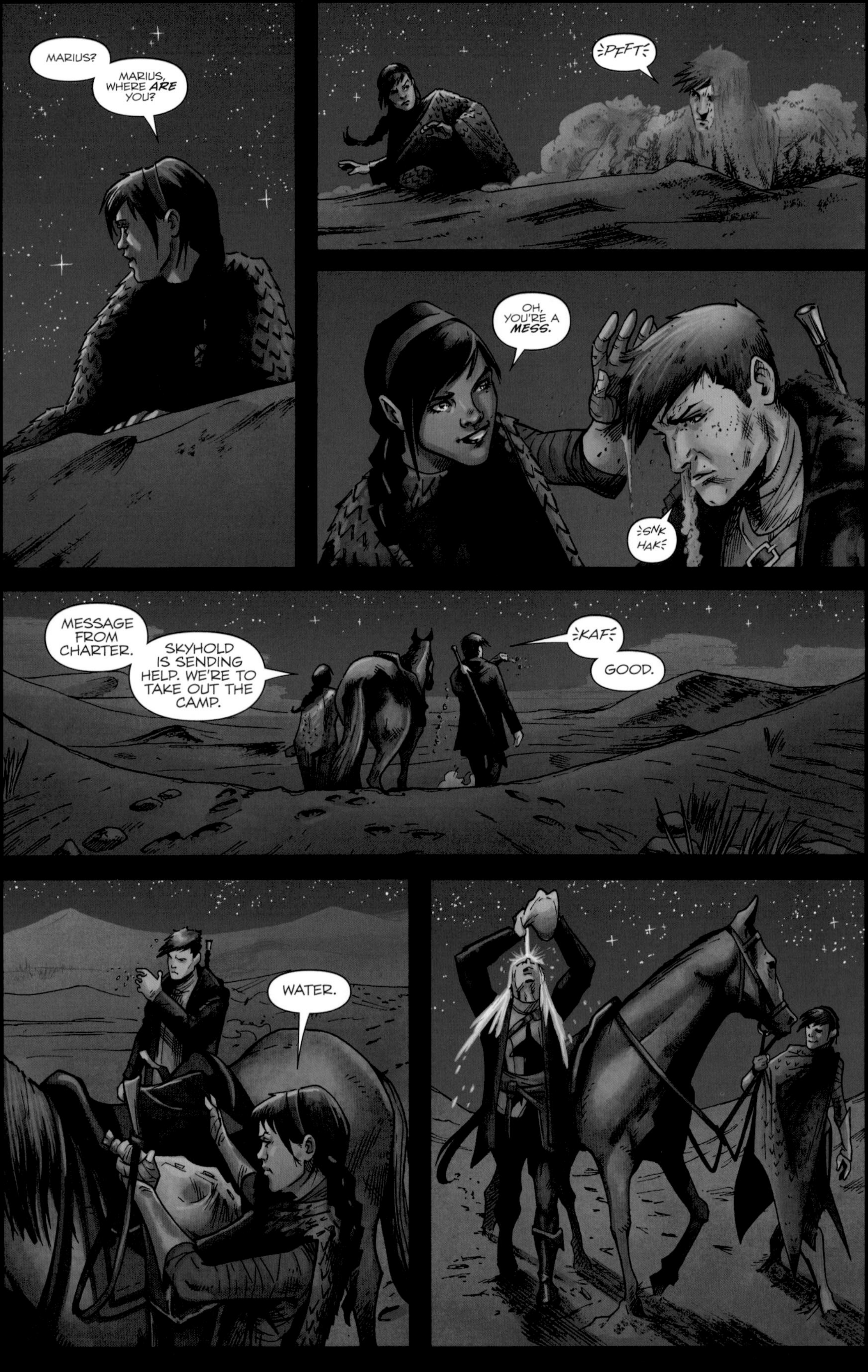
MARIUS?
MARIUS, WHERE ARE YOU?
PFFT
OH, YOU'RE A MESS.
SNK HAK
MESSAGE FROM CHARTER.
SKYHOLD IS SENDING HELP. WE'RE TO TAKE OUT THE CAMP.
KAF
GOOD.
WATER.

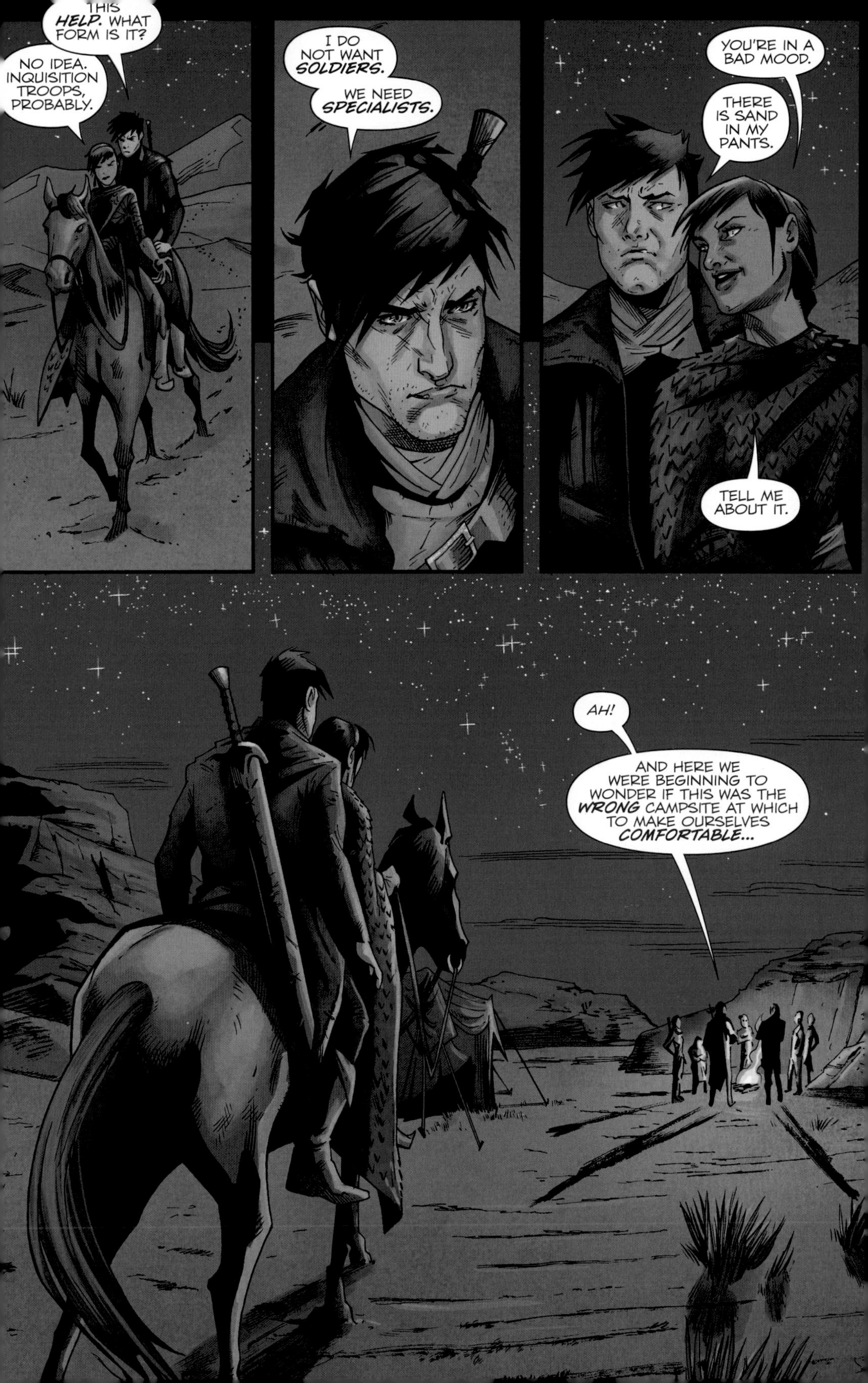
THIS HELP. WHAT FORM IS IT?
NO IDEA. INQUISITION TROOPS, PROBABLY.
I DO NOT WANT SOLDIERS.
WE NEED SPECIALISTS.
YOU'RE IN A BAD MOOD.
THERE IS SAND IN MY PANTS.
TELL ME ABOUT IT.
AH!
AND HERE WE WERE BEGINNING TO WONDER IF THIS WAS THE WRONG CAMPSITE AT WHICH TO MAKE OURSELVES COMFORTABLE...

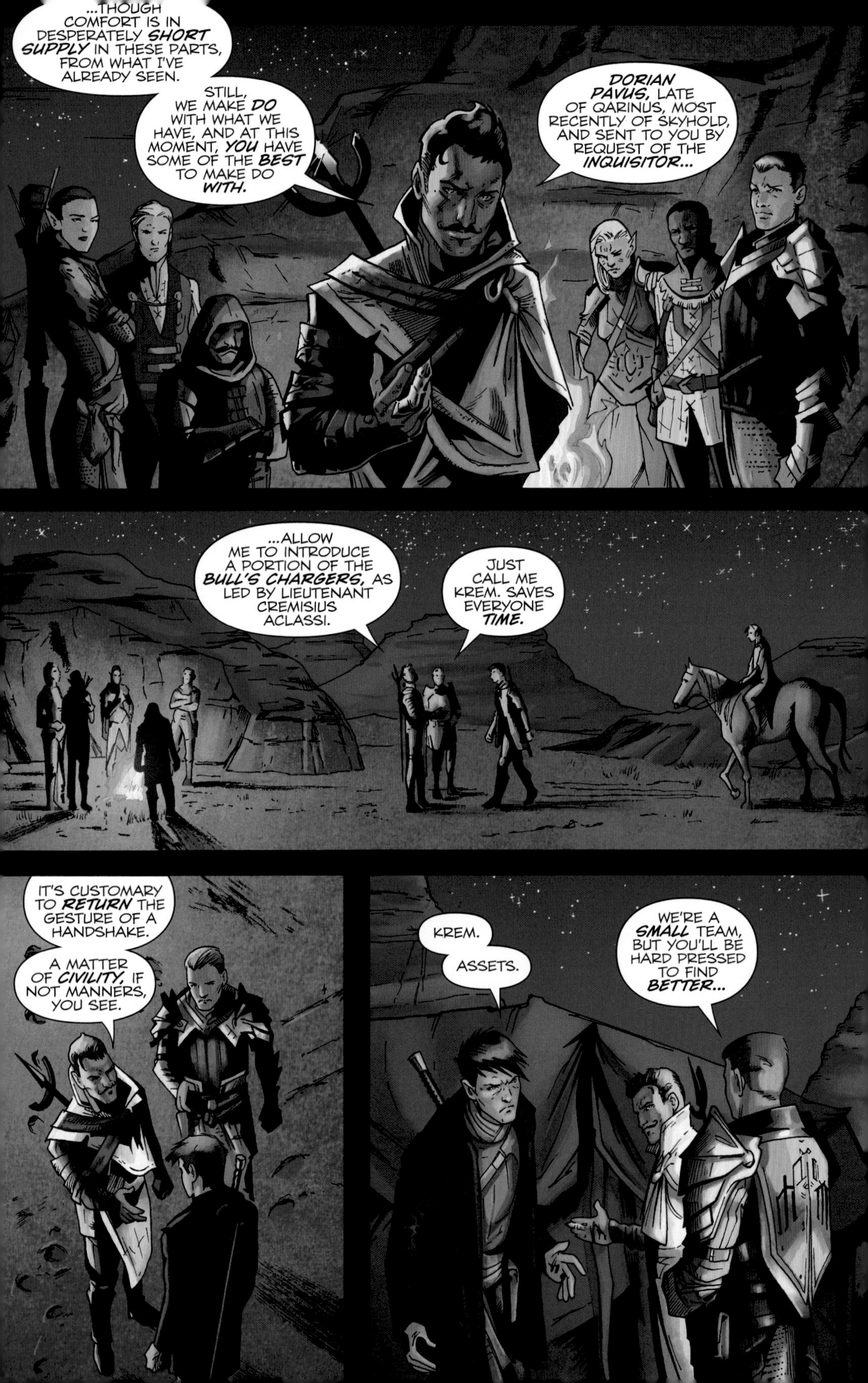
...THOUGH COMFORT IS IN DESPERATELY SHORT SUPPLY IN THESE PARTS, FROM WHAT I'VE ALREADY SEEN.
STILL, WE MAKE DO WITH WHAT WE HAVE, AND AT THIS MOMENT, YOU HAVE SOME OF THE BEST TO MAKE DO WITH.
DORIAN PAVUS, LATE OF QARINUS, MOST RECENTLY OF SKYHOLD, AND SENT TO YOU BY REQUEST OF THE INQUISITOR...
...ALLOW ME TO INTRODUCE A PORTION OF THE BULL'S CHARGERS, AS LED BY LIEUTENANT CREMISIUS ACLASSI.
JUST CALL ME KREM. SAVES EVERYONE TIME.
IT'S CUSTOMARY TO RETURN THE GESTURE OF A HANDSHAKE.
A MATTER OF CIVILITY, IF NOT MANNERS, YOU SEE.
KREM.
ASSETS.
WE'RE A SMALL TEAM, BUT YOU'LL BE HARD PRESSED TO FIND BETTER...

...SAPPER, HEALER, INFILTRATOR, ONE MAGE--

I'M NOT A MAGE! IT'S A *BOW*, I KEEP TELLING YOU...

DON'T MIND HIM.

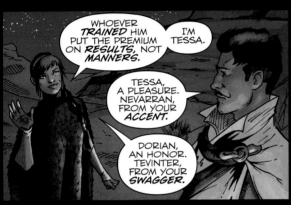

WHOEVER *TRAINED* HIM PUT THE PREMIUM ON *RESULTS*, NOT *MANNERS*.

I'M TESSA.

TESSA, A PLEASURE. NEVARRAN, FROM YOUR *ACCENT*.

DORIAN, AN HONOR. TEVINTER, FROM YOUR *SWAGGER*.

OH, *THAT'S* ONLY ONE OF THE *MANY* REASONS WHY I SWAGGER, TESSA.

YOU TWO JUST GOING TO MAKE *NICE*...

...OR ARE WE GOING TO GET TO *BUSINESS?*

CAN'T WE DO *BOTH?*

NO.

THIS IS THE *SITUATION*...

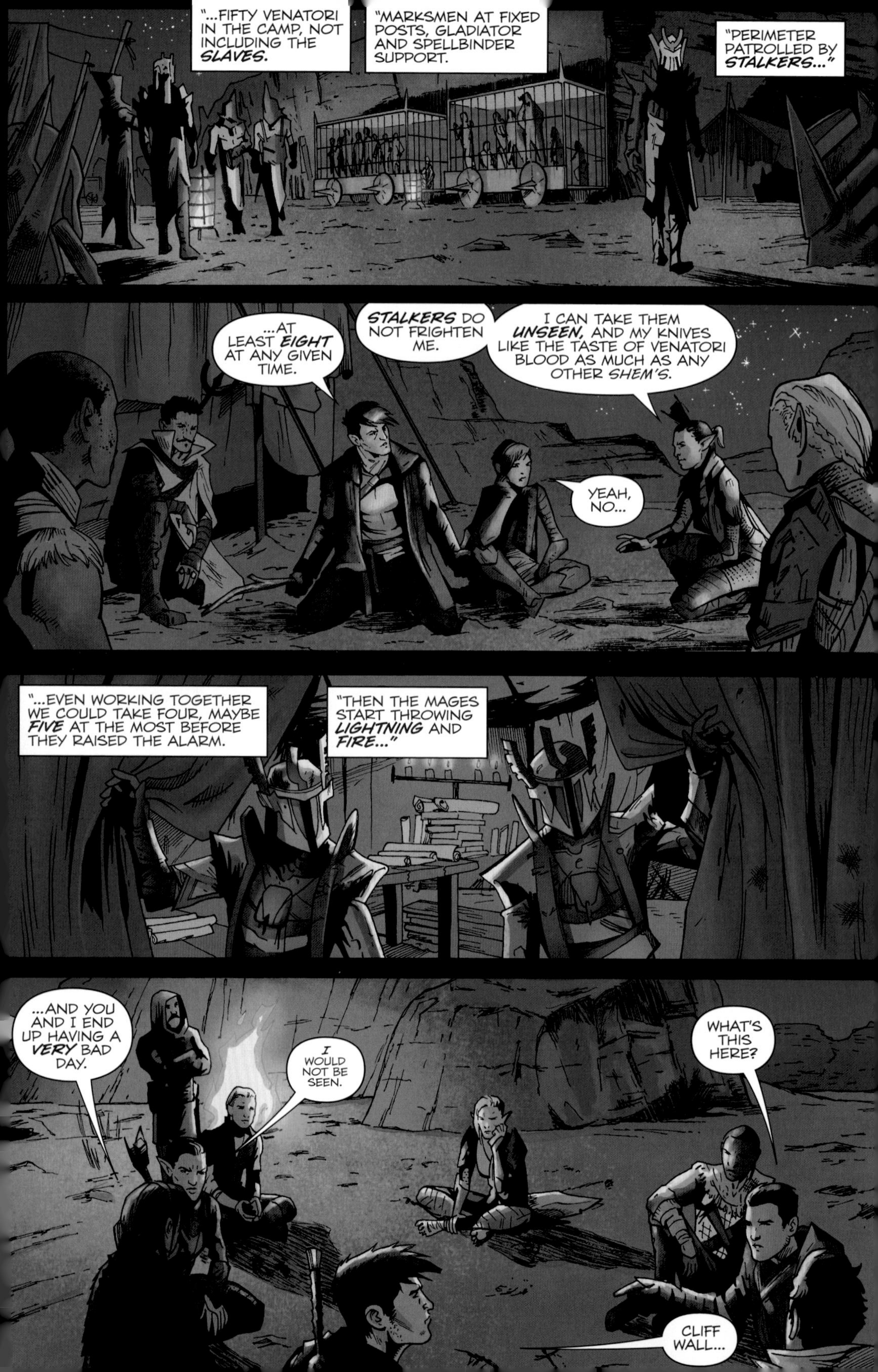
"...FIFTY VENATORI IN THE CAMP, NOT INCLUDING THE SLAVES.
"MARKSMEN AT FIXED POSTS, GLADIATOR AND SPELLBINDER SUPPORT.
"PERIMETER PATROLLED BY STALKERS..."
...AT LEAST EIGHT AT ANY GIVEN TIME.
STALKERS DO NOT FRIGHTEN ME.
I CAN TAKE THEM UNSEEN, AND MY KNIVES LIKE THE TASTE OF VENATORI BLOOD AS MUCH AS ANY OTHER SHEM'S.
YEAH, NO...
"...EVEN WORKING TOGETHER WE COULD TAKE FOUR, MAYBE FIVE AT THE MOST BEFORE THEY RAISED THE ALARM.
"THEN THE MAGES START THROWING LIGHTNING AND FIRE..."
...AND YOU AND I END UP HAVING A VERY BAD DAY.
I WOULD NOT BE SEEN.
WHAT'S THIS HERE?
CLIFF WALL...

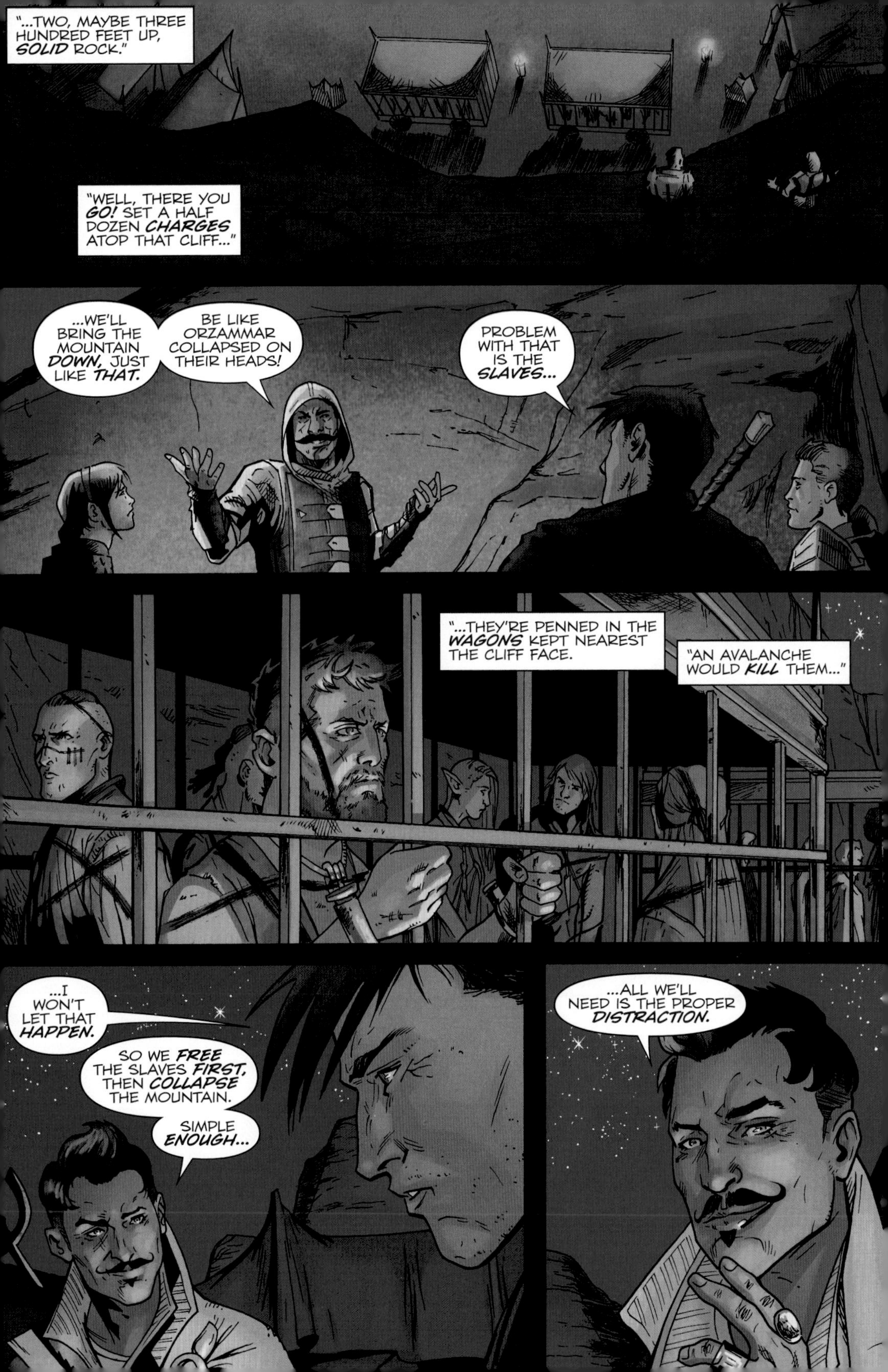
"...TWO, MAYBE THREE HUNDRED FEET UP, SOLID ROCK."
"WELL, THERE YOU GO! SET A HALF DOZEN CHARGES ATOP THAT CLIFF..."
...WE'LL BRING THE MOUNTAIN DOWN, JUST LIKE THAT.
BE LIKE ORZAMMAR COLLAPSED ON THEIR HEADS!
PROBLEM WITH THAT IS THE SLAVES...
"...THEY'RE PENNED IN THE WAGONS KEPT NEAREST THE CLIFF FACE.
"AN AVALANCHE WOULD KILL THEM..."
...I WON'T LET THAT HAPPEN.
SO WE FREE THE SLAVES FIRST, THEN COLLAPSE THE MOUNTAIN.
SIMPLE ENOUGH...
...ALL WE'LL NEED IS THE PROPER DISTRACTION.

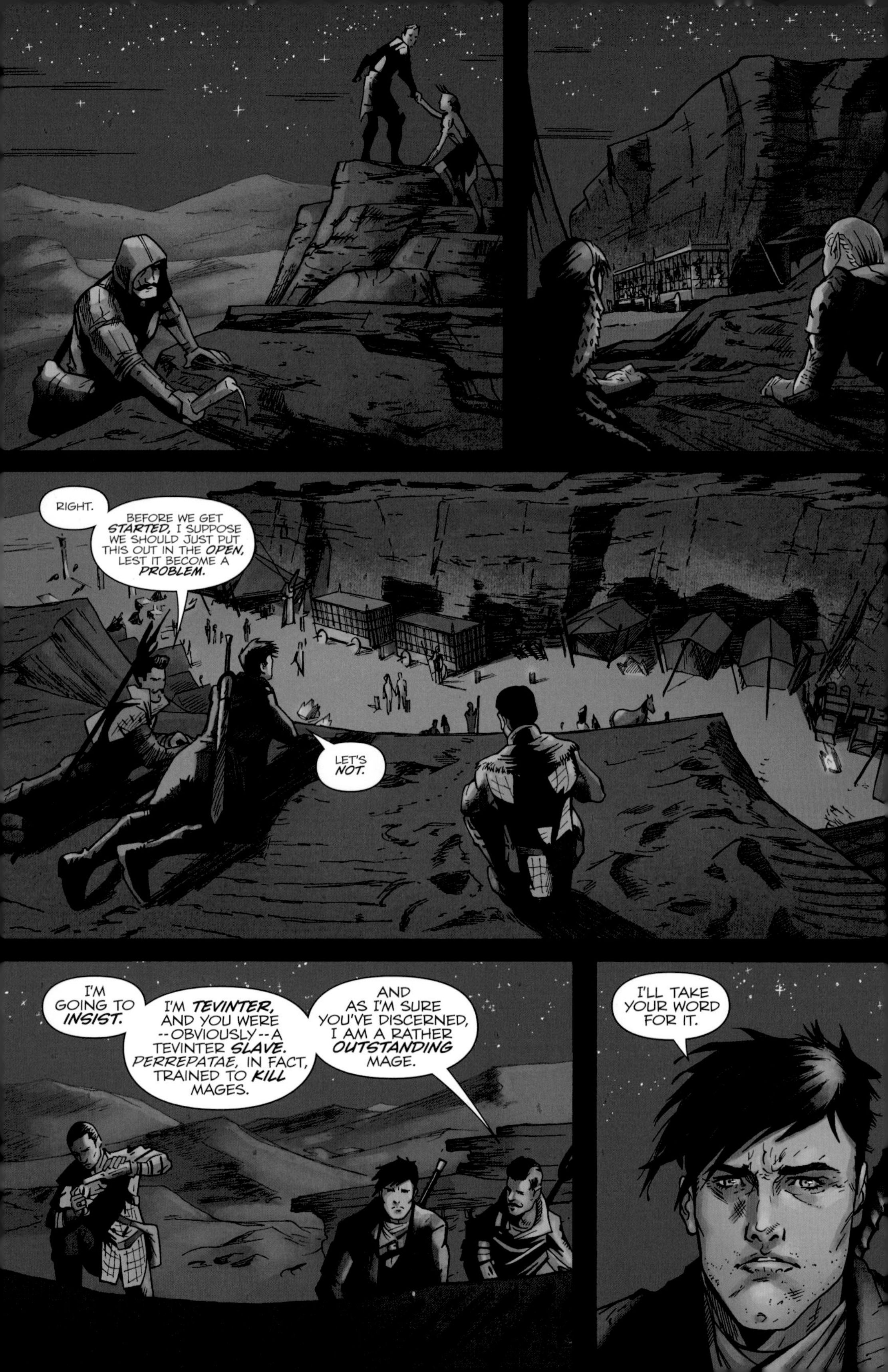
RIGHT.
BEFORE WE GET STARTED, I SUPPOSE WE SHOULD JUST PUT THIS OUT IN THE OPEN, LEST IT BECOME A PROBLEM.
LET'S NOT.
I'M GOING TO INSIST.
I'M TEVINTER, AND YOU WERE --OBVIOUSLY--A TEVINTER SLAVE. PERREPATAE, IN FACT, TRAINED TO KILL MAGES.
AND AS I'M SURE YOU'VE DISCERNED, I AM A RATHER OUTSTANDING MAGE.
I'LL TAKE YOUR WORD FOR IT.

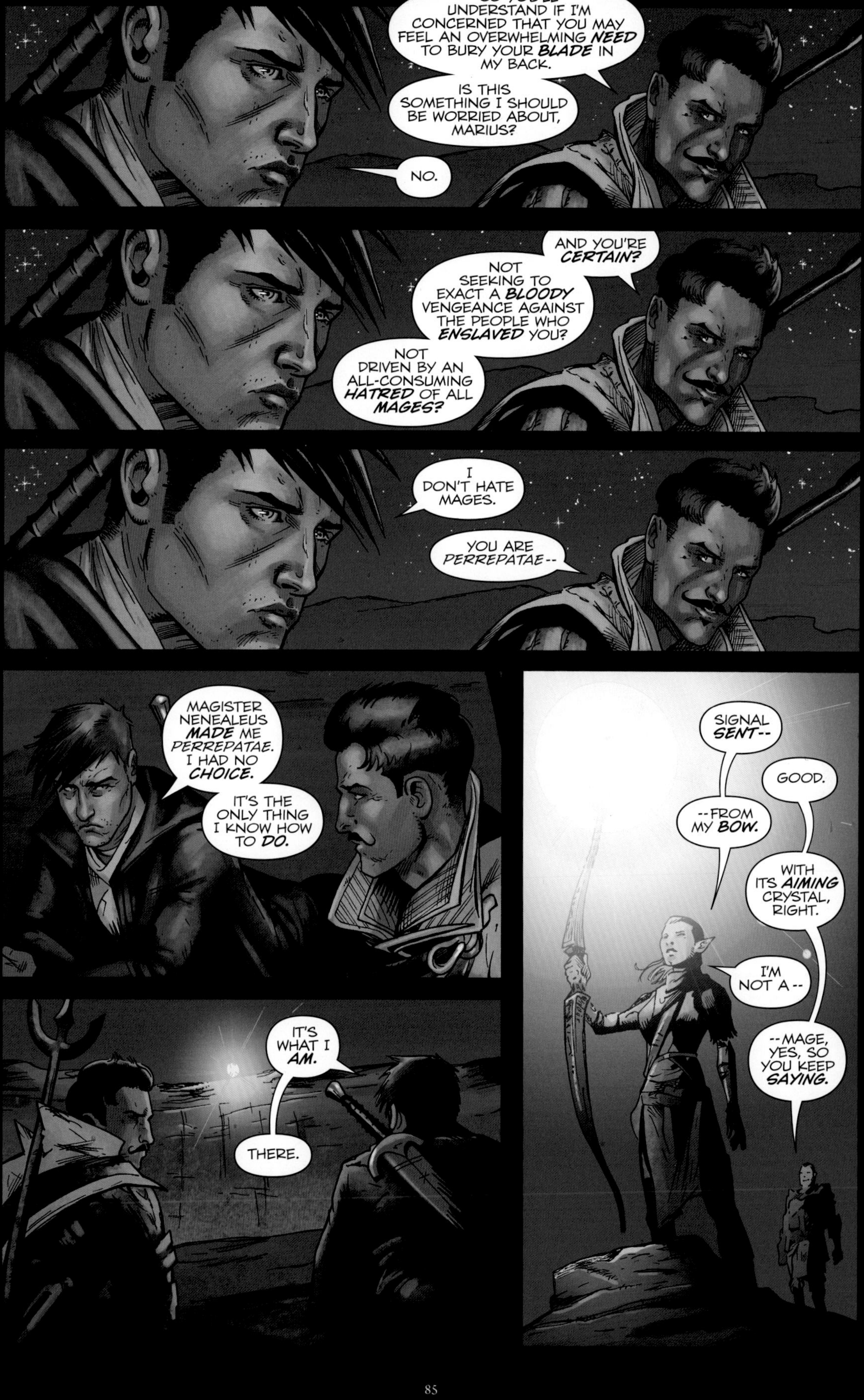
SO YOU'LL UNDERSTAND IF I'M CONCERNED THAT YOU MAY FEEL AN OVERWHELMING **NEED** TO BURY YOUR **BLADE** IN MY BACK.
IS THIS SOMETHING I SHOULD BE WORRIED ABOUT, MARIUS?
NO.
AND YOU'RE **CERTAIN?**
NOT SEEKING TO EXACT A **BLOODY** VENGEANCE AGAINST THE PEOPLE WHO **ENSLAVED** YOU?
NOT DRIVEN BY AN ALL-CONSUMING **HATRED** OF ALL **MAGES?**
I DON'T HATE MAGES.
YOU ARE *PERREPATAE*--
MAGISTER NENEALEUS **MADE** ME *PERREPATAE.* I HAD NO **CHOICE.**
IT'S THE ONLY THING I KNOW HOW TO **DO.**
IT'S WHAT I **AM.**
THERE.
SIGNAL **SENT**--
--FROM MY **BOW.**
GOOD.
WITH ITS **AIMING** CRYSTAL, RIGHT.
I'M NOT A --
--MAGE, YES, SO YOU KEEP **SAYING.**

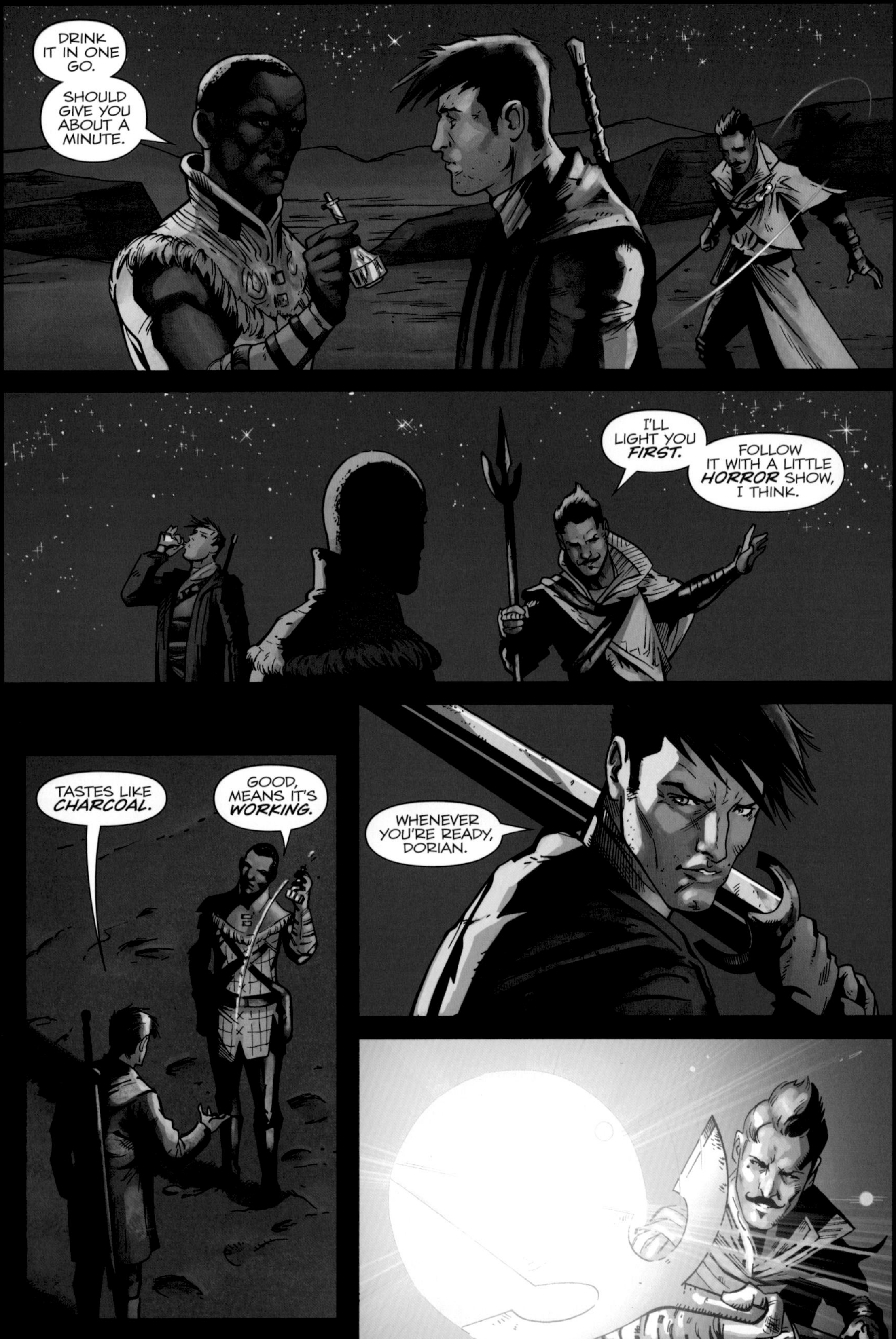
DRINK IT IN ONE GO.
SHOULD GIVE YOU ABOUT A MINUTE.
I'LL LIGHT YOU FIRST.
FOLLOW IT WITH A LITTLE HORROR SHOW, I THINK.
TASTES LIKE CHARCOAL.
GOOD, MEANS IT'S WORKING.
WHENEVER YOU'RE READY, DORIAN.

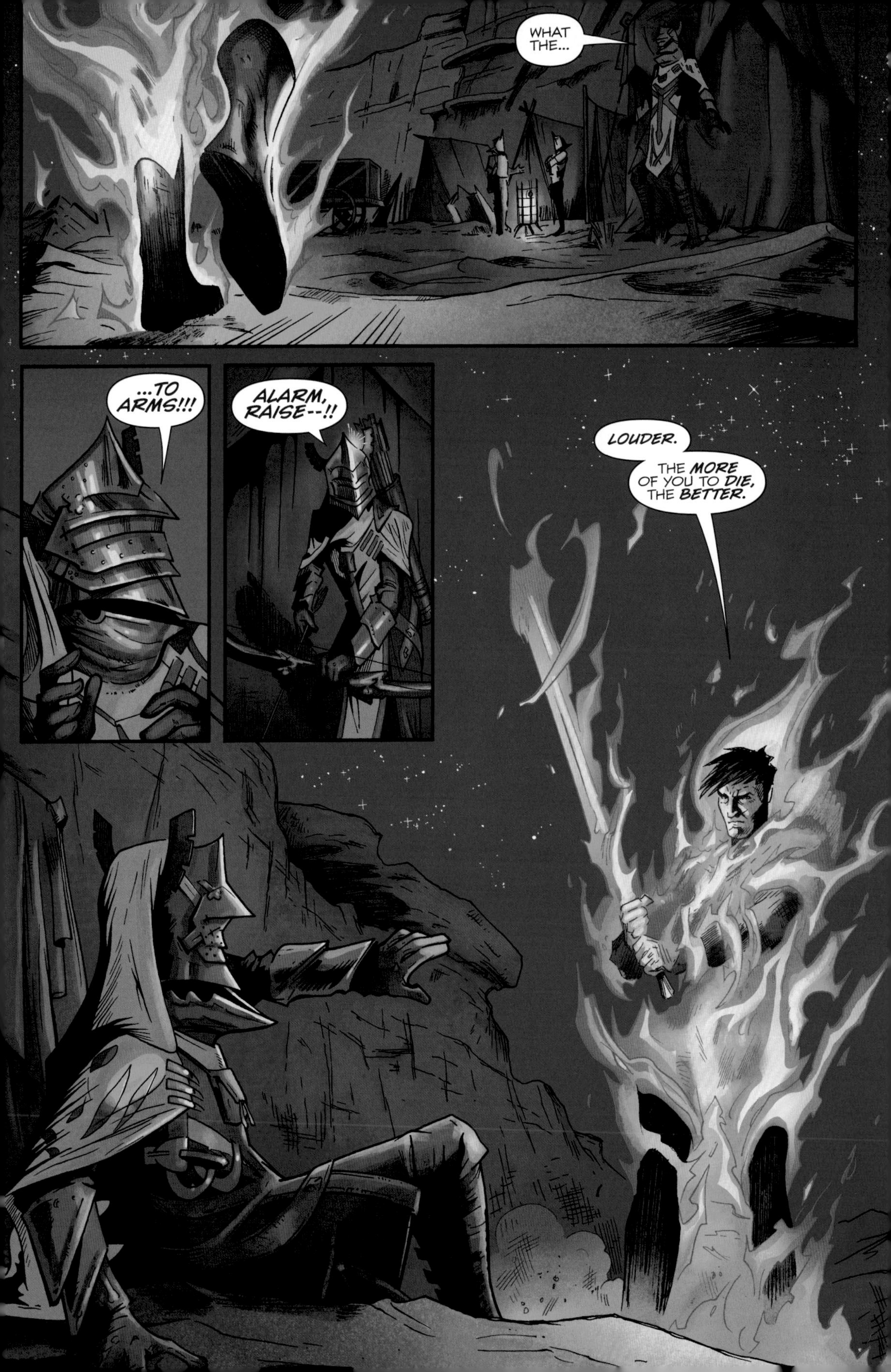
WHAT THE...
...TO ARMS!!!
ALARM, RAISE--!!
LOUDER.
THE MORE OF YOU TO DIE, THE BETTER.

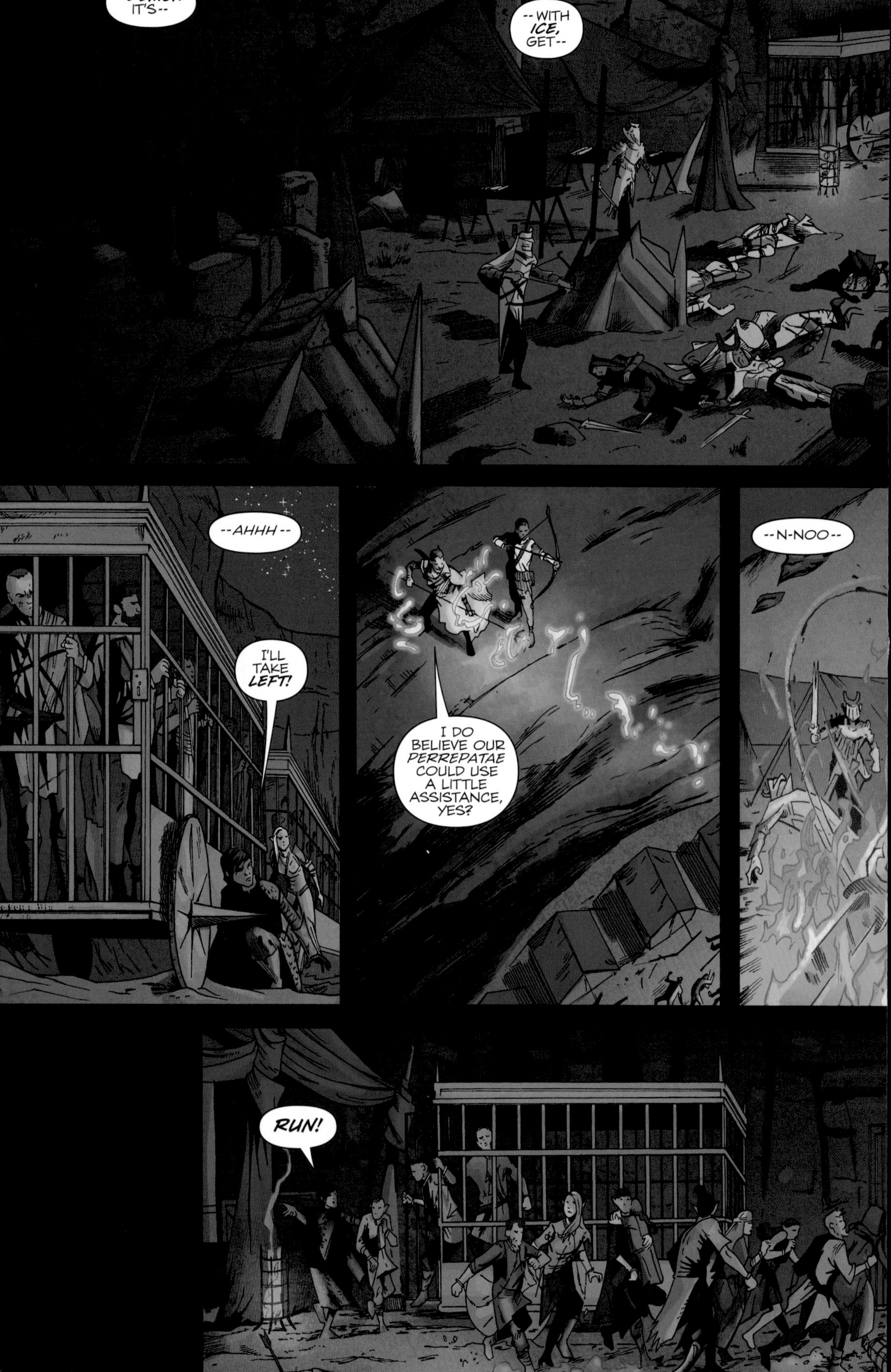
IT'S--
--WITH *ICE,* GET--
--*AHHH*--
I'LL TAKE ***LEFT!***
I DO BELIEVE OUR *PERREPATAE* COULD USE A LITTLE ASSISTANCE, YES?
--N-NOO--
RUN!

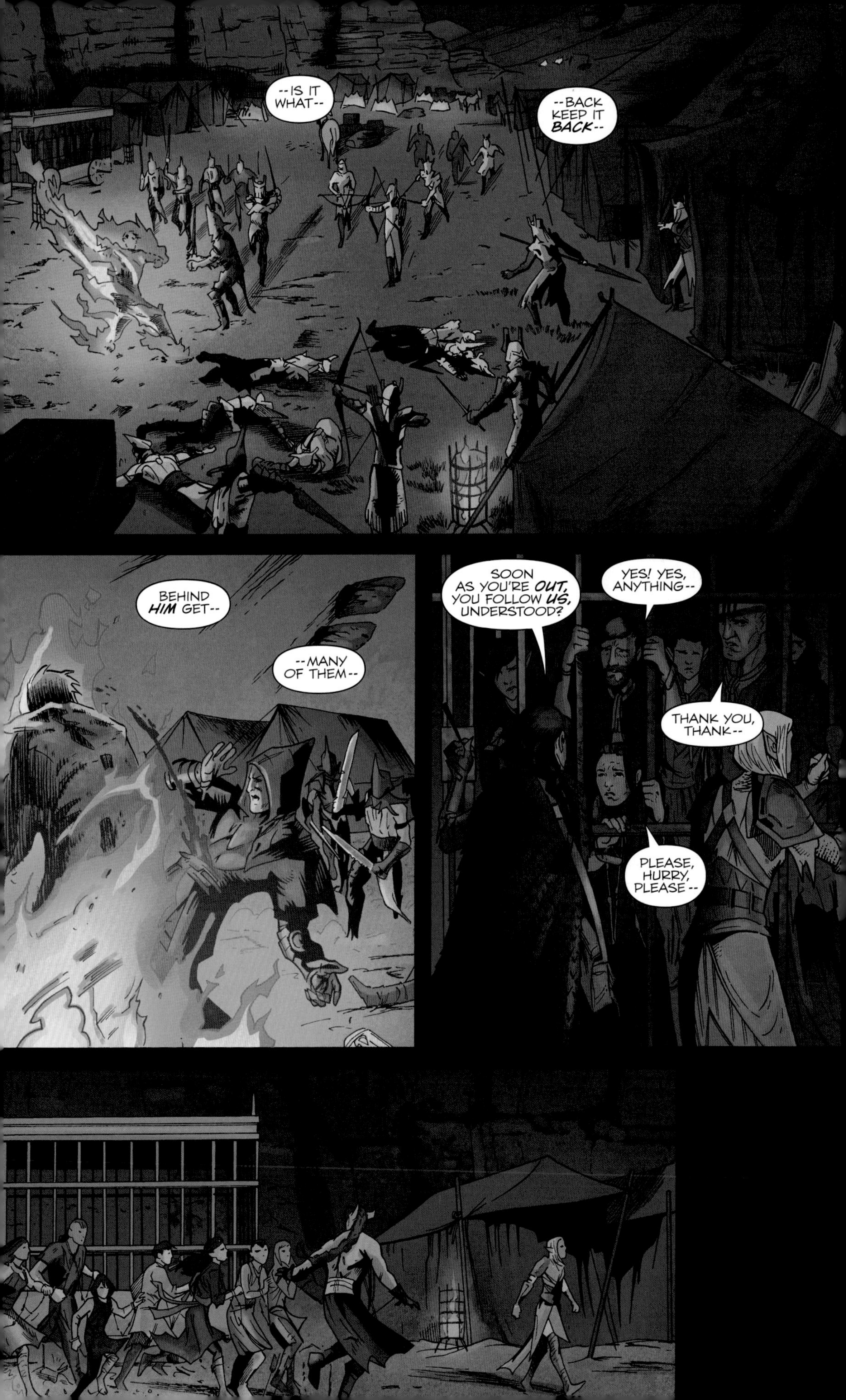
--IS IT WHAT--
--BACK KEEP IT BACK--
BEHIND HIM GET--
--MANY OF THEM--
SOON AS YOU'RE OUT, YOU FOLLOW US, UNDERSTOOD?
YES! YES, ANYTHING--
THANK YOU, THANK--
PLEASE, HURRY, PLEASE--

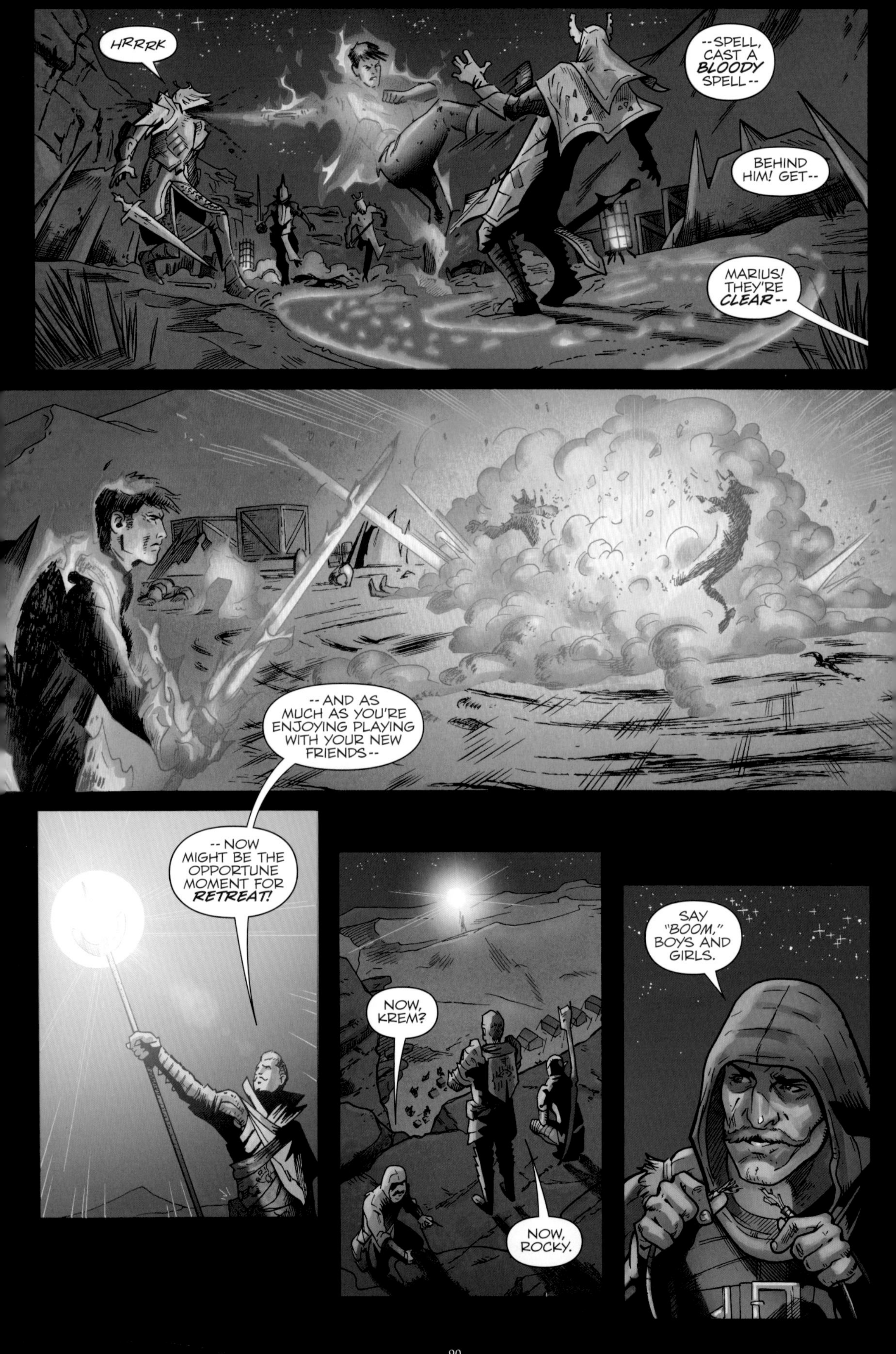
HRRRK
--SPELL, CAST A BLOODY SPELL--
BEHIND HIM! GET--
MARIUS! THEY'RE CLEAR--
--AND AS MUCH AS YOU'RE ENJOYING PLAYING WITH YOUR NEW FRIENDS--
-- NOW MIGHT BE THE OPPORTUNE MOMENT FOR RETREAT!
NOW, KREM?
NOW, ROCKY.
SAY "BOOM," BOYS AND GIRLS.

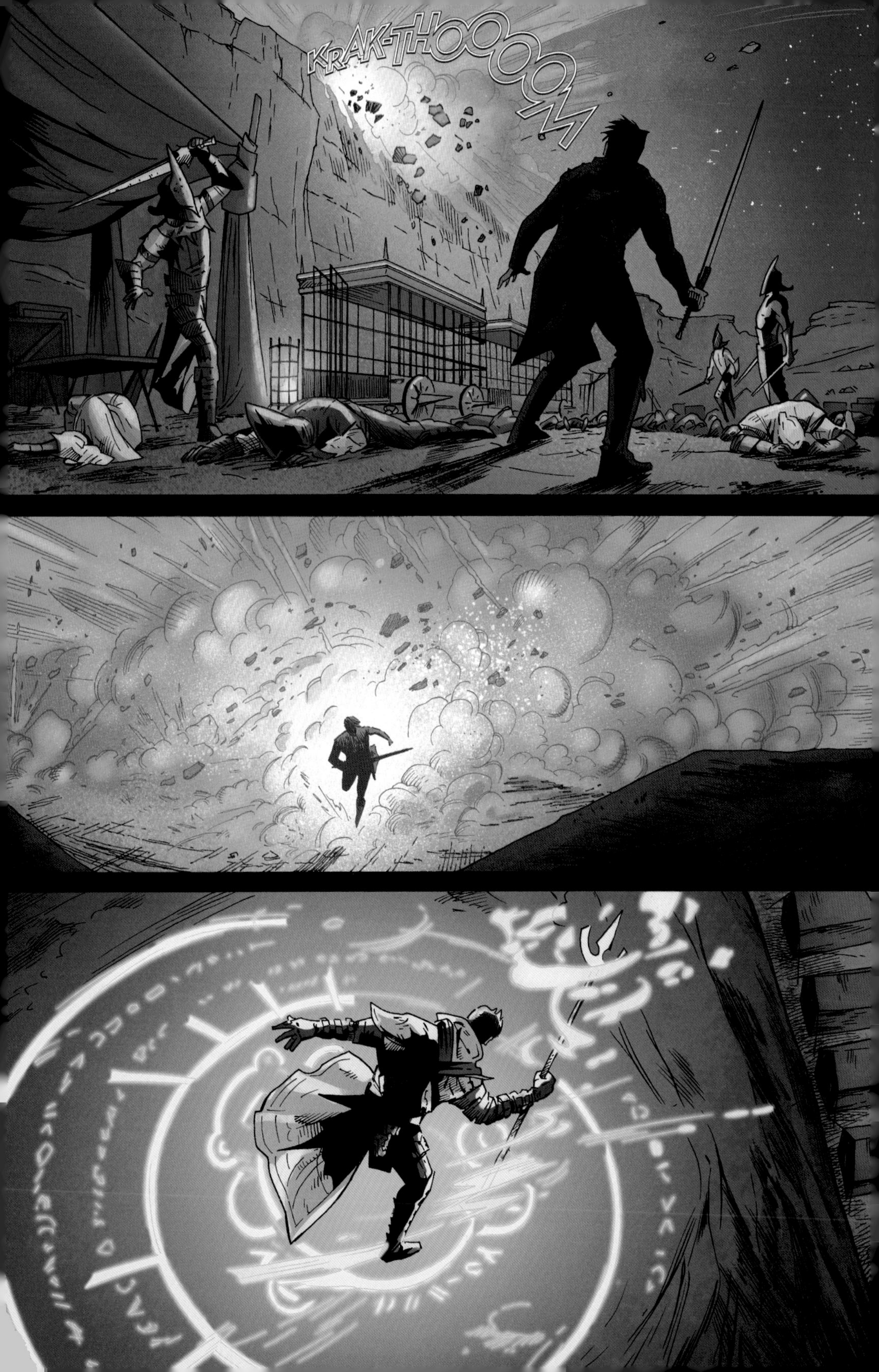
KRAK-THOOOOOM

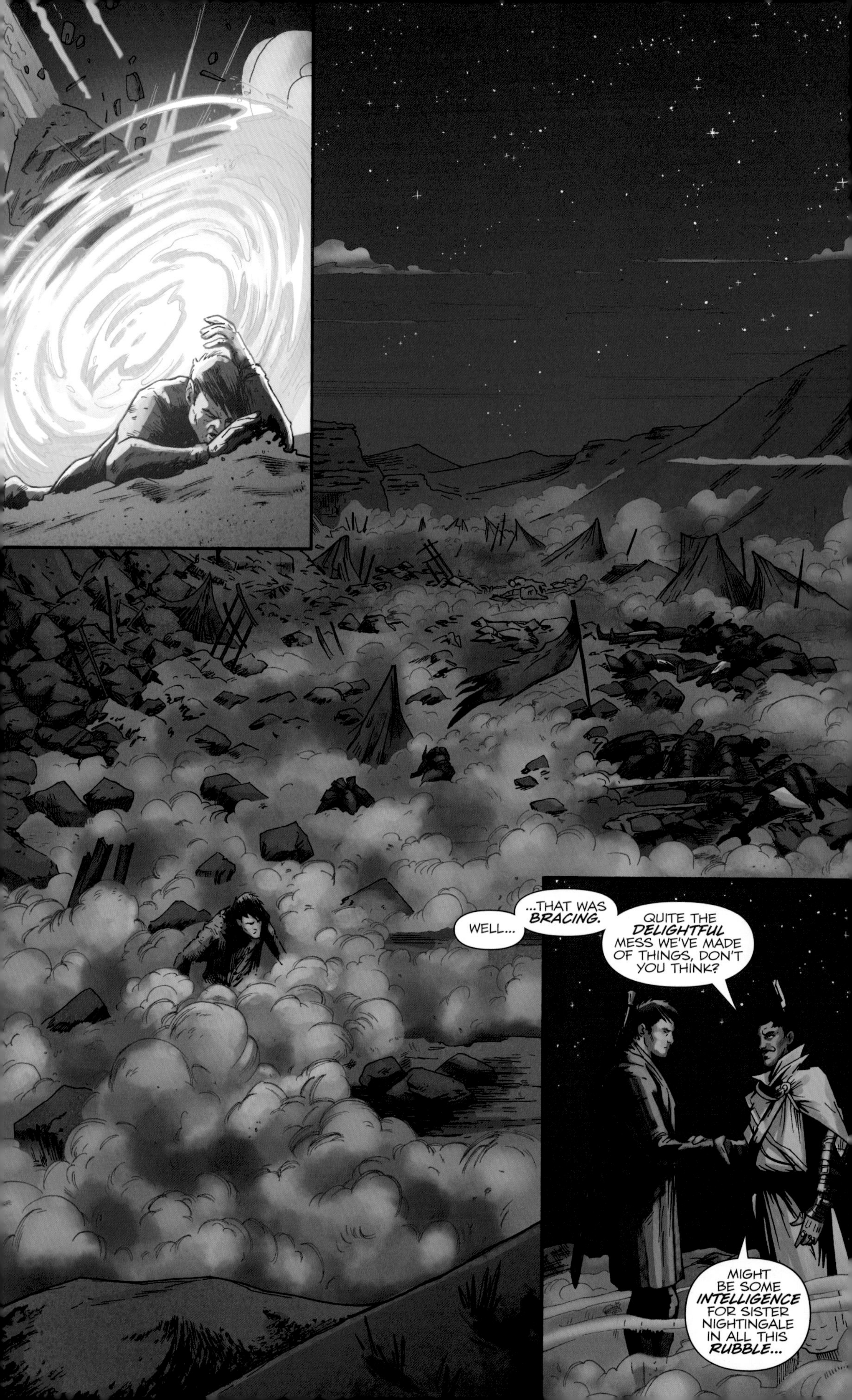
WELL...
...THAT WAS BRACING.
QUITE THE DELIGHTFUL MESS WE'VE MADE OF THINGS, DON'T YOU THINK?
MIGHT BE SOME INTELLIGENCE FOR SISTER NIGHTINGALE IN ALL THIS RUBBLE...

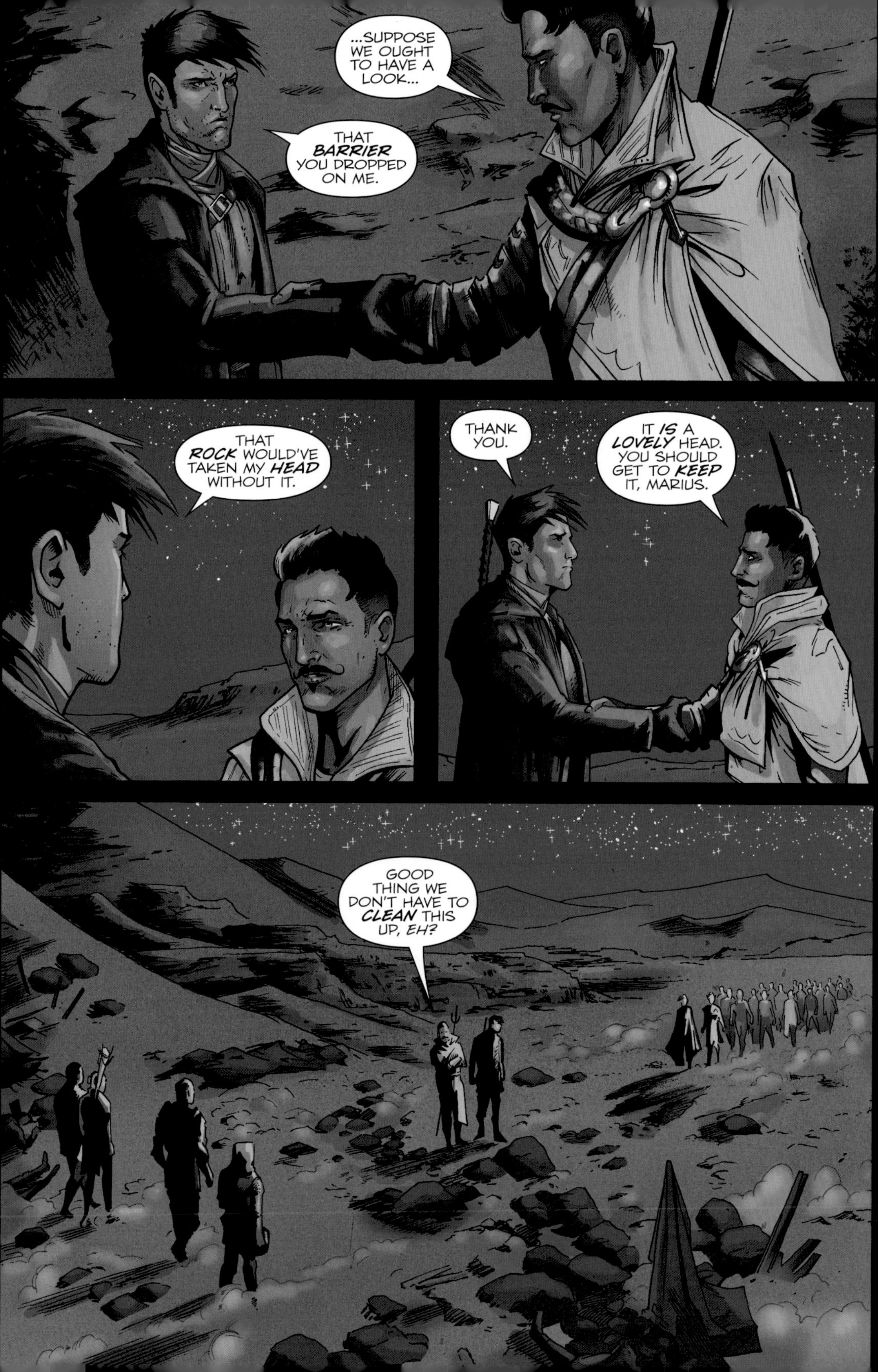
...SUPPOSE WE OUGHT TO HAVE A LOOK...
THAT BARRIER YOU DROPPED ON ME.
THAT ROCK WOULD'VE TAKEN MY HEAD WITHOUT IT.
THANK YOU.
IT IS A LOVELY HEAD. YOU SHOULD GET TO KEEP IT, MARIUS.
GOOD THING WE DON'T HAVE TO CLEAN THIS UP, EH?

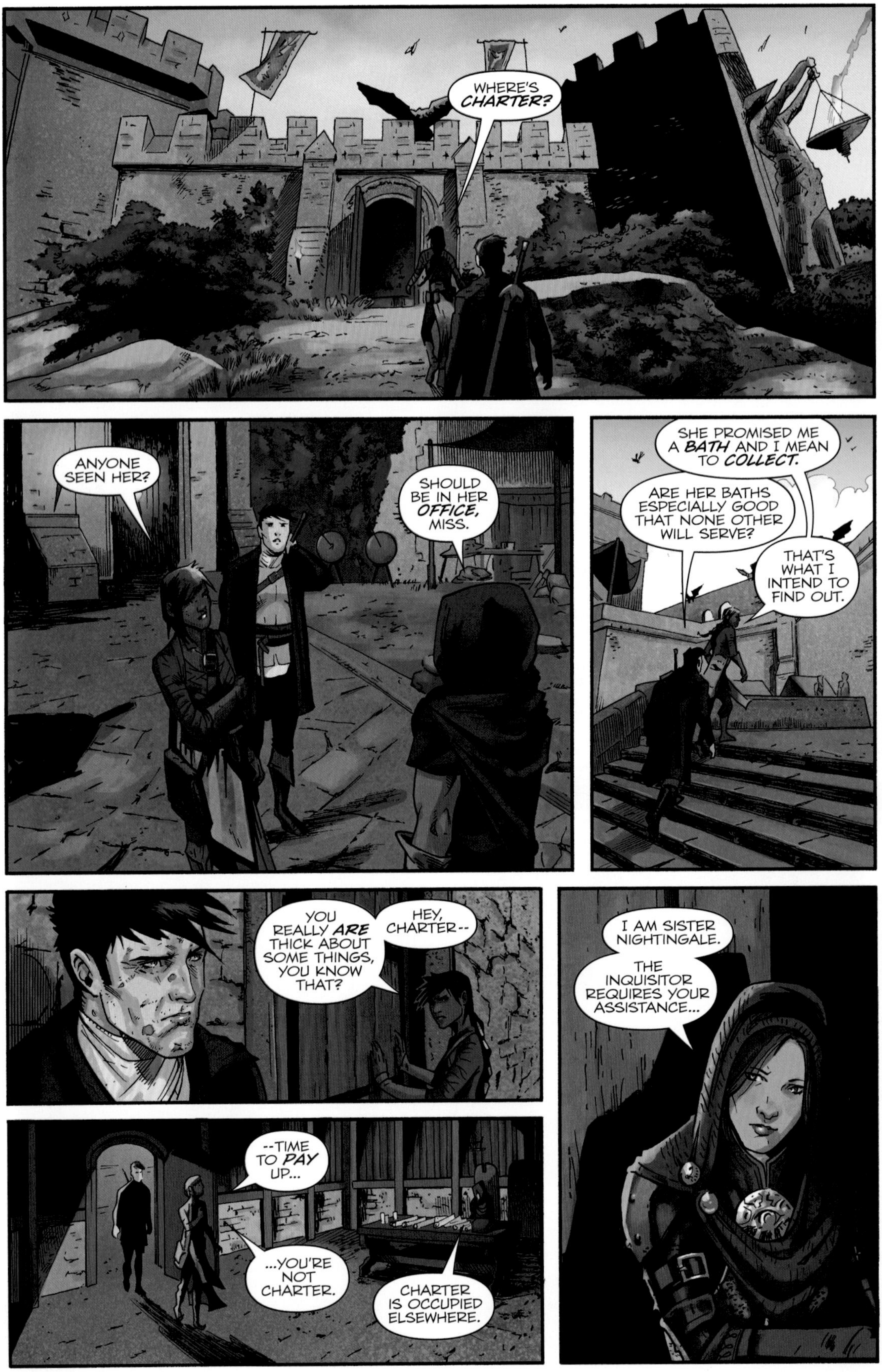
WHERE'S CHARTER?
ANYONE SEEN HER?
SHOULD BE IN HER OFFICE, MISS.
SHE PROMISED ME A BATH AND I MEAN TO COLLECT.
ARE HER BATHS ESPECIALLY GOOD THAT NONE OTHER WILL SERVE?
THAT'S WHAT I INTEND TO FIND OUT.
HEY, CHARTER--
YOU REALLY ARE THICK ABOUT SOME THINGS, YOU KNOW THAT?
--TIME TO PAY UP...
...YOU'RE NOT CHARTER.
CHARTER IS OCCUPIED ELSEWHERE.
I AM SISTER NIGHTINGALE.
THE INQUISITOR REQUIRES YOUR ASSISTANCE...

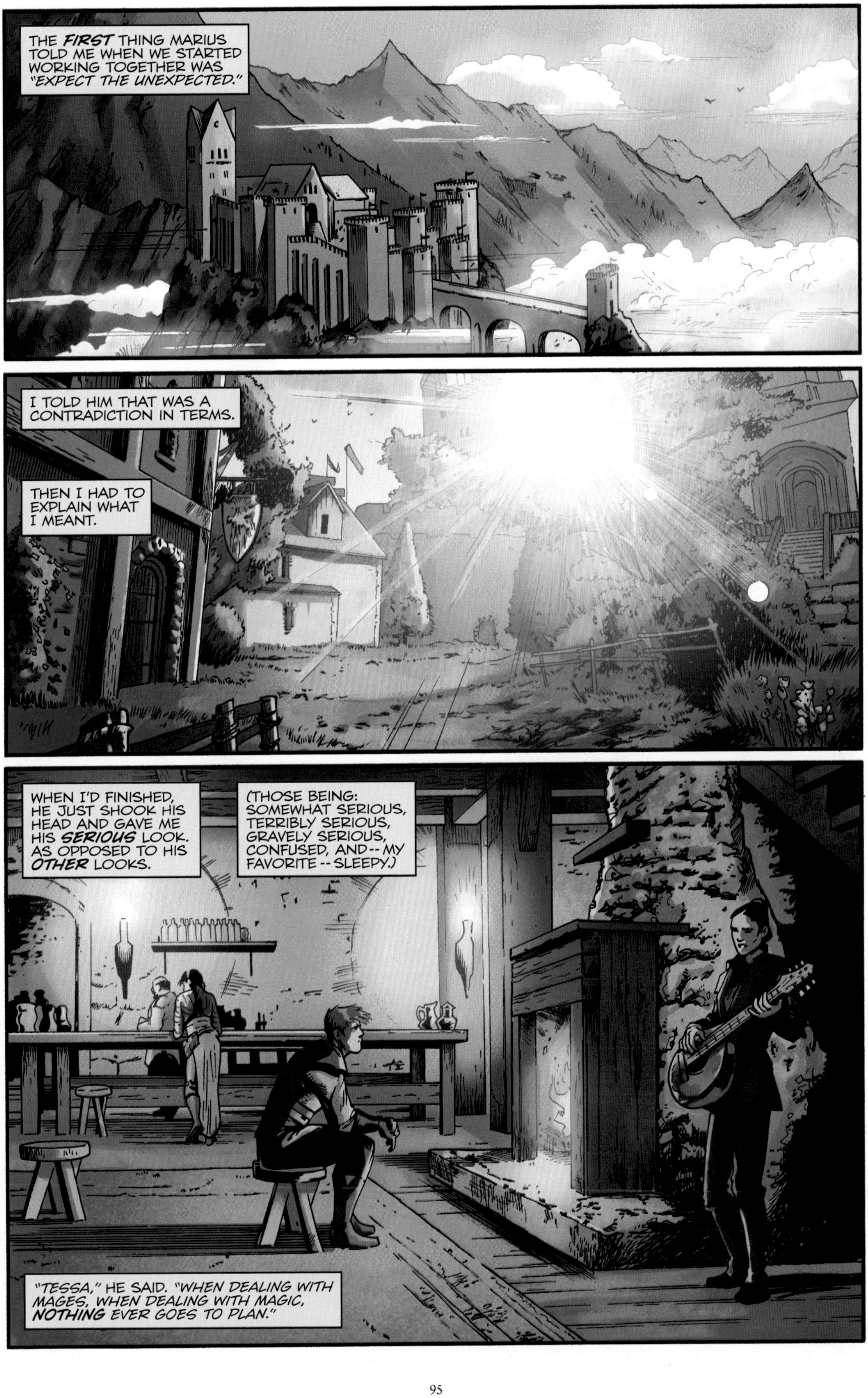
THE *FIRST* THING MARIUS TOLD ME WHEN WE STARTED WORKING TOGETHER WAS *"EXPECT THE UNEXPECTED."*
I TOLD HIM THAT WAS A CONTRADICTION IN TERMS.
THEN I HAD TO EXPLAIN WHAT I MEANT.
WHEN I'D FINISHED, HE JUST SHOOK HIS HEAD AND GAVE ME HIS *SERIOUS* LOOK. AS OPPOSED TO HIS *OTHER* LOOKS.
(THOSE BEING: SOMEWHAT SERIOUS, TERRIBLY SERIOUS, GRAVELY SERIOUS, CONFUSED, AND -- MY FAVORITE -- SLEEPY.)
"TESSA," HE SAID. *"WHEN DEALING WITH MAGES, WHEN DEALING WITH MAGIC,* ***NOTHING*** *EVER GOES TO PLAN."*

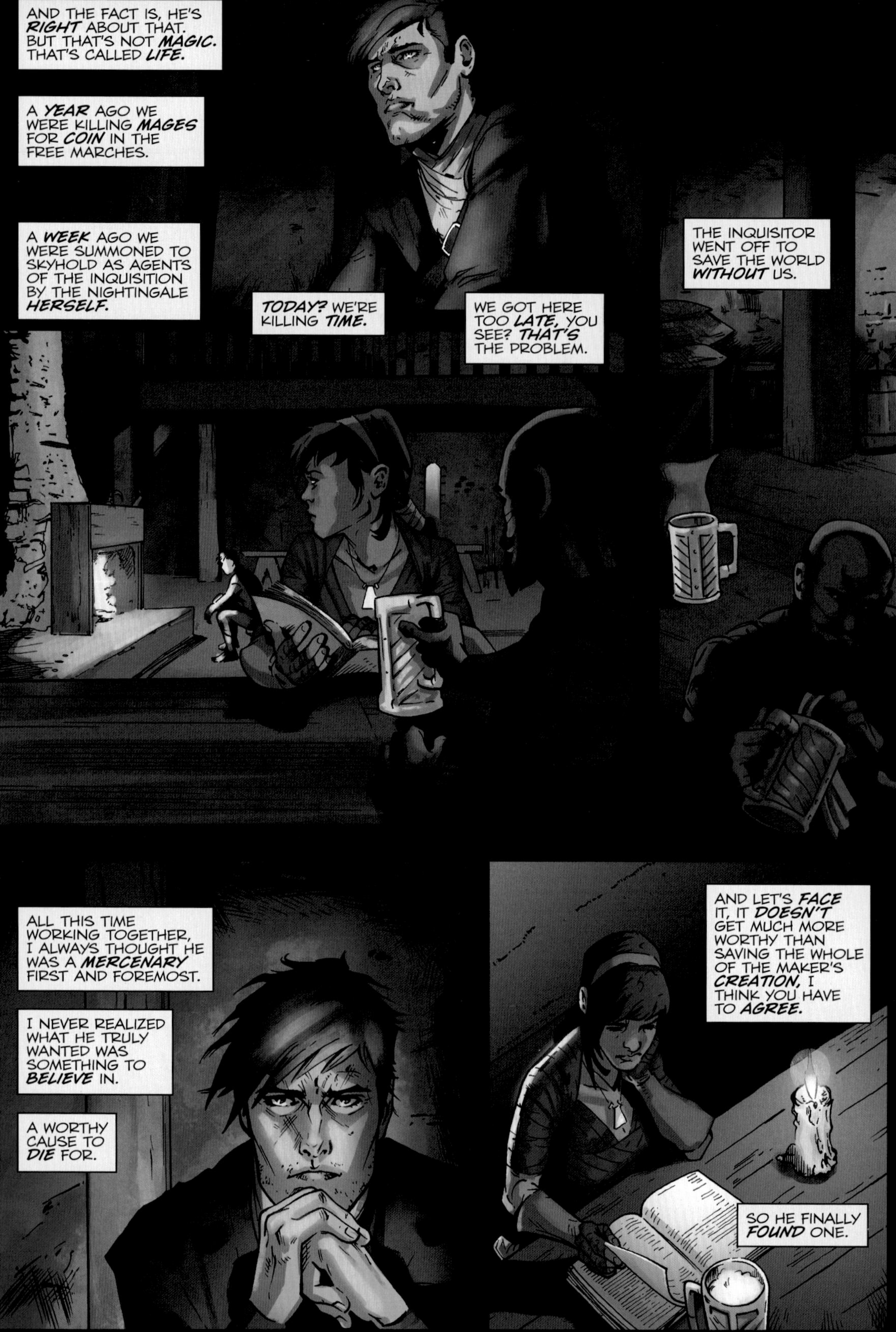
AND THE FACT IS, HE'S RIGHT ABOUT THAT. BUT THAT'S NOT MAGIC. THAT'S CALLED LIFE.
A YEAR AGO WE WERE KILLING MAGES FOR COIN IN THE FREE MARCHES.
A WEEK AGO WE WERE SUMMONED TO SKYHOLD AS AGENTS OF THE INQUISITION BY THE NIGHTINGALE HERSELF.
TODAY? WE'RE KILLING TIME.
WE GOT HERE TOO LATE, YOU SEE? THAT'S THE PROBLEM.
THE INQUISITOR WENT OFF TO SAVE THE WORLD WITHOUT US.
ALL THIS TIME WORKING TOGETHER, I ALWAYS THOUGHT HE WAS A MERCENARY FIRST AND FOREMOST.
I NEVER REALIZED WHAT HE TRULY WANTED WAS SOMETHING TO BELIEVE IN.
A WORTHY CAUSE TO DIE FOR.
AND LET'S FACE IT, IT DOESN'T GET MUCH MORE WORTHY THAN SAVING THE WHOLE OF THE MAKER'S CREATION, I THINK YOU HAVE TO AGREE.
SO HE FINALLY FOUND ONE.

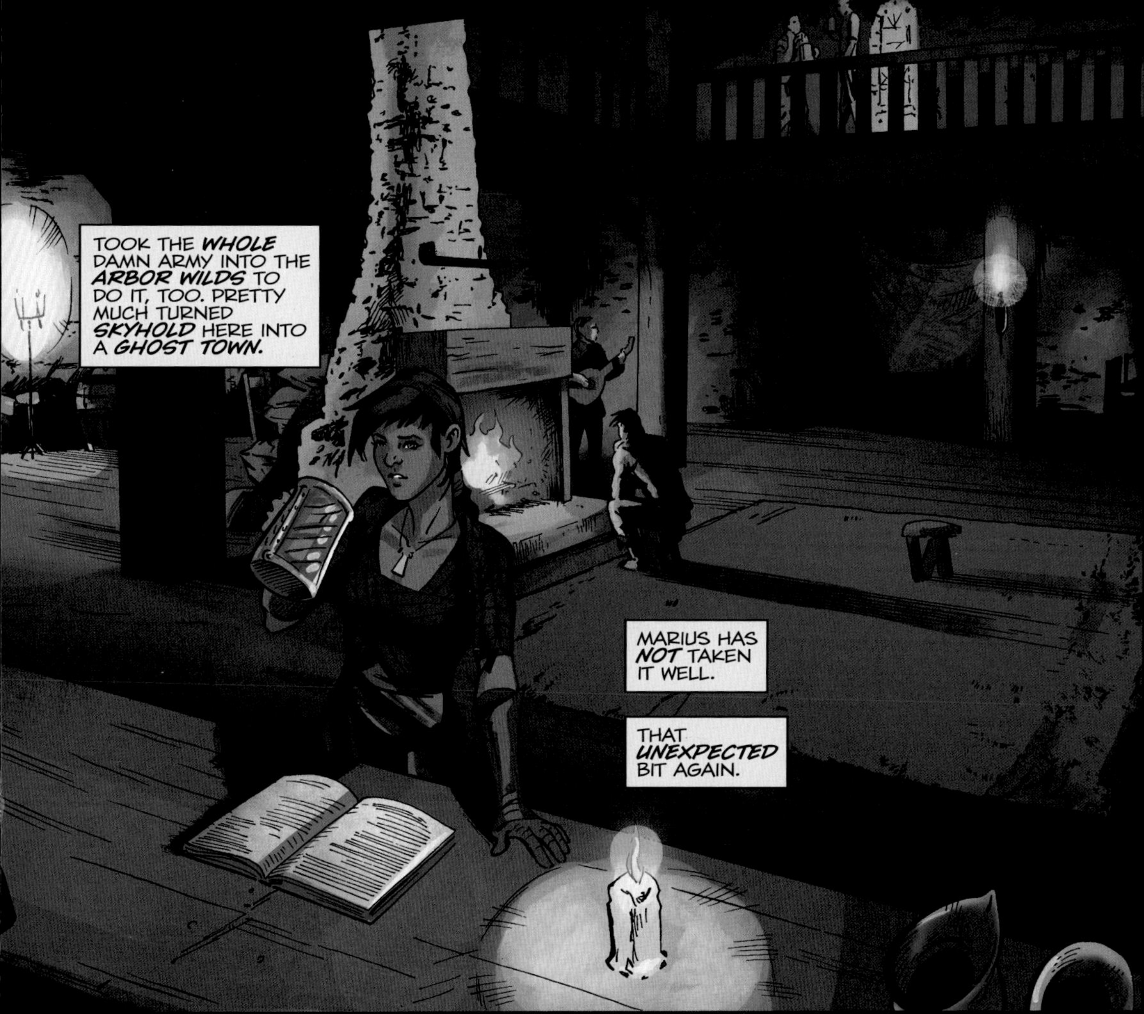
TOOK THE WHOLE DAMN ARMY INTO THE ARBOR WILDS TO DO IT, TOO. PRETTY MUCH TURNED SKYHOLD HERE INTO A GHOST TOWN.
MARIUS HAS NOT TAKEN IT WELL.
THAT UNEXPECTED BIT AGAIN.

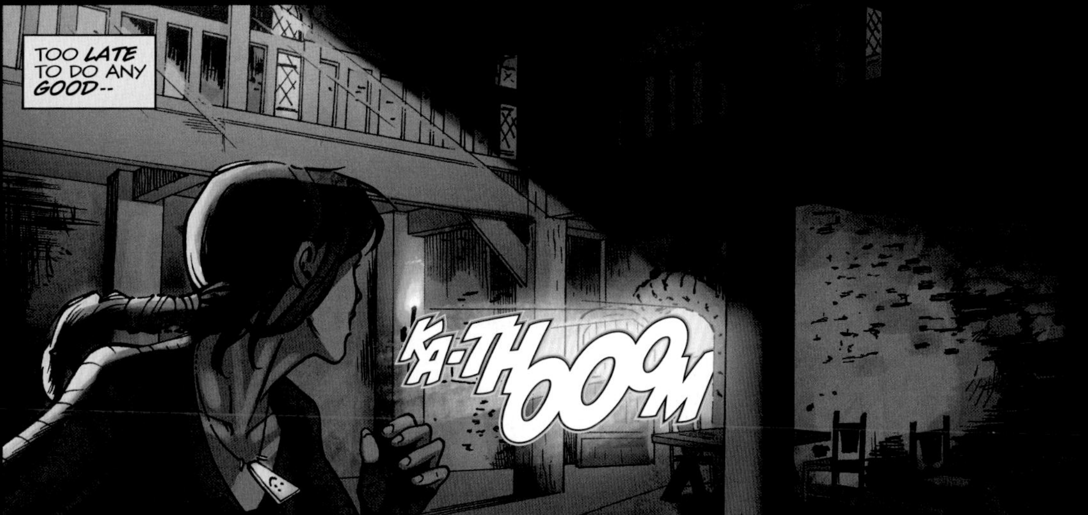
TOO LATE TO DO ANY GOOD--
KA-THOOM

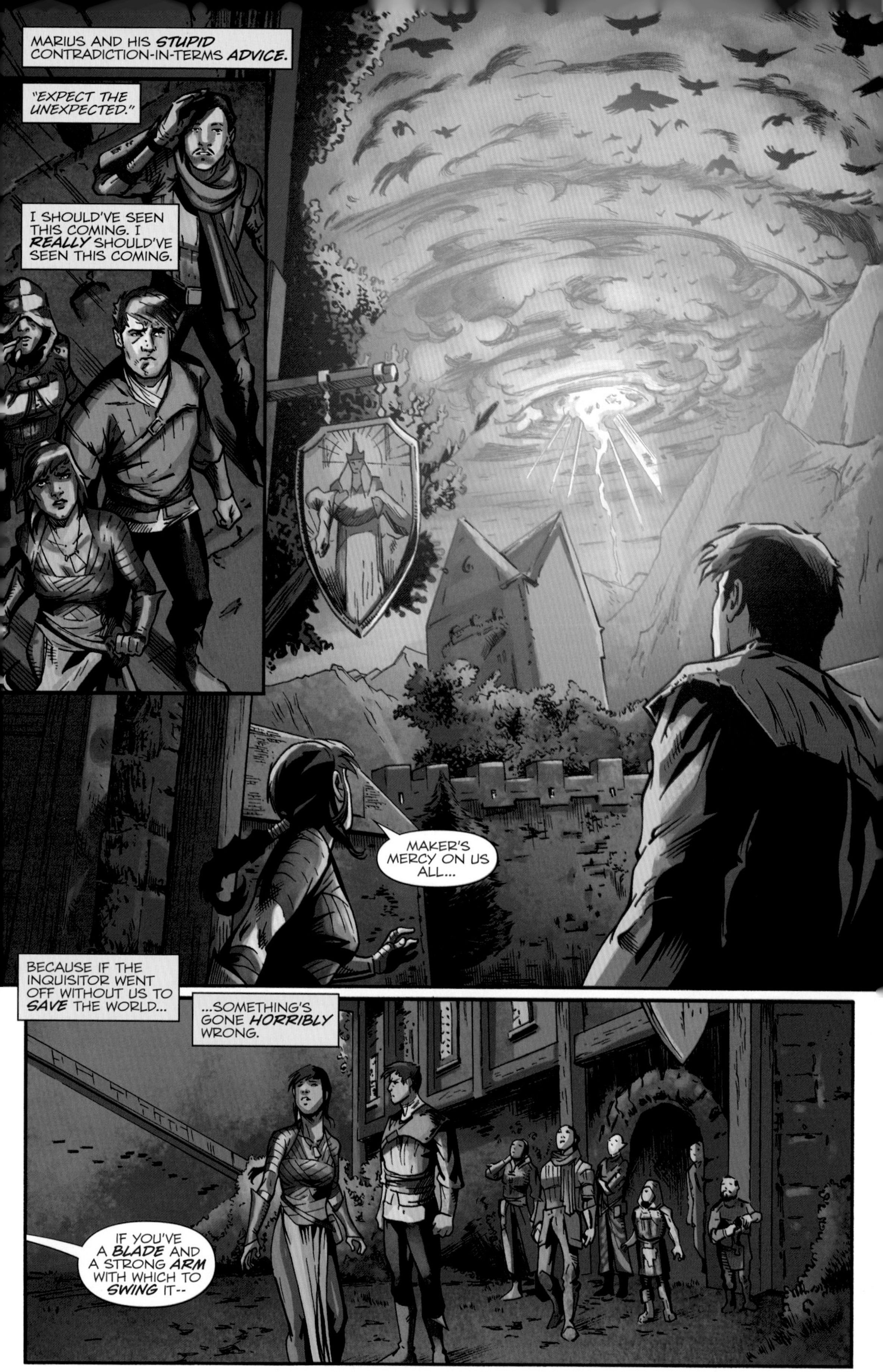
MARIUS AND HIS STUPID CONTRADICTION-IN-TERMS ADVICE.
"EXPECT THE UNEXPECTED."
I SHOULD'VE SEEN THIS COMING. I REALLY SHOULD'VE SEEN THIS COMING.
MAKER'S MERCY ON US ALL...
BECAUSE IF THE INQUISITOR WENT OFF WITHOUT US TO SAVE THE WORLD...
...SOMETHING'S GONE HORRIBLY WRONG.
IF YOU'VE A BLADE AND A STRONG ARM WITH WHICH TO SWING IT--

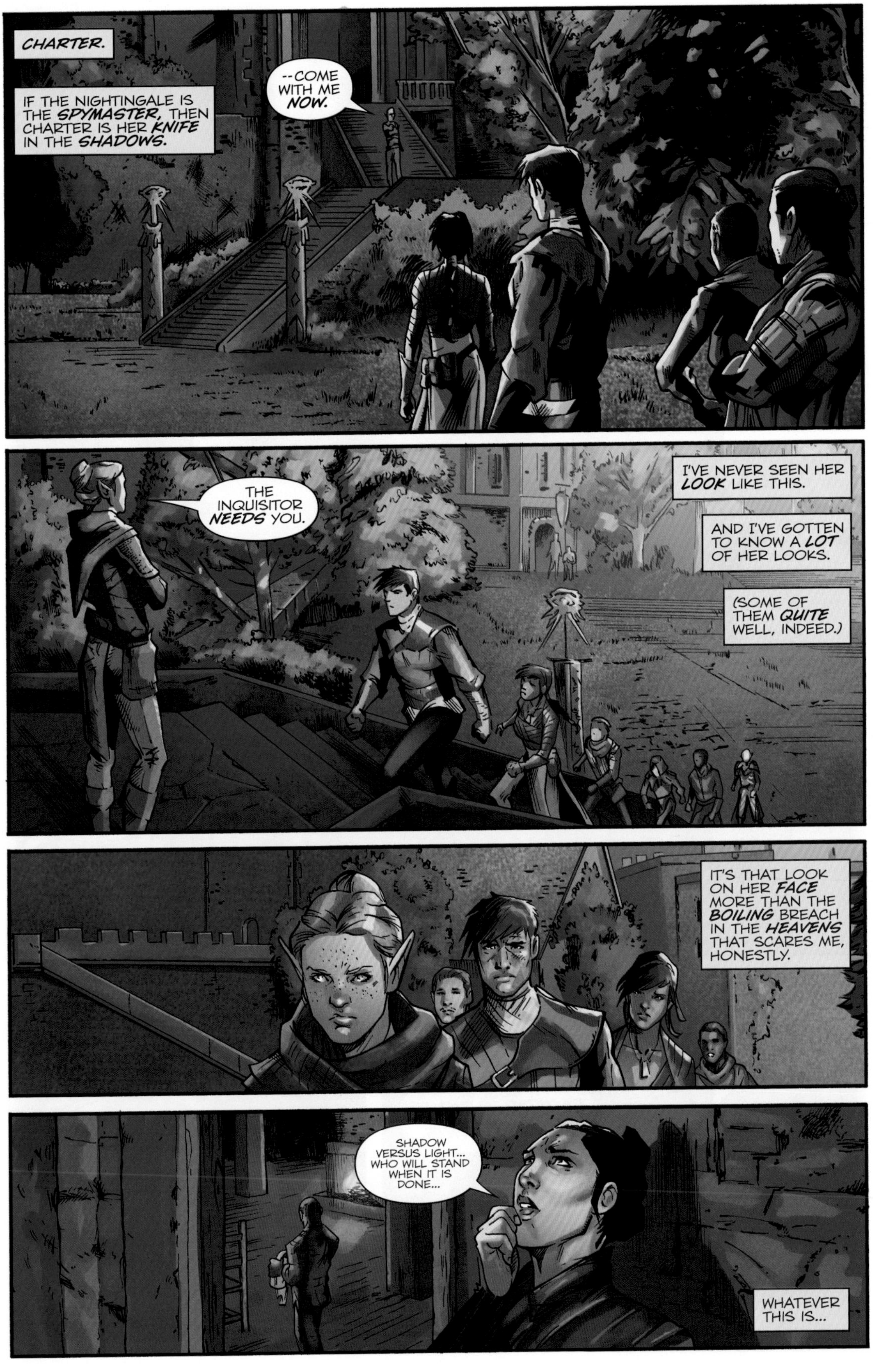
CHARTER.
IF THE NIGHTINGALE IS THE SPYMASTER, THEN CHARTER IS HER KNIFE IN THE SHADOWS.
--COME WITH ME NOW.
THE INQUISITOR NEEDS YOU.
I'VE NEVER SEEN HER LOOK LIKE THIS.
AND I'VE GOTTEN TO KNOW A LOT OF HER LOOKS.
(SOME OF THEM QUITE WELL, INDEED.)
IT'S THAT LOOK ON HER FACE MORE THAN THE BOILING BREACH IN THE HEAVENS THAT SCARES ME, HONESTLY.
SHADOW VERSUS LIGHT... WHO WILL STAND WHEN IT IS DONE...
WHATEVER THIS IS...

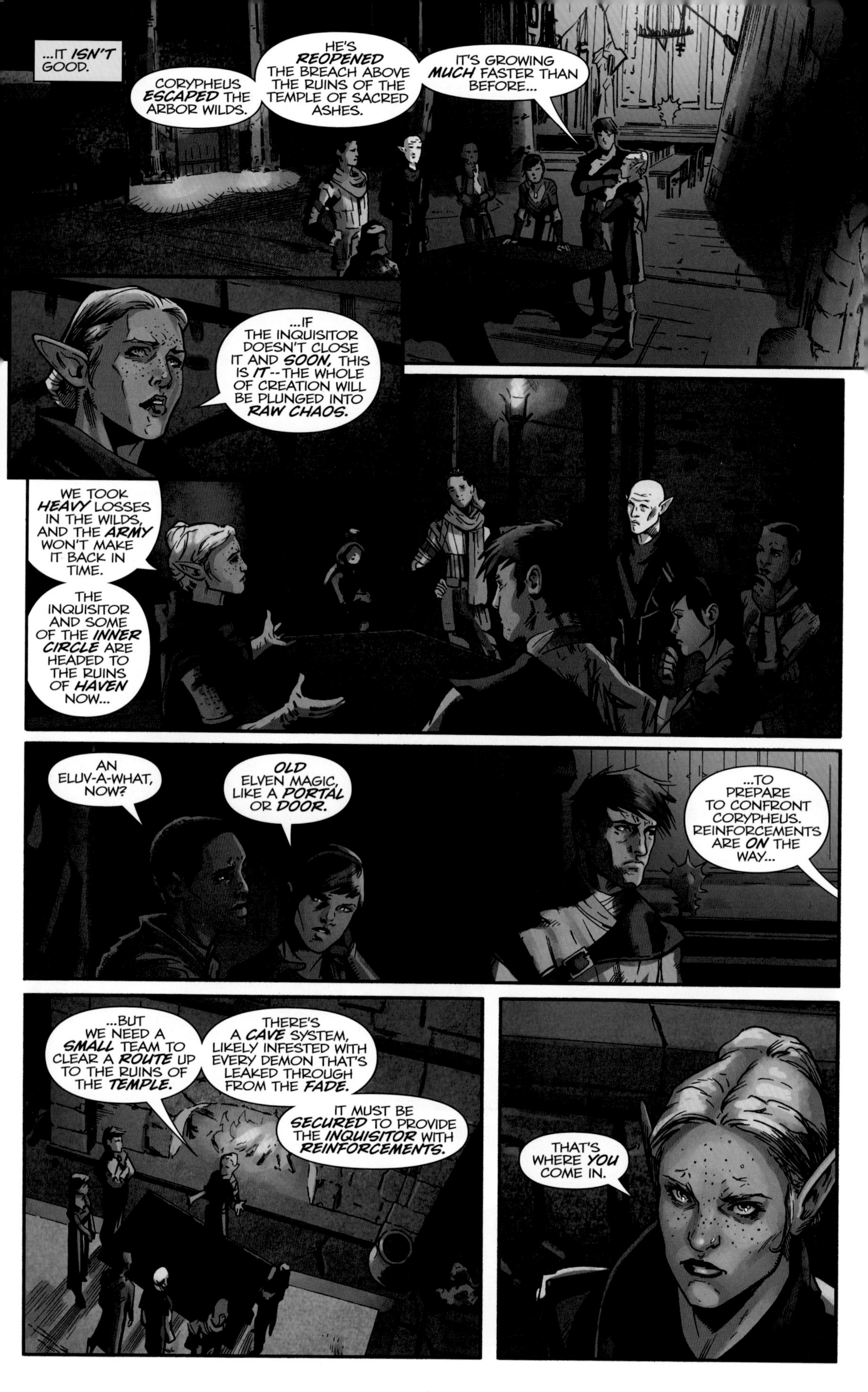
...IT ISN'T GOOD.
CORYPHEUS ESCAPED THE ARBOR WILDS.
HE'S REOPENED THE BREACH ABOVE THE RUINS OF THE TEMPLE OF SACRED ASHES.
IT'S GROWING MUCH FASTER THAN BEFORE...
...IF THE INQUISITOR DOESN'T CLOSE IT AND SOON, THIS IS IT--THE WHOLE OF CREATION WILL BE PLUNGED INTO RAW CHAOS.
WE TOOK HEAVY LOSSES IN THE WILDS, AND THE ARMY WON'T MAKE IT BACK IN TIME.
THE INQUISITOR AND SOME OF THE INNER CIRCLE ARE HEADED TO THE RUINS OF HAVEN NOW...
AN ELUV-A-WHAT, NOW?
OLD ELVEN MAGIC, LIKE A PORTAL OR DOOR.
...TO PREPARE TO CONFRONT CORYPHEUS. REINFORCEMENTS ARE ON THE WAY...
...BUT WE NEED A SMALL TEAM TO CLEAR A ROUTE UP TO THE RUINS OF THE TEMPLE.
THERE'S A CAVE SYSTEM, LIKELY INFESTED WITH EVERY DEMON THAT'S LEAKED THROUGH FROM THE FADE.
IT MUST BE SECURED TO PROVIDE THE INQUISITOR WITH REINFORCEMENTS.
THAT'S WHERE YOU COME IN.

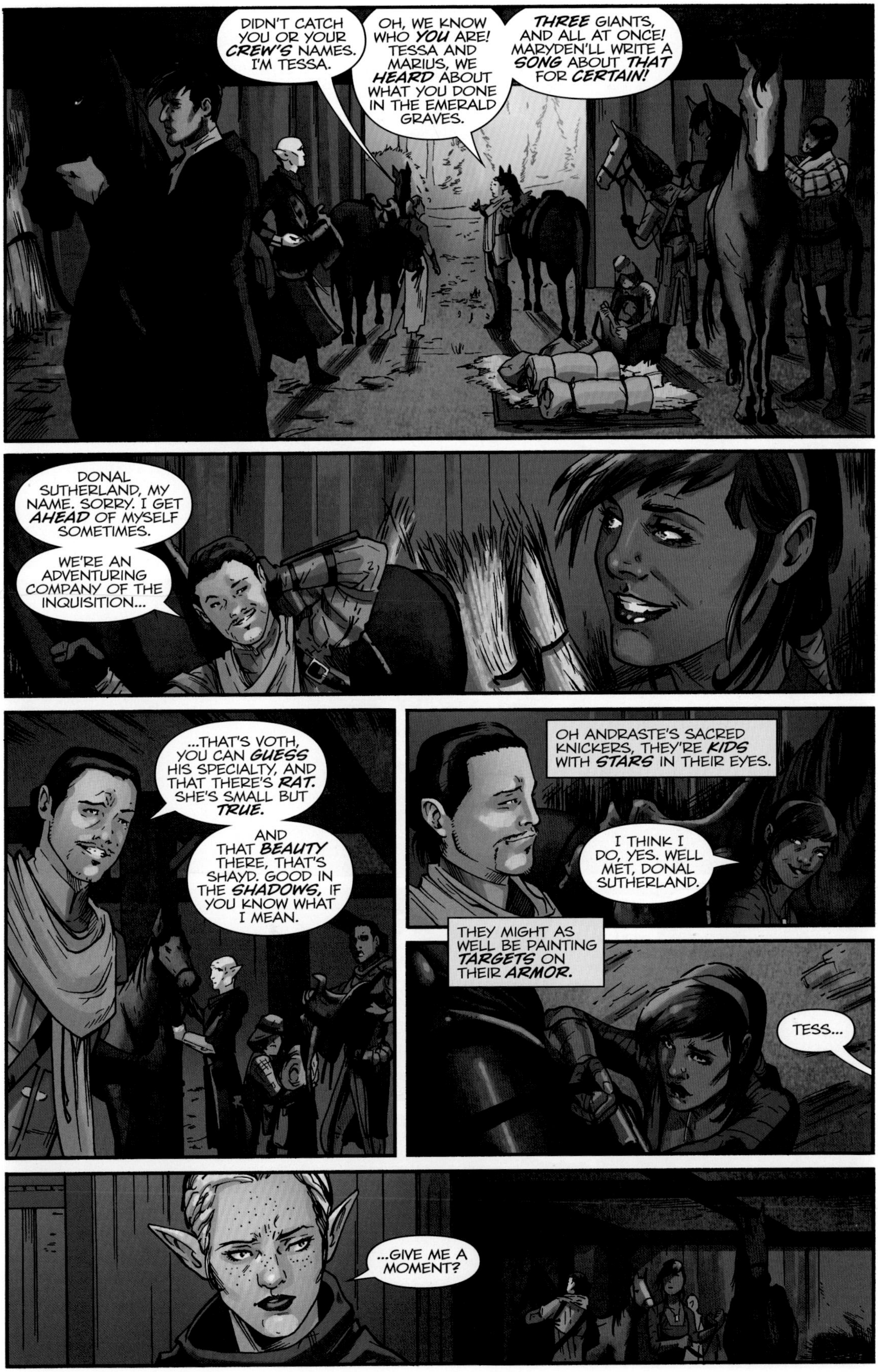
DIDN'T CATCH YOU OR YOUR CREW'S NAMES. I'M TESSA.
OH, WE KNOW WHO YOU ARE! TESSA AND MARIUS, WE HEARD ABOUT WHAT YOU DONE IN THE EMERALD GRAVES.
THREE GIANTS, AND ALL AT ONCE! MARYDEN'LL WRITE A SONG ABOUT THAT FOR CERTAIN!
DONAL SUTHERLAND, MY NAME. SORRY. I GET AHEAD OF MYSELF SOMETIMES.
WE'RE AN ADVENTURING COMPANY OF THE INQUISITION...
...THAT'S VOTH, YOU CAN GUESS HIS SPECIALTY, AND THAT THERE'S RAT. SHE'S SMALL BUT TRUE.
AND THAT BEAUTY THERE, THAT'S SHAYD. GOOD IN THE SHADOWS, IF YOU KNOW WHAT I MEAN.
OH ANDRASTE'S SACRED KNICKERS, THEY'RE KIDS WITH STARS IN THEIR EYES.
I THINK I DO, YES. WELL MET, DONAL SUTHERLAND.
THEY MIGHT AS WELL BE PAINTING TARGETS ON THEIR ARMOR.
TESS...
...GIVE ME A MOMENT?

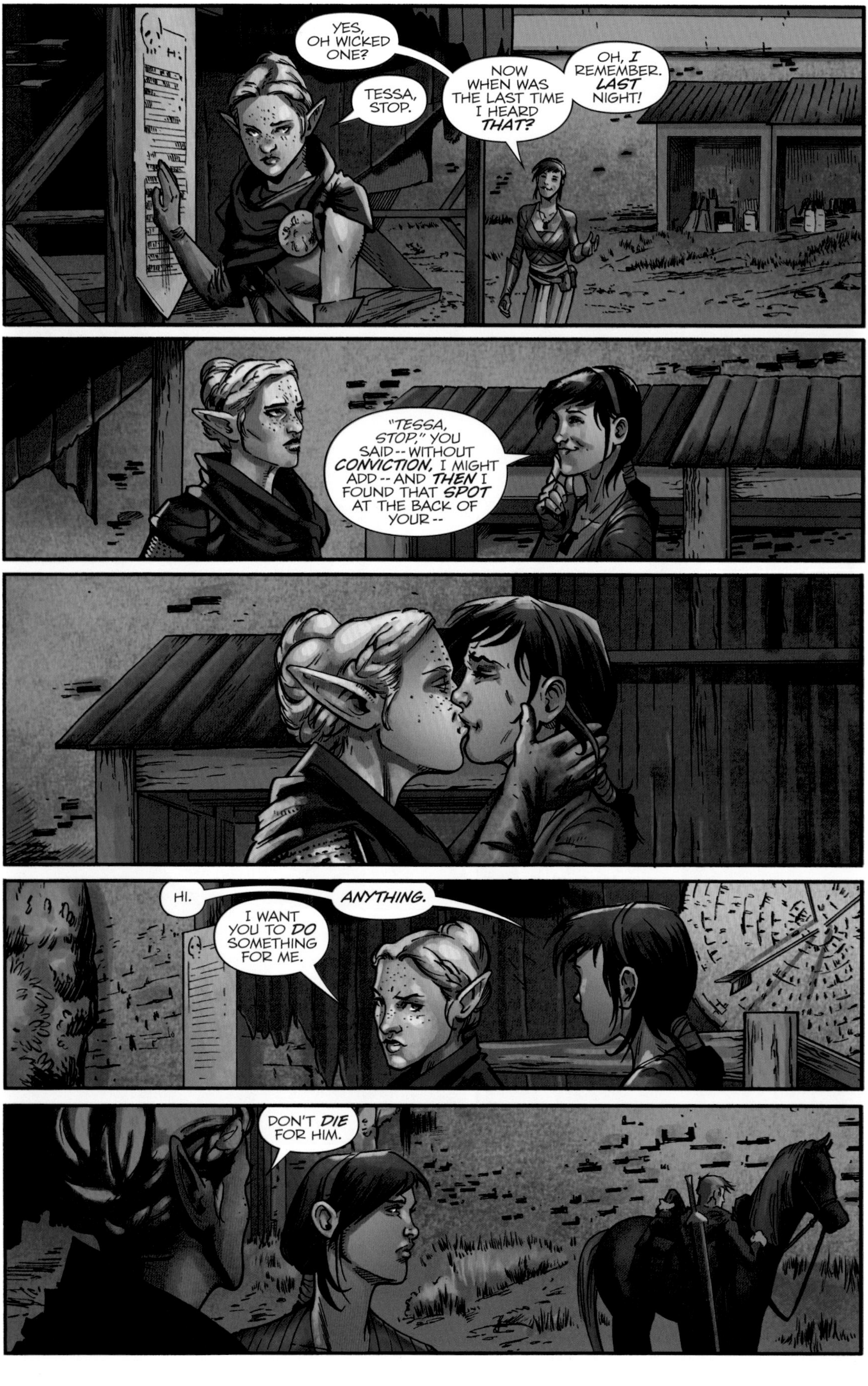
YES, OH WICKED ONE?
TESSA, STOP.
NOW WHEN WAS THE LAST TIME I HEARD THAT?
OH, I REMEMBER. LAST NIGHT!
"TESSA, STOP," YOU SAID -- WITHOUT CONVICTION, I MIGHT ADD -- AND THEN I FOUND THAT SPOT AT THE BACK OF YOUR --
HI.
ANYTHING.
I WANT YOU TO DO SOMETHING FOR ME.
DON'T DIE FOR HIM.

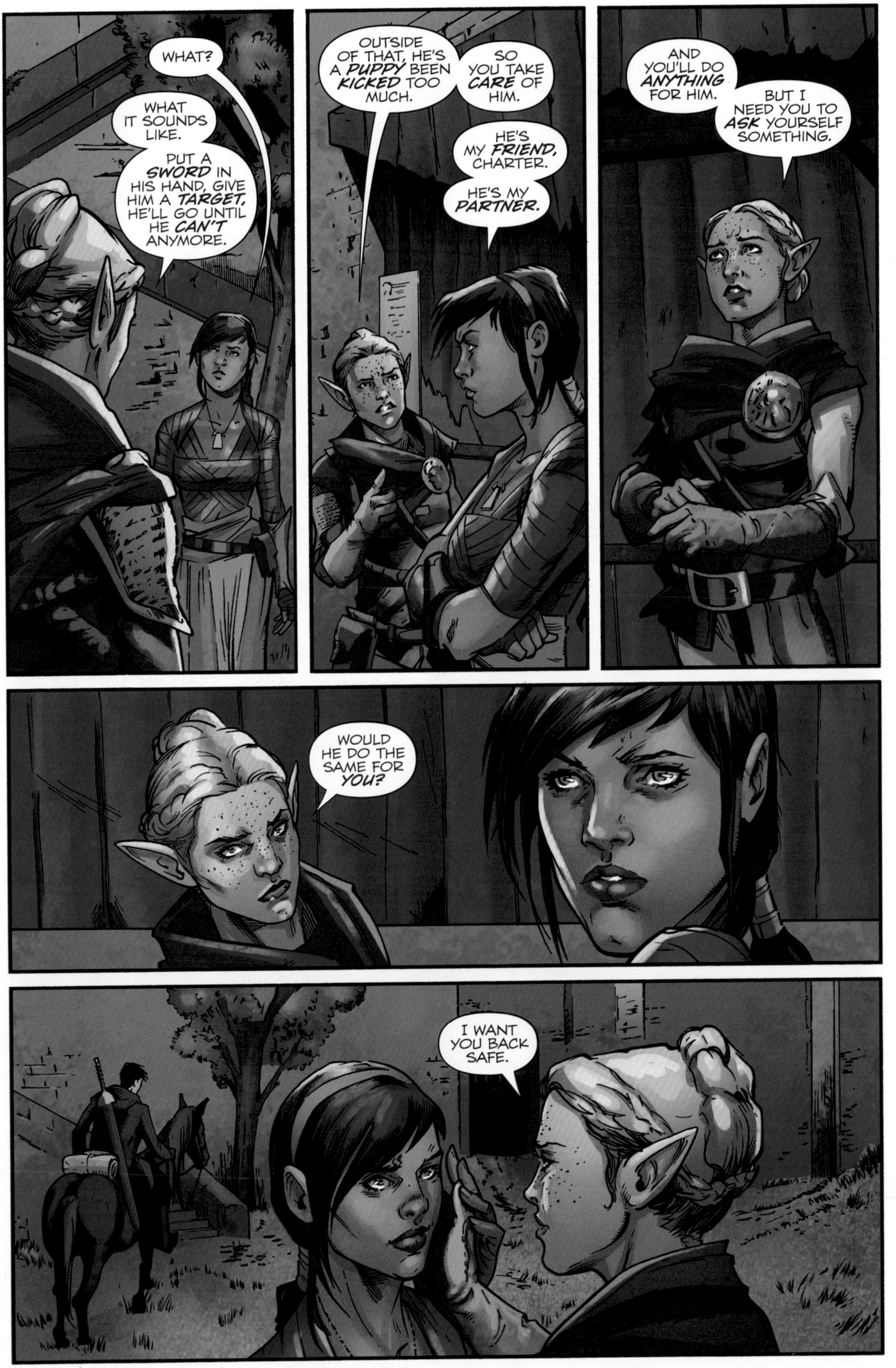
WHAT?
WHAT IT SOUNDS LIKE.
PUT A SWORD IN HIS HAND, GIVE HIM A TARGET, HE'LL GO UNTIL HE CAN'T ANYMORE.
OUTSIDE OF THAT, HE'S A PUPPY BEEN KICKED TOO MUCH.
SO YOU TAKE CARE OF HIM.
HE'S MY FRIEND, CHARTER.
HE'S MY PARTNER.
AND YOU'LL DO ANYTHING FOR HIM.
BUT I NEED YOU TO ASK YOURSELF SOMETHING.
WOULD HE DO THE SAME FOR YOU?
I WANT YOU BACK SAFE.

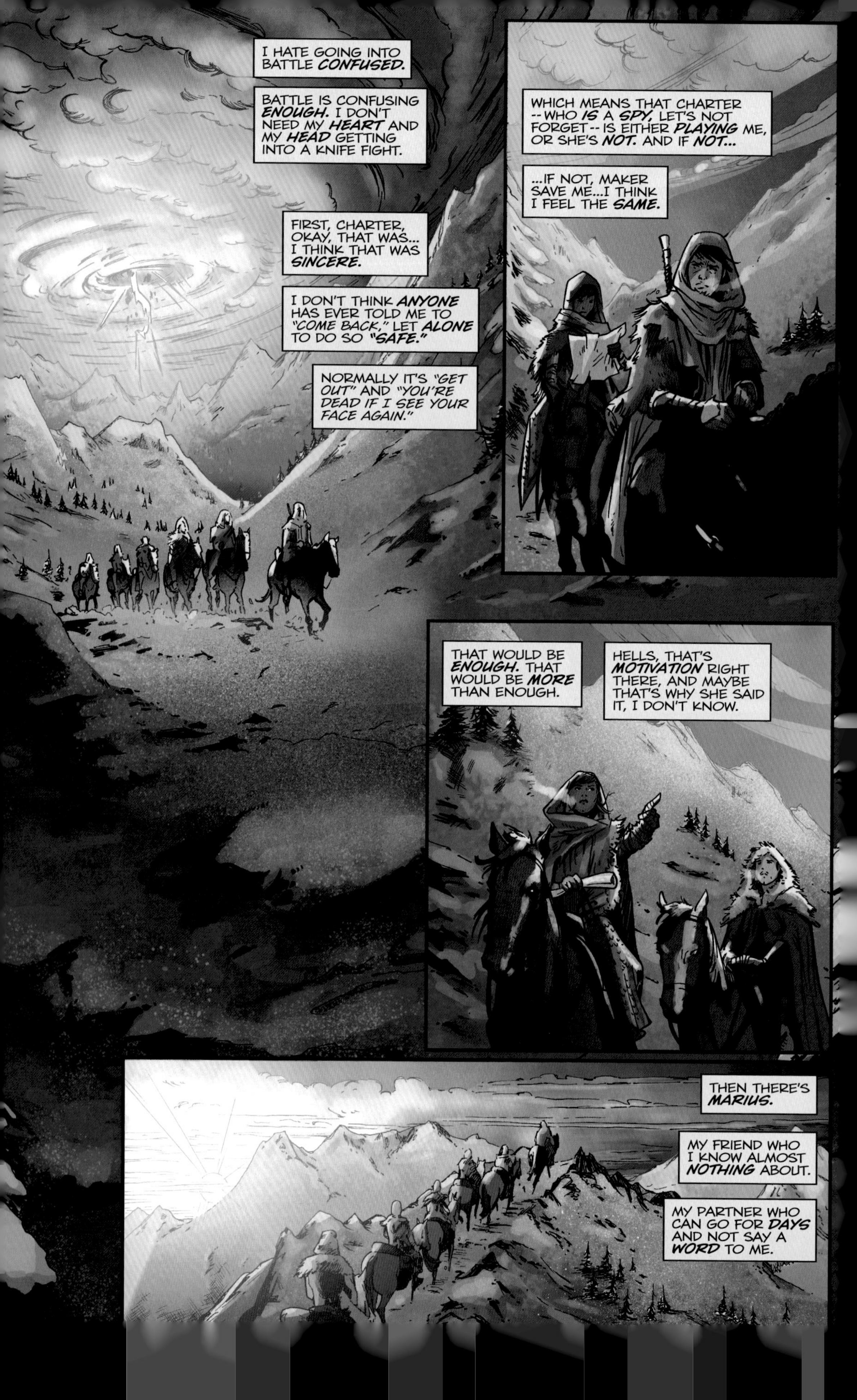
I HATE GOING INTO BATTLE CONFUSED.
BATTLE IS CONFUSING ENOUGH. I DON'T NEED MY HEART AND MY HEAD GETTING INTO A KNIFE FIGHT.
FIRST, CHARTER, OKAY, THAT WAS... I THINK THAT WAS SINCERE.
I DON'T THINK ANYONE HAS EVER TOLD ME TO "COME BACK," LET ALONE TO DO SO "SAFE."
NORMALLY IT'S "GET OUT" AND "YOU'RE DEAD IF I SEE YOUR FACE AGAIN."
WHICH MEANS THAT CHARTER --WHO IS A SPY, LET'S NOT FORGET-- IS EITHER PLAYING ME, OR SHE'S NOT. AND IF NOT...
...IF NOT, MAKER SAVE ME...I THINK I FEEL THE SAME.
THAT WOULD BE ENOUGH. THAT WOULD BE MORE THAN ENOUGH.
HELLS, THAT'S MOTIVATION RIGHT THERE, AND MAYBE THAT'S WHY SHE SAID IT, I DON'T KNOW.
THEN THERE'S MARIUS.
MY FRIEND WHO I KNOW ALMOST NOTHING ABOUT.
MY PARTNER WHO CAN GO FOR DAYS AND NOT SAY A WORD TO ME.

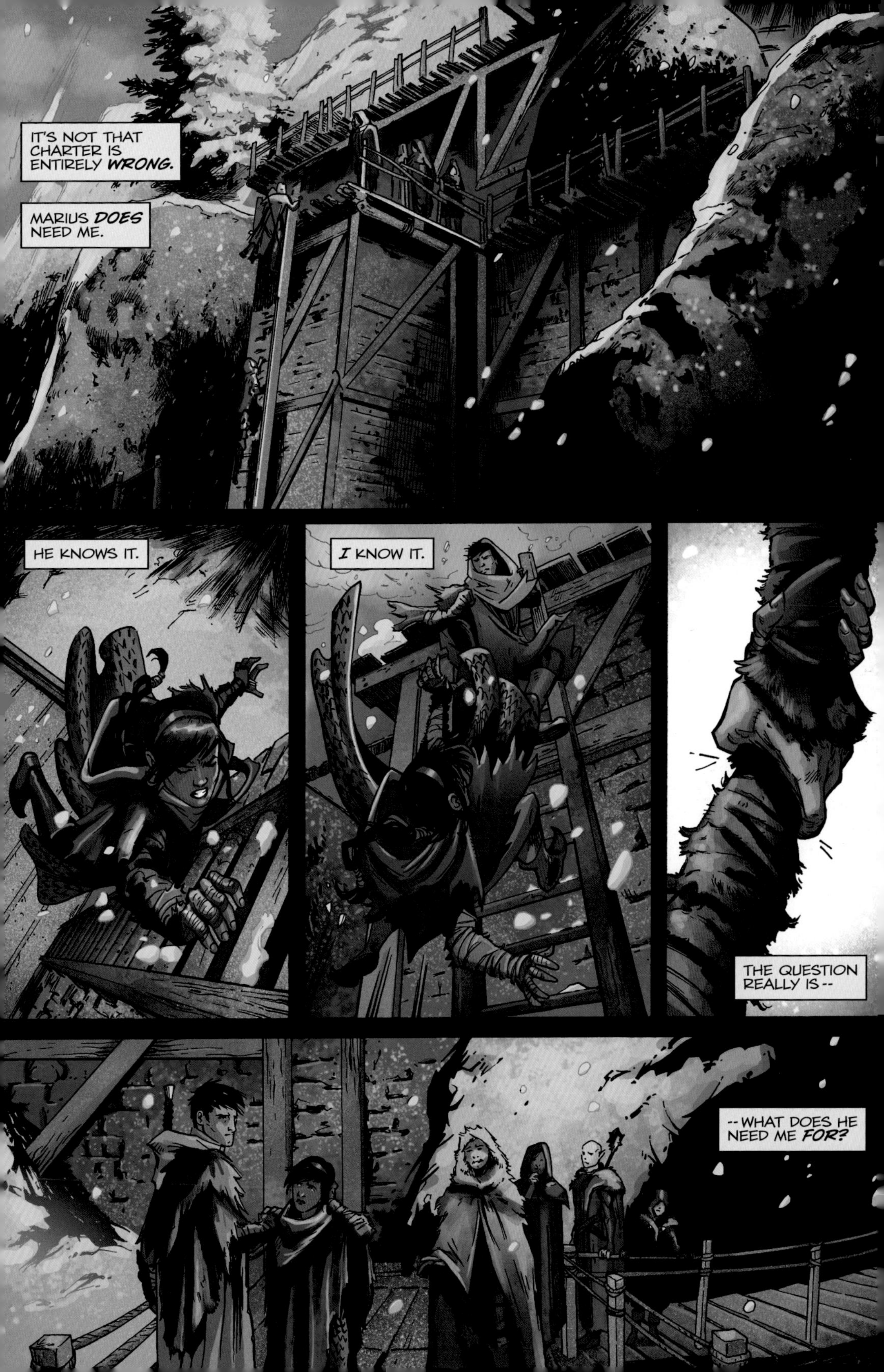
IT'S NOT THAT CHARTER IS ENTIRELY WRONG.
MARIUS DOES NEED ME.
HE KNOWS IT.
I KNOW IT.
THE QUESTION REALLY IS --
-- WHAT DOES HE NEED ME FOR?

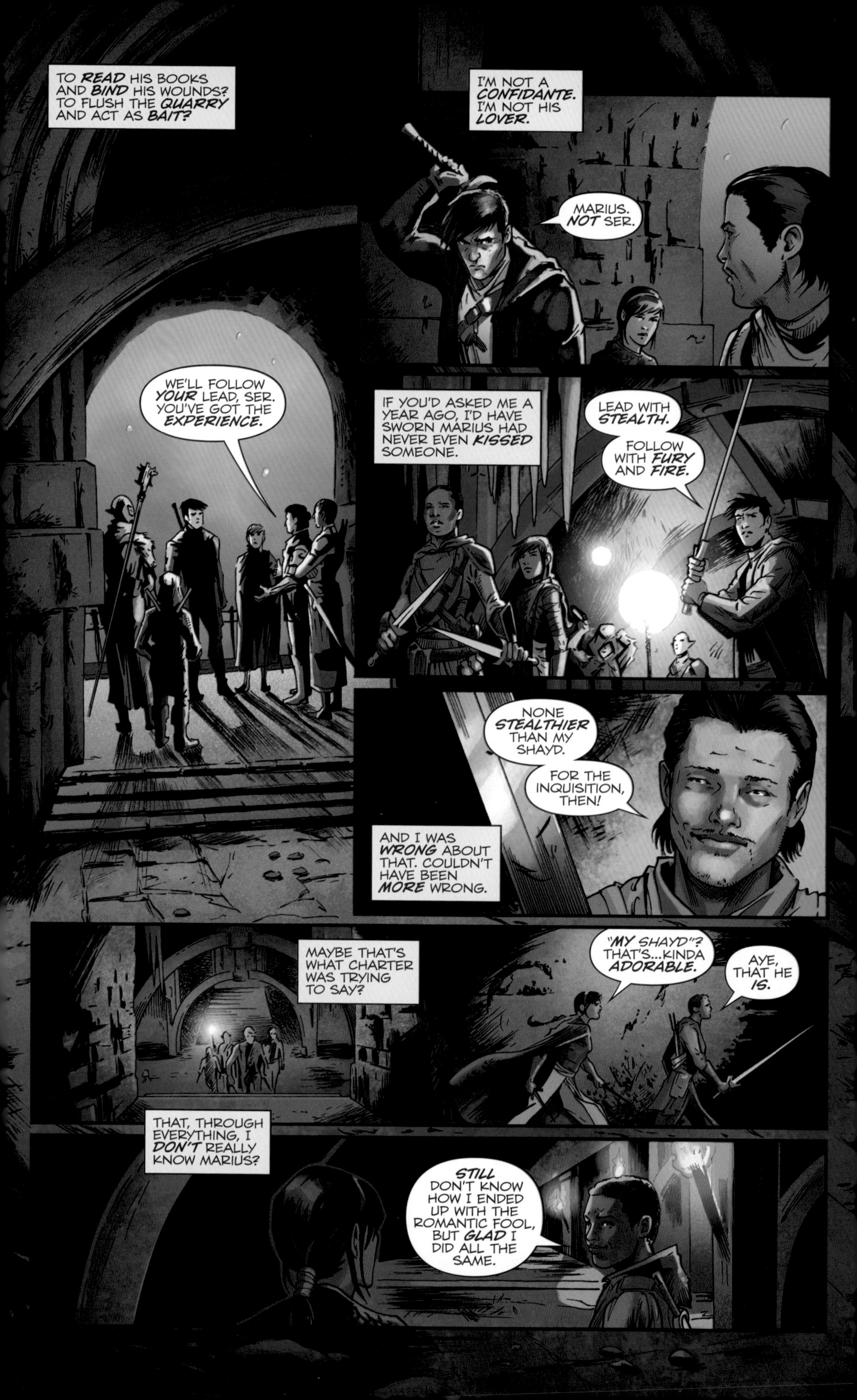
TO READ HIS BOOKS AND BIND HIS WOUNDS? TO FLUSH THE QUARRY AND ACT AS BAIT?
WE'LL FOLLOW YOUR LEAD, SER. YOU'VE GOT THE EXPERIENCE.
I'M NOT A CONFIDANTE. I'M NOT HIS LOVER.
MARIUS. NOT SER.
IF YOU'D ASKED ME A YEAR AGO, I'D HAVE SWORN MARIUS HAD NEVER EVEN KISSED SOMEONE.
LEAD WITH STEALTH.
FOLLOW WITH FURY AND FIRE.
NONE STEALTHIER THAN MY SHAYD.
FOR THE INQUISITION, THEN!
AND I WAS WRONG ABOUT THAT. COULDN'T HAVE BEEN MORE WRONG.
MAYBE THAT'S WHAT CHARTER WAS TRYING TO SAY?
"MY SHAYD"? THAT'S...KINDA ADORABLE.
AYE, THAT HE IS.
THAT, THROUGH EVERYTHING, I DON'T REALLY KNOW MARIUS?
STILL DON'T KNOW HOW I ENDED UP WITH THE ROMANTIC FOOL, BUT GLAD I DID ALL THE SAME.

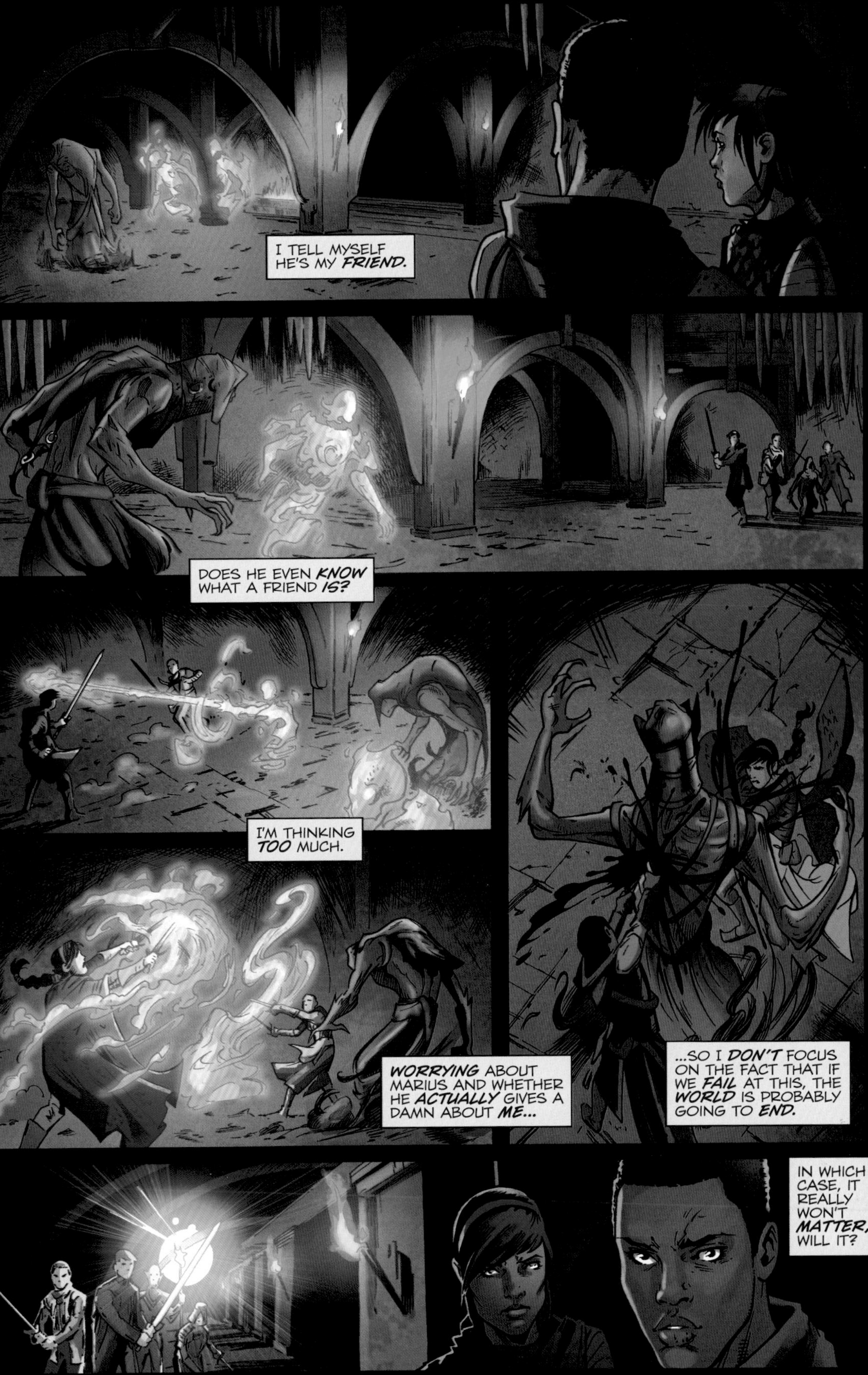

I TELL MYSELF HE'S MY *FRIEND.*
DOES HE EVEN *KNOW* WHAT A FRIEND *IS?*
I'M THINKING *TOO* MUCH.
WORRYING ABOUT MARIUS AND WHETHER HE *ACTUALLY* GIVES A DAMN ABOUT *ME...*
...SO I *DON'T* FOCUS ON THE FACT THAT IF WE *FAIL* AT THIS, THE *WORLD* IS PROBABLY GOING TO *END.*
IN WHICH CASE, IT REALLY WON'T *MATTER,* WILL IT?

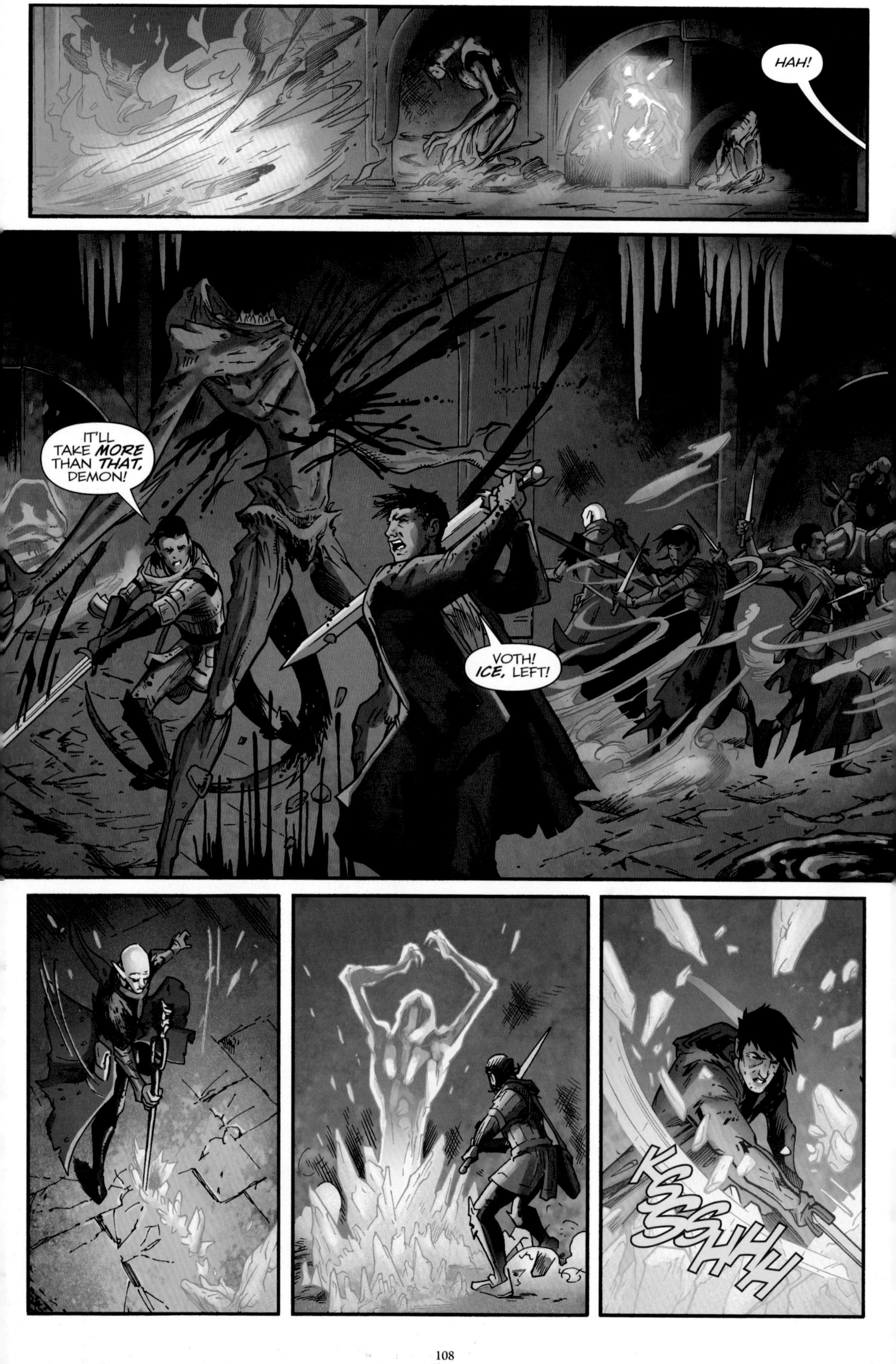
HAH!
IT'LL TAKE MORE THAN THAT, DEMON!
VOTH! ICE, LEFT!
KSSHHH

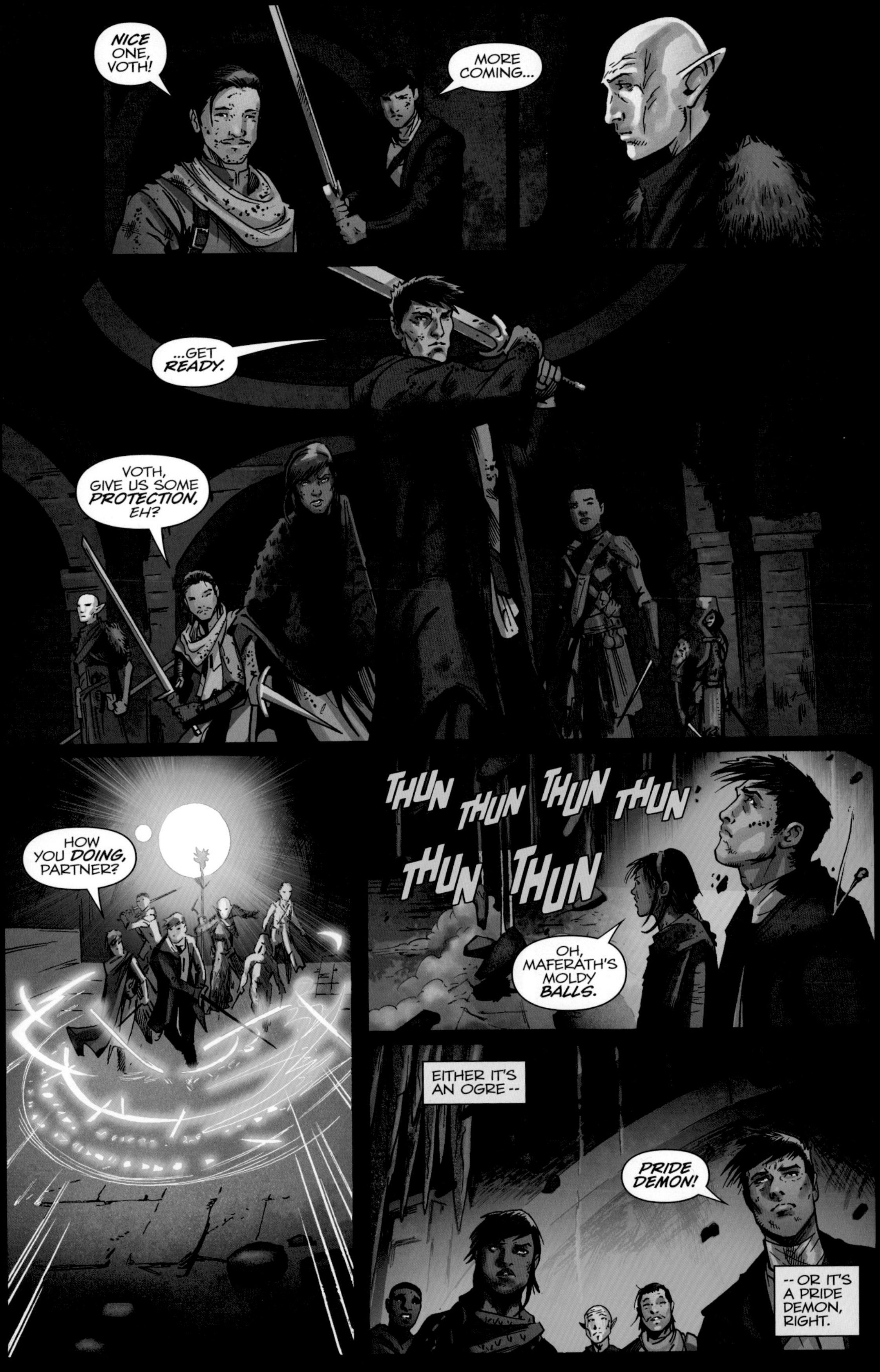
NICE ONE, VOTH!
MORE COMING...
...GET READY.
VOTH, GIVE US SOME PROTECTION, EH?
HOW YOU DOING, PARTNER?
THUN THUN THUN THUN
THUN THUN
OH, MAFERATH'S MOLDY BALLS.
EITHER IT'S AN OGRE --
PRIDE DEMON!
-- OR IT'S A PRIDE DEMON, RIGHT.

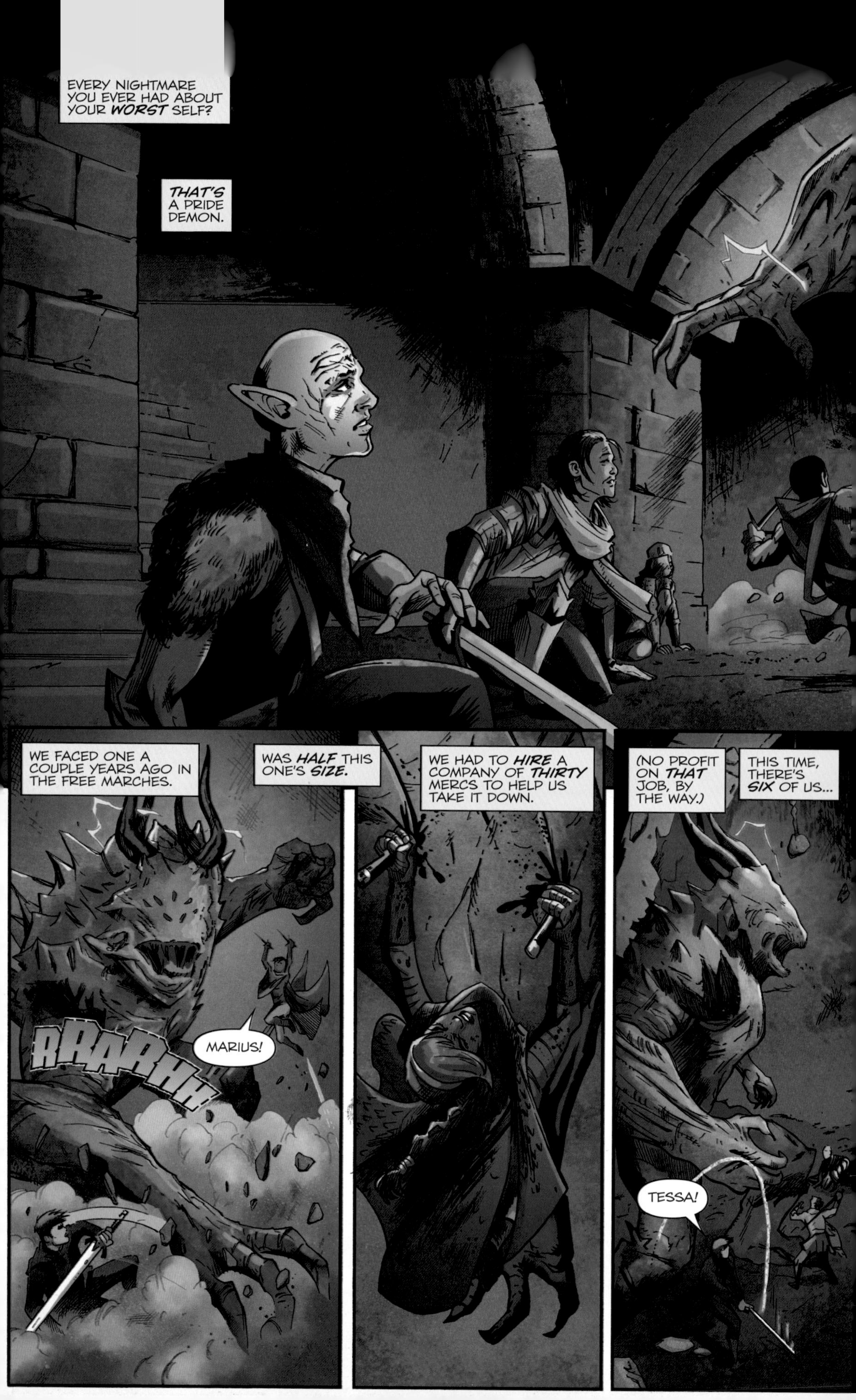
EVERY NIGHTMARE YOU EVER HAD ABOUT YOUR *WORST* SELF?
THAT'S A PRIDE DEMON.
WE FACED ONE A COUPLE YEARS AGO IN THE FREE MARCHES.
RRARHH
MARIUS!
WAS *HALF* THIS ONE'S *SIZE.*
WE HAD TO *HIRE* A COMPANY OF *THIRTY* MERCS TO HELP US TAKE IT DOWN.
(NO PROFIT ON *THAT* JOB, BY THE WAY.)
THIS TIME, THERE'S *SIX* OF US...
TESSA!

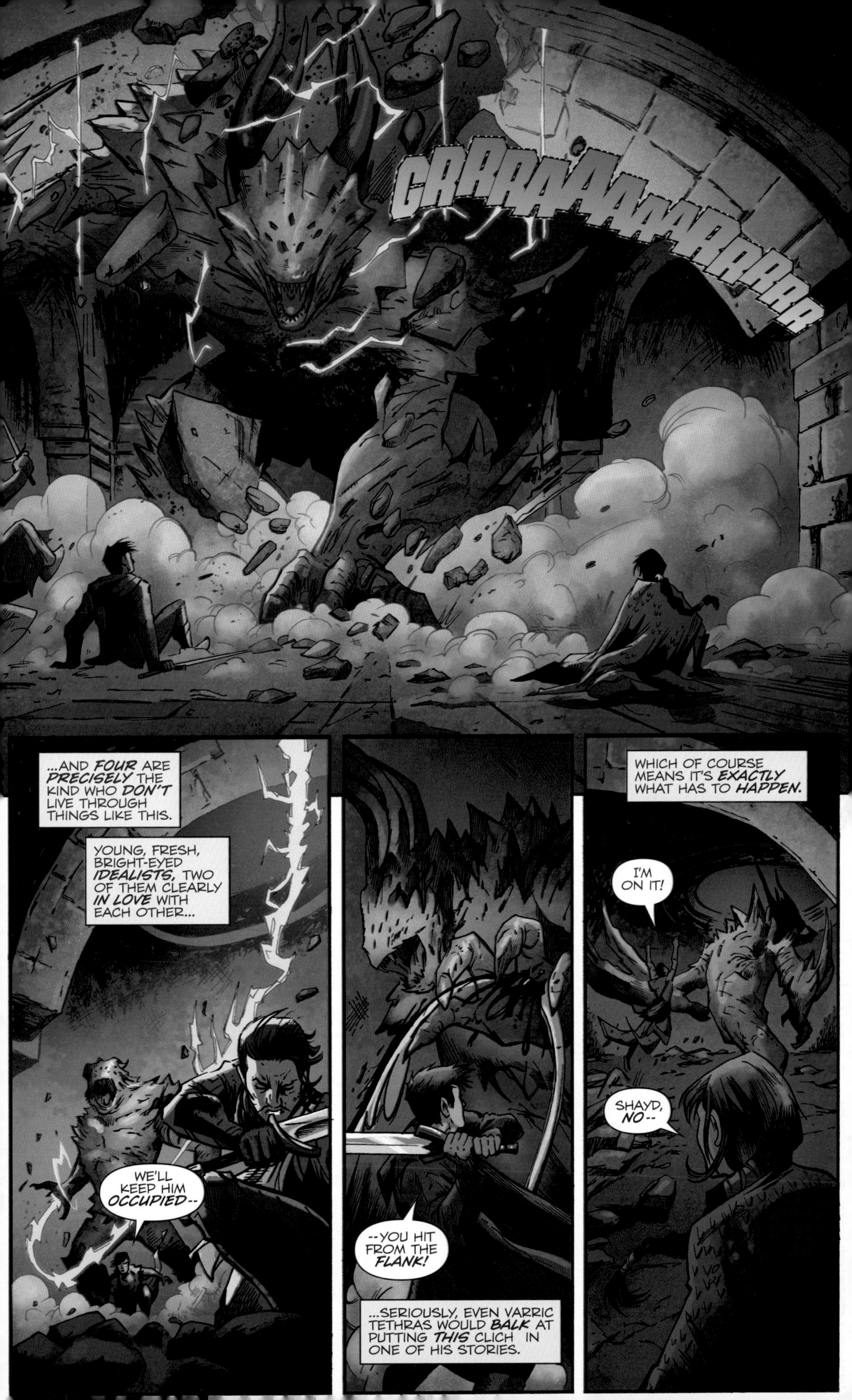

GRRRAAAAAARRRRR
...AND FOUR ARE PRECISELY THE KIND WHO DON'T LIVE THROUGH THINGS LIKE THIS.
YOUNG, FRESH, BRIGHT-EYED IDEALISTS, TWO OF THEM CLEARLY IN LOVE WITH EACH OTHER...
WE'LL KEEP HIM OCCUPIED--
--YOU HIT FROM THE FLANK!
...SERIOUSLY, EVEN VARRIC TETHRAS WOULD BALK AT PUTTING THIS CLICH IN ONE OF HIS STORIES.
WHICH OF COURSE MEANS IT'S EXACTLY WHAT HAS TO HAPPEN.
I'M ON IT!
SHAYD, NO--

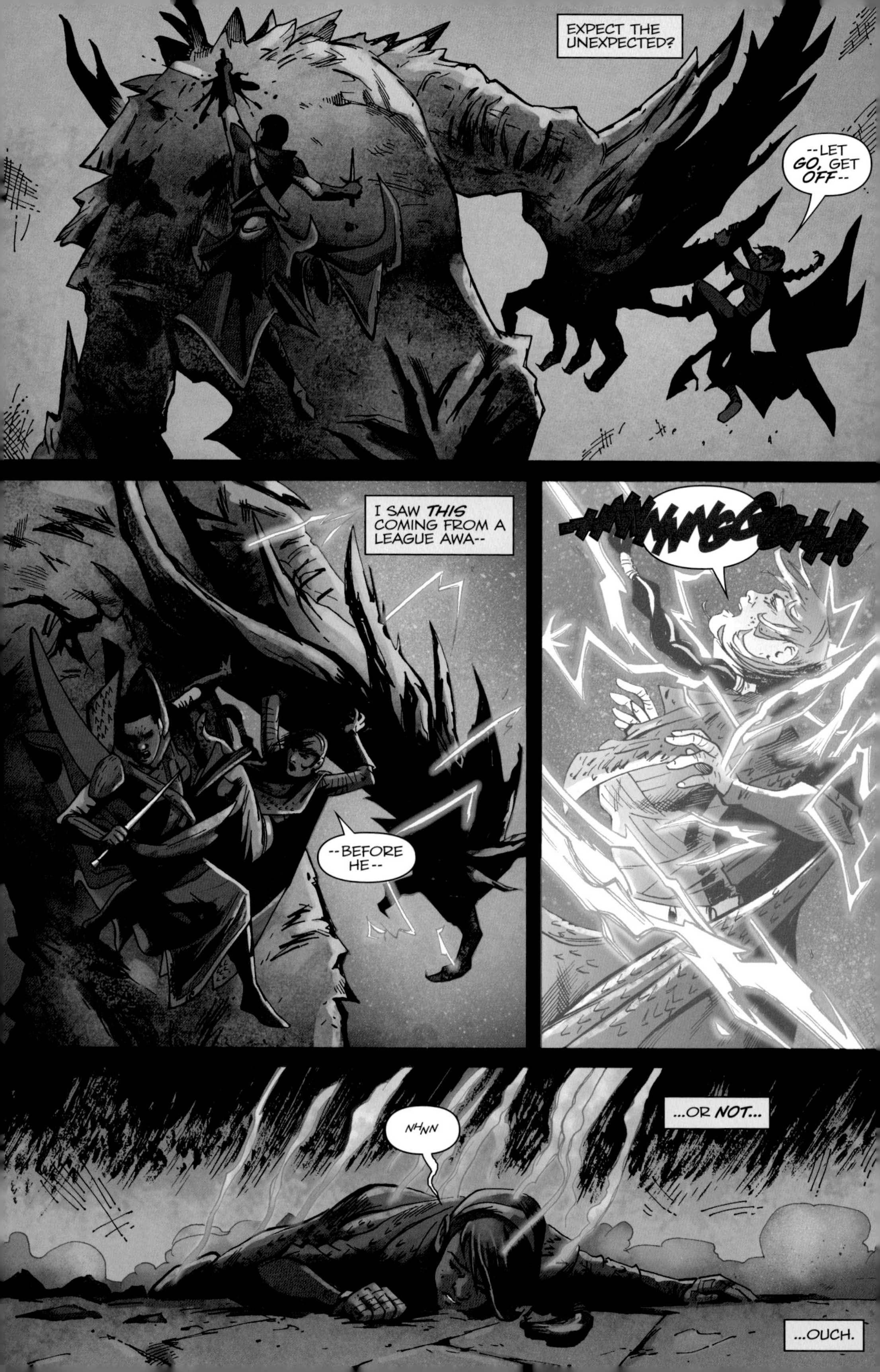
EXPECT THE UNEXPECTED?
--LET GO, GET OFF--
I SAW THIS COMING FROM A LEAGUE AWA--
--BEFORE HE--
...OR NOT...
NHNN
...OUCH.

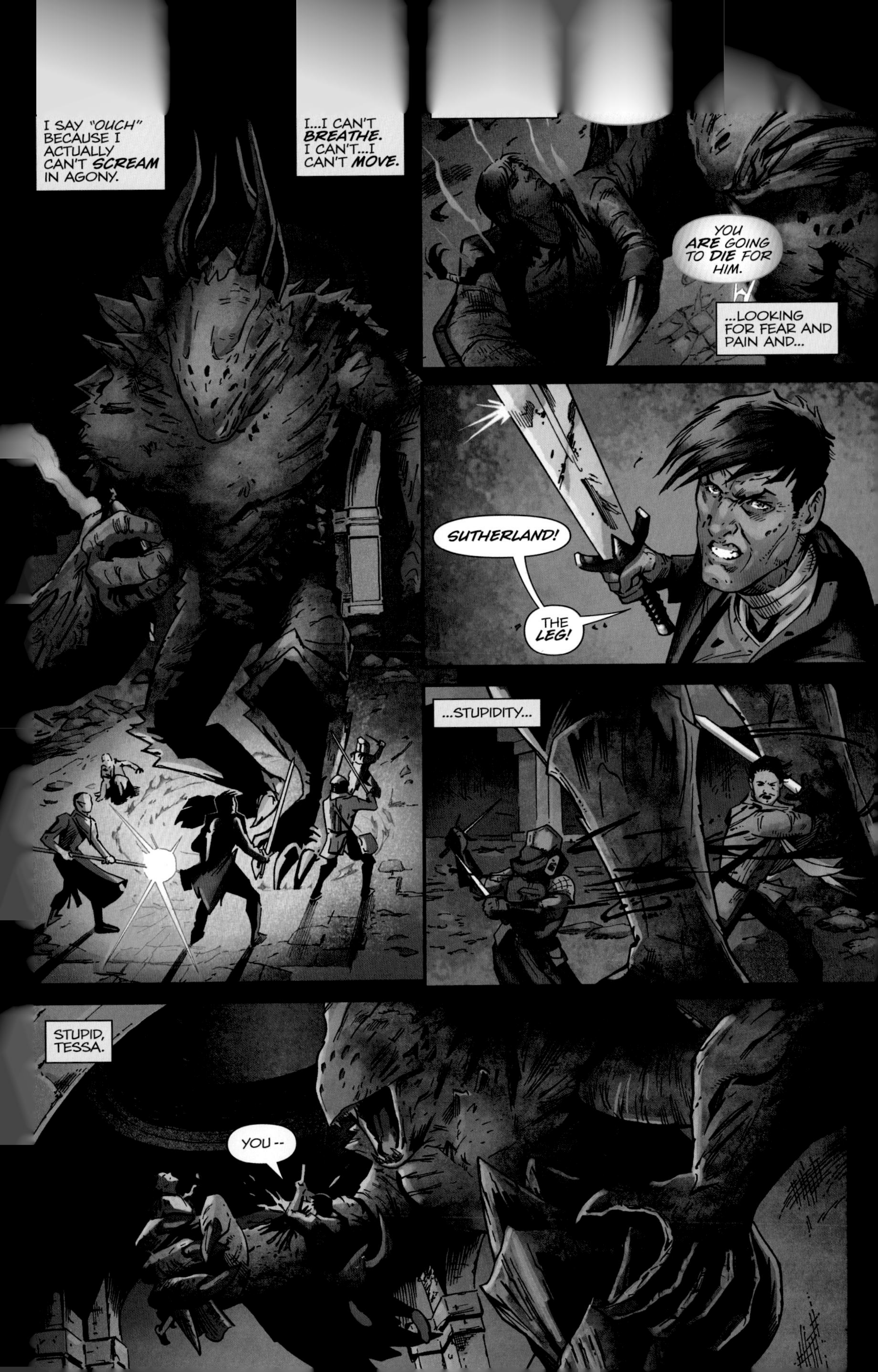

I SAY "OUCH" BECAUSE I ACTUALLY CAN'T SCREAM IN AGONY.
I...I CAN'T BREATHE. I CAN'T...I CAN'T MOVE.
YOU ARE GOING TO DIE FOR HIM.
...LOOKING FOR FEAR AND PAIN AND...
SUTHERLAND!
THE LEG!
...STUPIDITY...
STUPID, TESSA.
YOU --

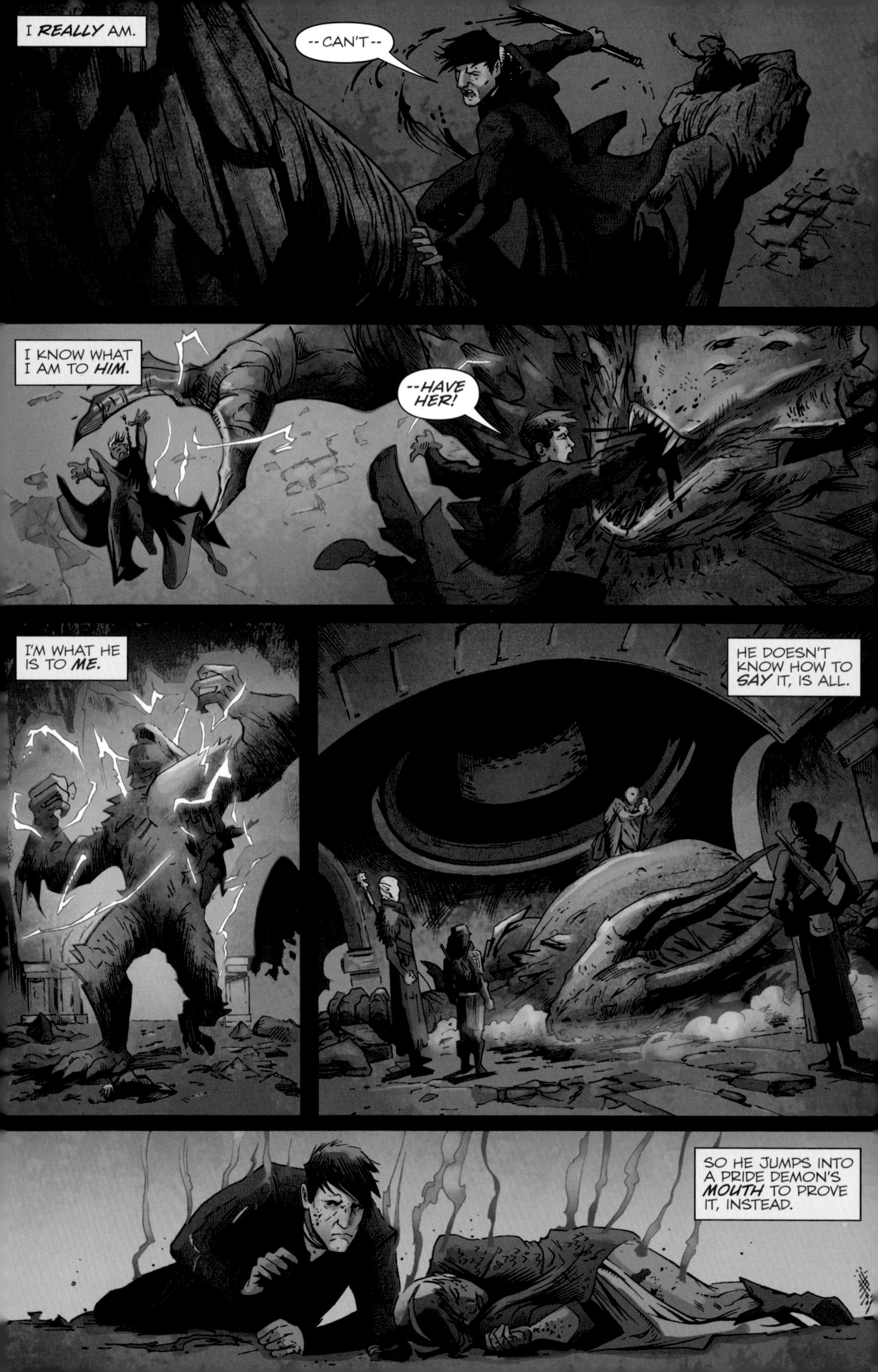
I REALLY AM.
--CAN'T--
I KNOW WHAT I AM TO HIM.
--HAVE HER!
I'M WHAT HE IS TO ME.
HE DOESN'T KNOW HOW TO SAY IT, IS ALL.
SO HE JUMPS INTO A PRIDE DEMON'S MOUTH TO PROVE IT, INSTEAD.

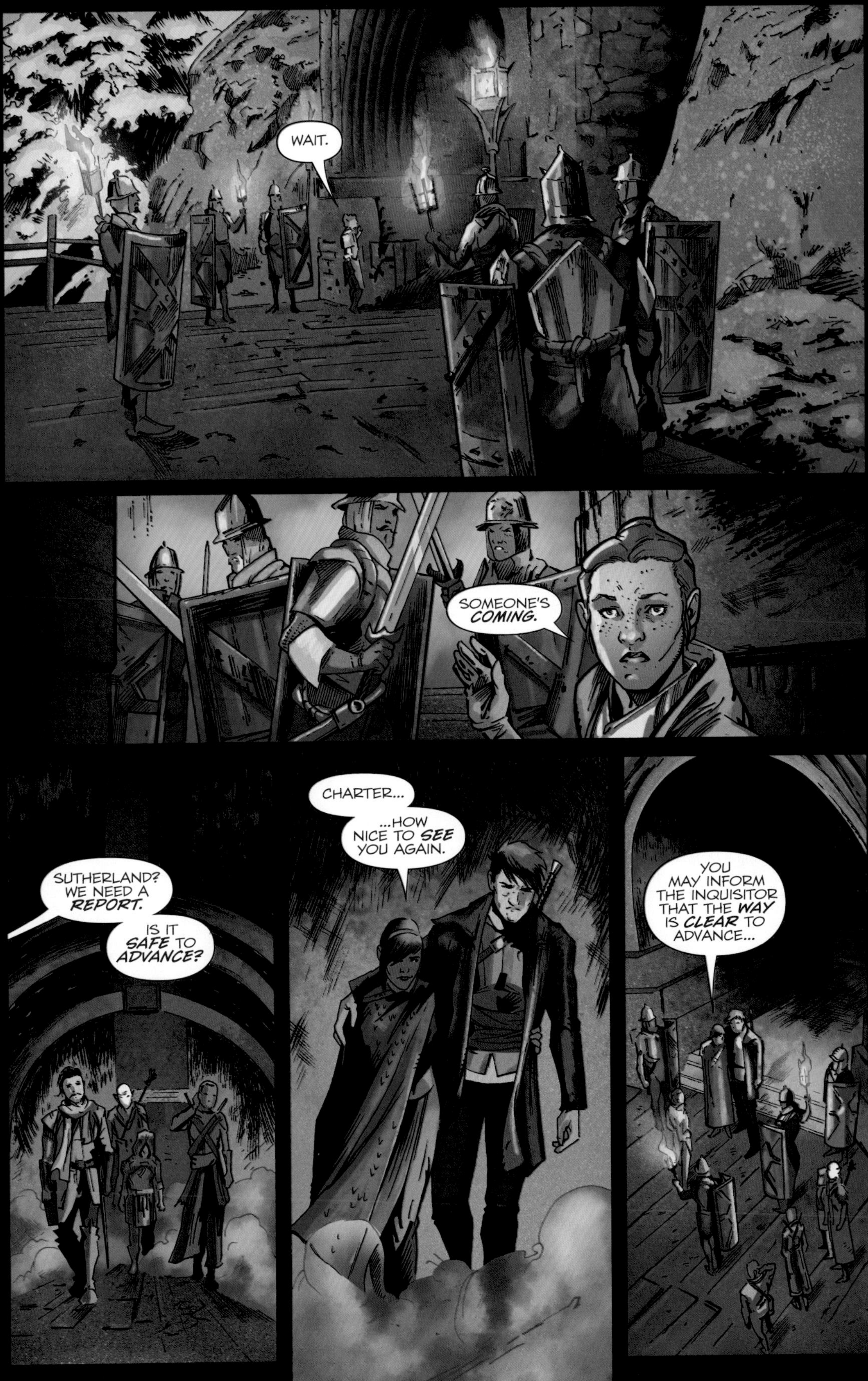
WAIT.
SOMEONE'S COMING.
SUTHERLAND? WE NEED A REPORT.
IS IT SAFE TO ADVANCE?
CHARTER...
...HOW NICE TO SEE YOU AGAIN.
YOU MAY INFORM THE INQUISITOR THAT THE WAY IS CLEAR TO ADVANCE...

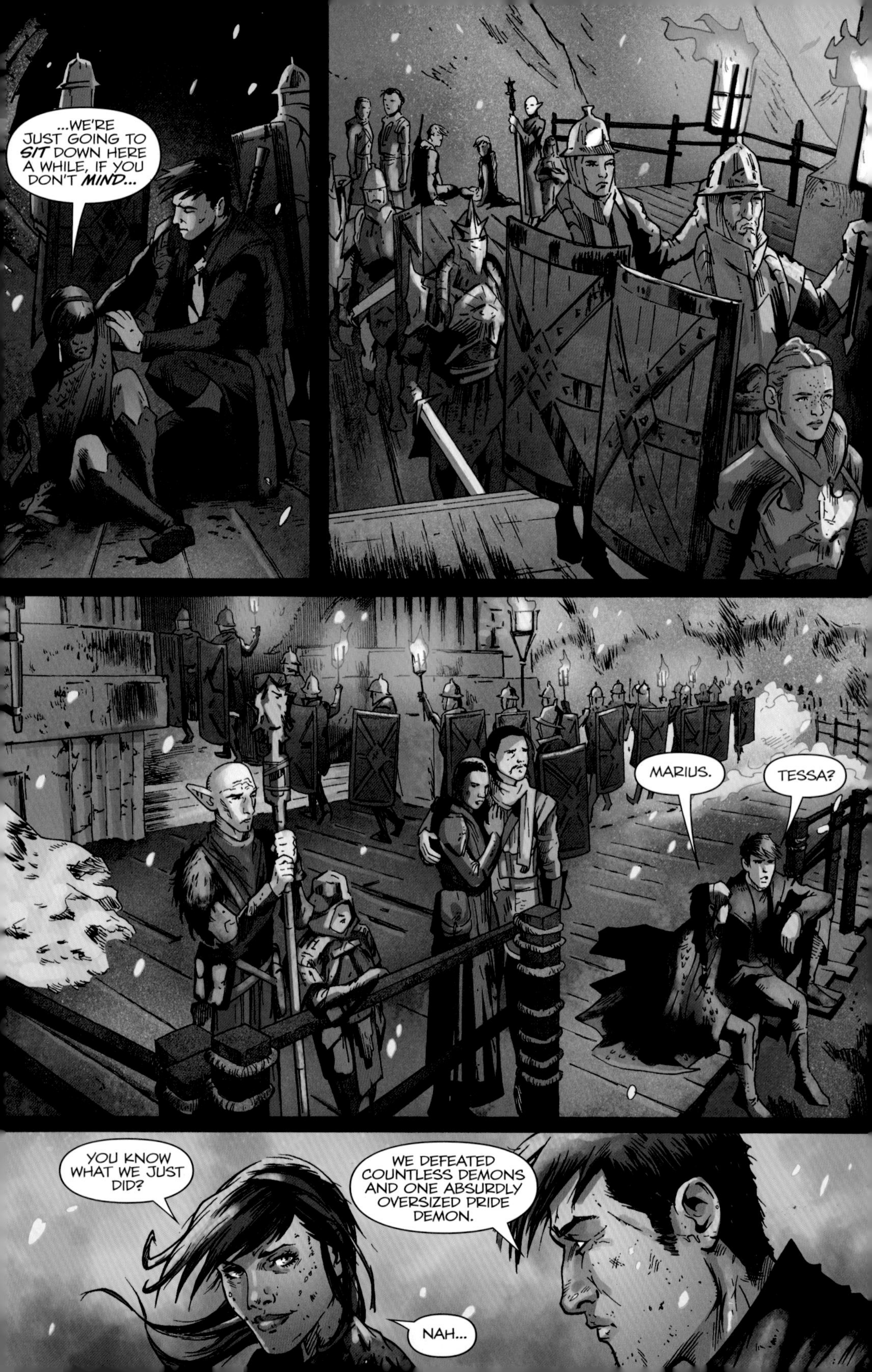
...WE'RE JUST GOING TO *SIT* DOWN HERE A WHILE, IF YOU DON'T *MIND*...
MARIUS.
TESSA?
YOU KNOW WHAT WE JUST DID?
WE DEFEATED COUNTLESS DEMONS AND ONE ABSURDLY OVERSIZED PRIDE DEMON.
NAH...

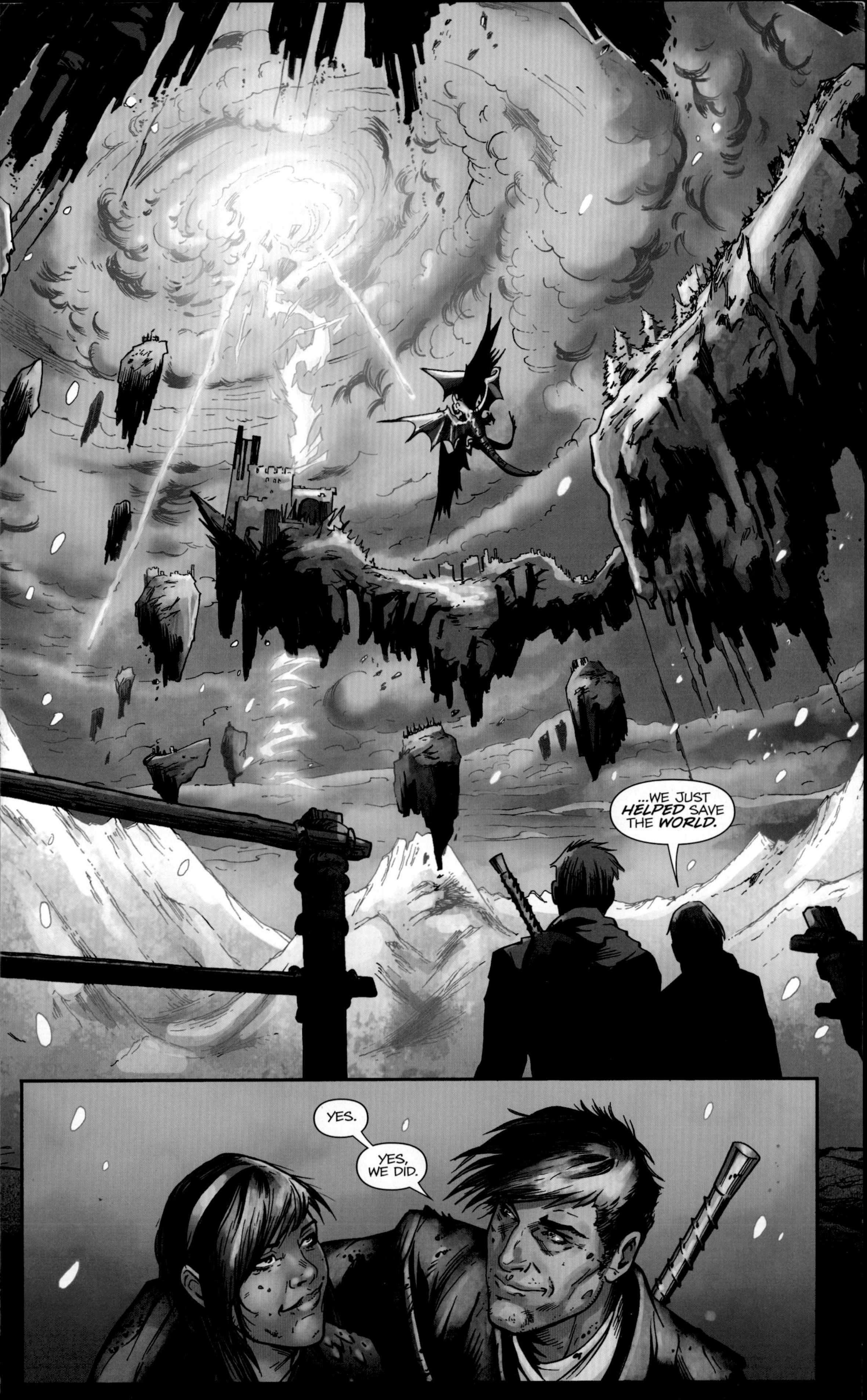
...WE JUST HELPED SAVE THE WORLD.
YES.
YES, WE DID.

Illustration by
SACHIN TENG

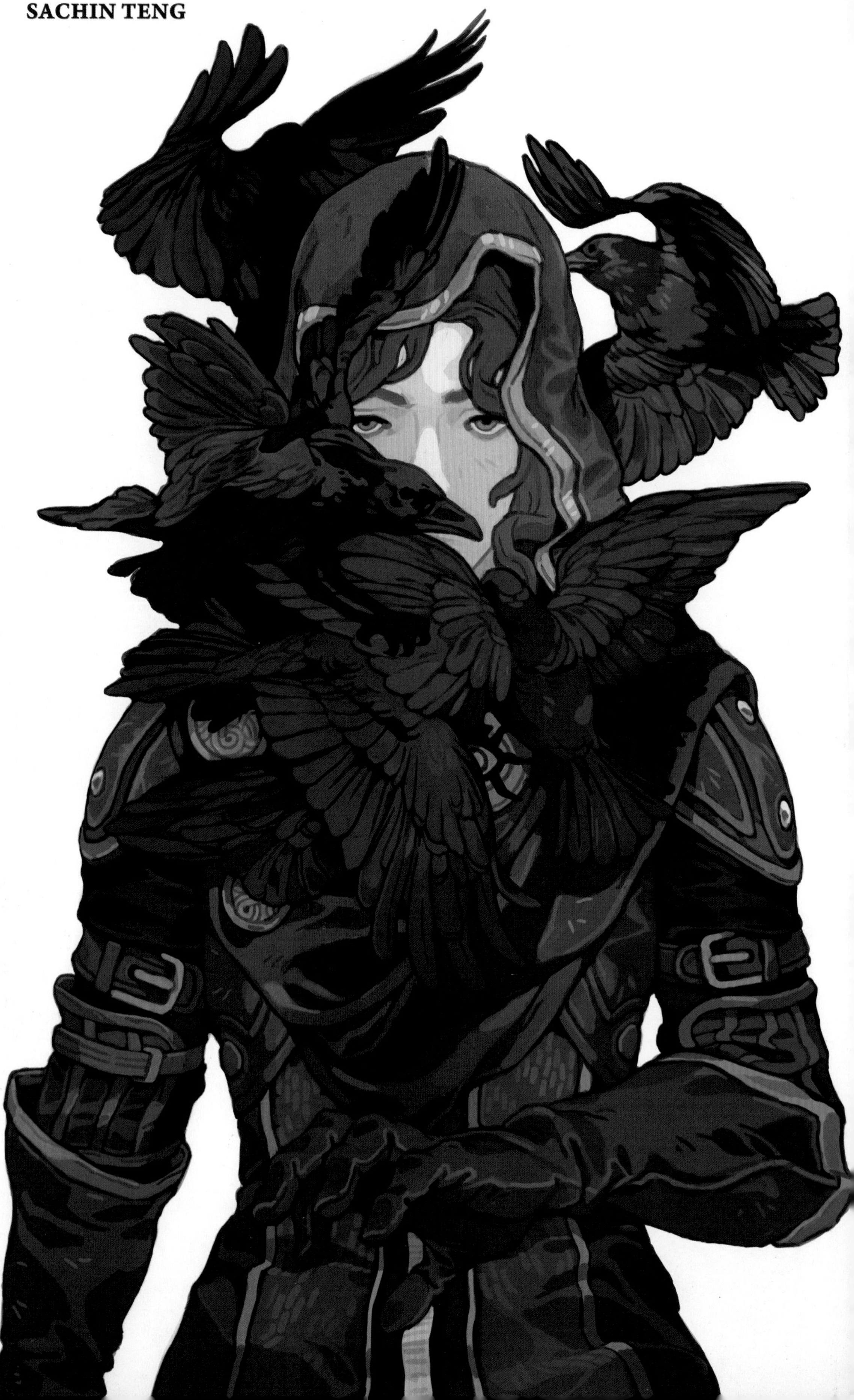

ALSO FROM DARK HORSE AND BIOWARE

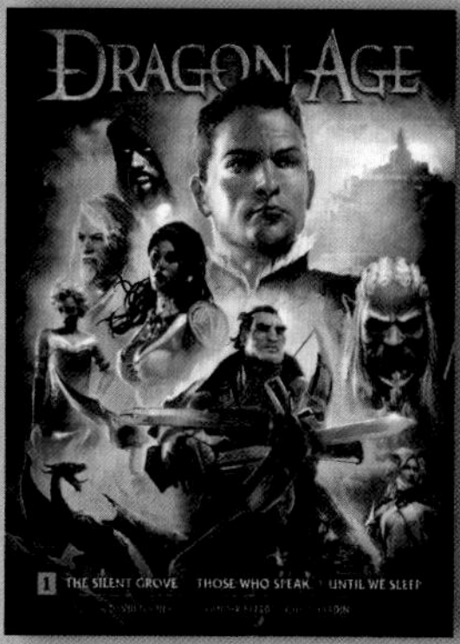
DRAGON AGE
THE SILENT GROVE · THOSE WHO SPEAK · UNTIL WE SLEEP

DRAGON AGE LIBRARY EDITION

This deluxe oversized hardcover collects every Dark Horse *Dragon Age* comic to date—*The Silent Grove, Those Who Speak*, and *Until We Sleep*—an epic trilogy complete in one volume, written by *Dragon Age* lead writer David Gaider!

$39.99
ISBN 978-1-61655-384-5

Also available:

DRAGON AGE: THE SILENT GROVE
$14.99 | ISBN 978-1-59582-916-0

DRAGON AGE: THOSE WHO SPEAK
$14.99 | ISBN 978-1-61655-053-0

DRAGON AGE: UNTIL WE SLEEP
$14.99 | ISBN 978-1-61655-219-0

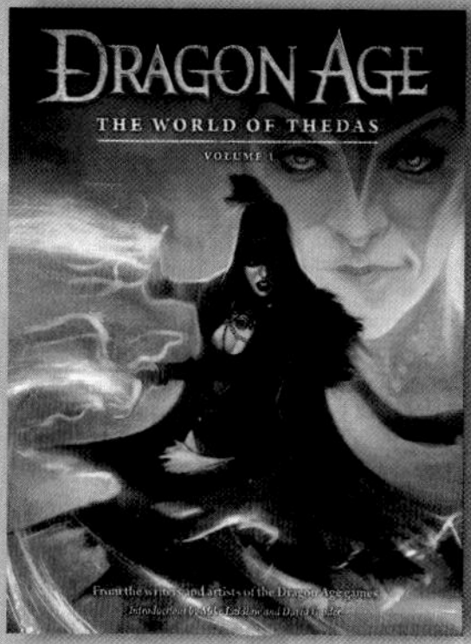
DRAGON AGE
THE WORLD OF THEDAS
VOLUME 1

DRAGON AGE: THE WORLD OF THEDAS VOLUME 1
$39.99 | ISBN 978-1-61655-115-5

DRAGON AGE: THE WORLD OF THEDAS VOLUME 2
$39.99 | ISBN 978-1-61655-501-6

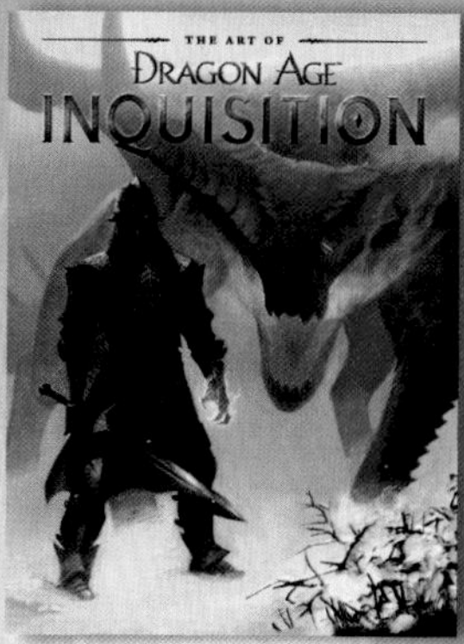
THE ART OF
DRAGON AGE
INQUISITION

THE ART OF DRAGON AGE: INQUISITION

Hardcover
$39.99 | ISBN 978-1-61655-186-5

Limited Edition Hardcover
$69.99 | ISBN 978-1-61655-728-7

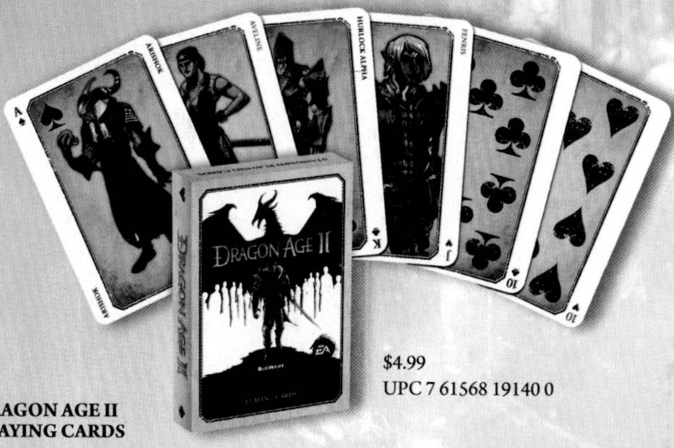
DRAGON AGE II

$4.99
UPC 7 61568 19140 0

DRAGON AGE II PLAYING CARDS

The BioWare development team helped Dark Horse design a fantastic deck of *Dragon Age II* playing cards. The detailed artwork captures the look and feel of the game, and the set is a perfect addition to your *Dragon Age* game collection!

DRAGON AGE II EMBROIDERED PATCHES
Chantry, Kirkwall, Qunari, Templars

Collect all four embroidered patches from BioWare's world of *Dragon Age II*. Each patch is beautifully embroidered with the logos representing the Qunari, the Chantry, Kirkwall, and the Templars. Each patch sold separately.

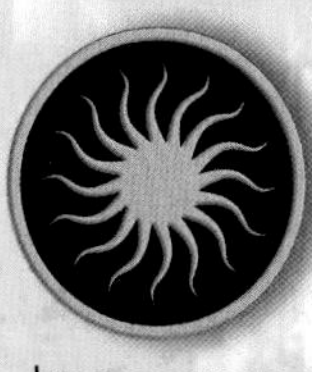

$4.99 | UPC 7 61568 21343 0

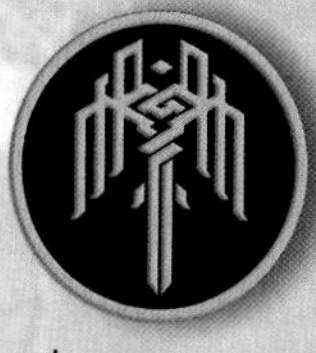

$4.99 | UPC 7 61568 21344 7

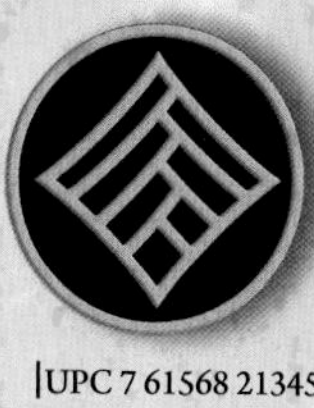

$4.99 | UPC 7 61568 21345 4

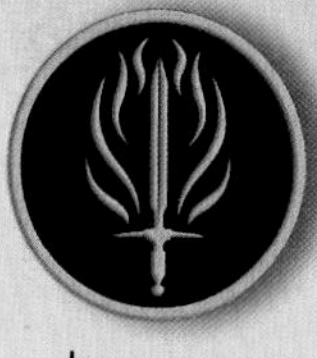

$4.99 | UPC 7 61568 21346 1

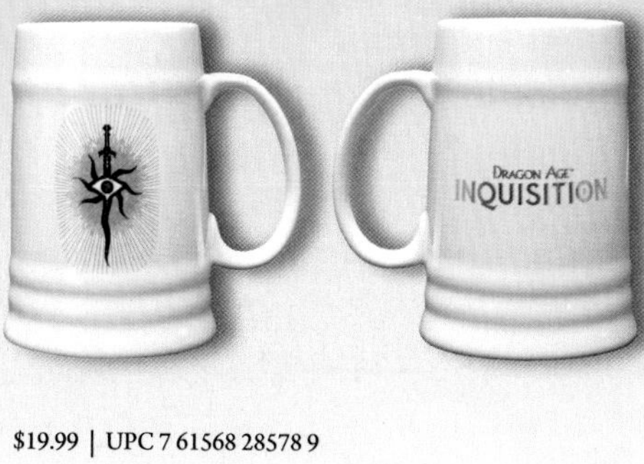
DRAGON AGE
INQUISITION

$19.99 | UPC 7 61568 28578 9

DRAGON AGE: INQUISITION STEIN
With this high-quality 22 oz. ceramic stein featuring the *Inquisition* symbol and the *Dragon Age: Inquisition* logo, you'll be ready to toast your victories.

Illustration by
SACHIN TENG

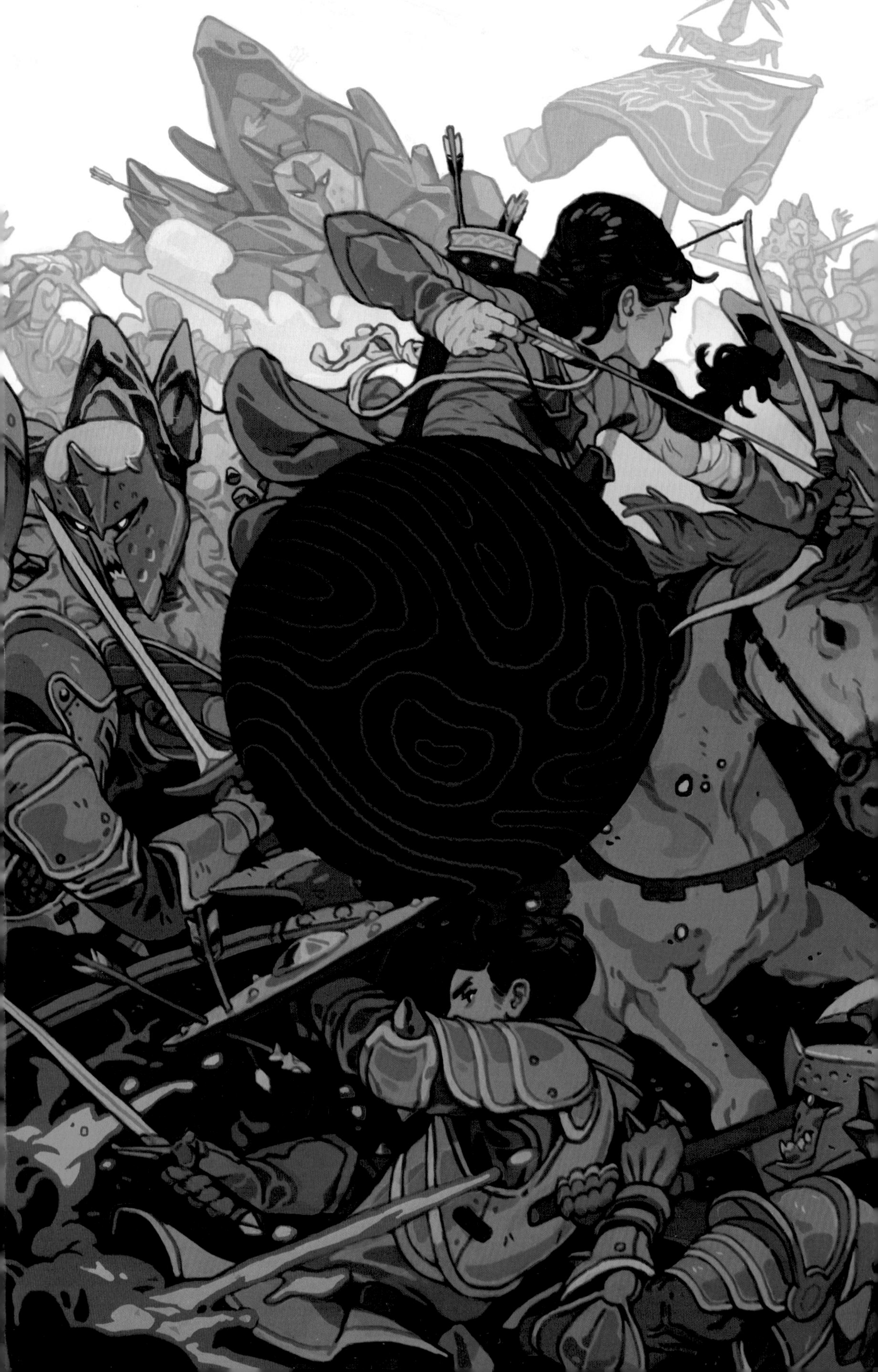